FORMAL LOGIC

FORMAL LOGIC

EDITED BY
JOHN H. PIET
AND
AYODHYA PRASAD

COSMO PUBLICATIONS
2000 INDIA

FORMAL LOGIC

First COSMO Print 2000

ISBN 81-7755-010-1

This indipendent and complete volume has been derived from the set -
Encyclopaedia of ETHICS AND LOGIC

Published by
MRS. RANI KAPOOR
for COSMO PUBLICATIONS Div. of
GENESIS PUBLISHING PVT. LTD.
24-B, Ansari Road,
Darya Ganj,
New Delhi-110 002, INDIA

Composed at
Cosmo Publications

Printed at
Mehra Offset Press

CONTENTS

Chapter-1

A History of the Philosophy of Logic

Chapter-1

I. INTRODUCTION

Metalogic is a level of reflection on Formal Logic which remains close to the experience of actually doing logic; its topics and problems are basically technical and their clarification does not commit one to extra-logical philosophical positions. There is room for a further kind of reflection which seeks more ultimate clarification of the nature of logic in general, of logical entities in particular, and of its situation within the corpus of human wisdom. This kind of reflection gives rise to topics and problems which, in this textbook, are collectively named Philosophy of Logic.

There are two other usages of the name. Philosophy of Logic (or Philosophical Logic). The first does not discriminate types of reflection on formal logic and includes any topic or problem arising at a *meta*-reflectivc level; in practice it deals predominantly with topics and problems that can be treated and solved, in principle, within logic although the relevant writings of, e.g. Quine (*Philosophy of Logic*) and Strawson (*Philosophical Logic*, which he edited and prefaced) do have important philosophical content. In its second usage the term denotes philosophical applications of logic. Thus, introducing his book *Logic, Language-Games and Information: Kantian Themes in the Philosophy of Logic* Jaakko Hintikka says:

> In this book, the consequences of certain logical insights for philosophical problems will be studied. This kind of enterprise has been given different names: philosophy of logic, philosophical logic, logical analysis in philosophy and so on ... In a rough and ready way, one can ... make a distinction between problems which are studied, at the present moment at least, primarily because of their significance for mathematical logic itself or for the

> foundations of mathematics, and problems which do not have much of this kind of interest (or not as much as some other subjects) but which are nevertheless of a genuine philosophical interest ... Although many concepts studied in the more technical parts of present-day logic have a clear-cut intuitive content, they are often fairly complicated and soon lead to considerable technical problems ... Nevertheless there are, it seems to me, certain concepts which have a great deal of philosophical interest but which can be explicated without too great technical difficulties. In this book, our attention will be focused on a few such relative non-technical concepts. They belong to the metatheory (syntax, semantics and pragmatics) of first-order logic (quantification theory), (pp. 1—3)

In *Topics in Philosophical Logic*, Nicholas Rescher interprets philosophical logic as branches of logical theory developed specifically with philosophical applications in mind and he analyses its contemporary content as ethical applications, metaphysical applications, epistemological applications with some specific uses made of inductive logic.

The view adopted in this textbook is that there is need of a section in the science which, seeking to bring ultimate clarifications to logic, is open to extra-logical considerations. These in practice will be mainly philosophical, and the section of logic, which is quite distinct from metalogic and applied logic, is suitably called Philosophy of Logic. The existence of such a section will preserve the clear-cut distinctions of formal logic, levels of reflection on formal logic (metalogical and philosophical), and applications of logic (collectively called Applied Logic). It will also help to preserve something that Rescher felt might be jeopardized by the notable contemporary development of philosophical applications — the aspect which logic has of being 'a unified discipline, exhibiting, across the whole of its great extent, a tight integrative cohesion'. (Topics in Philosophical Logic, p. 5)

Studying the mainstream of logical thought from the

Greeks, through medieval Arabian and European logic, on through shallow presentations by post-Renaissance logicians, through the development of modern mathematical logic and its emergence in the form of our contemporary science—is immediately struck by the fact that self-reflection of an ultimate kind is (relatively to other parts of logic) unextensive in content, indefinite in framework and insecure in quality. The Cartesian experiment, mixing mathematical thinking and philosophical explanation has been a special discouragement, perhaps, in modern times.

The other two traditions in logic—the Indian and the Chinese—have not been more forthcoming. The former seems, most of all, to embody dedication" to the purpose of developing a formal apparatus for writing on philosophy, grammar, ritual and science generally. (Of course Indian logic, covering twenty-three centuries, is only superficially known today and only a minute portion of its literature is edited.) Chinese thought, consistently moral and practical in quality, produced a logical tradition devoid of much formal system or abstract speculation and centred on the nature, use and problems of names. (It is surmised that the Chinese language was not one to promote a simultaneous growth of grammar and logic: that as speech with uninflected words it produced lexicographer, rather than grammarians.)

II. THE GREEK PERIOD

Principles of the general philosophy of Aristotle are undoubtedly relevant to the discussions in this section of logic but it is clear that he did not conceive the need of a philosophy of logic for situating logical knowledge within a plan of general human knowledge, or for explaining its ultimate reference, scope and value. For Aristotle and his school, apparently, logic was essentially a tool (*organon*) of science.

The Megarian-Stoic school, however, regarded it as a main branch of philosophy. The fragmentary knowledge we have does not include any indication that they had a philosophical doctrine about *lekton*. The fact that the Stoics were, in general, materialists and that their logic was closely associated with their theory of language would not tend to promote a *metaphysic* of lekton.

Thus Greece, so important for the development of Formal Logic, Metalogic and Applied Logic, did not achieve a Philosophy of Logic.

III. THE MEDIEVAL PERIOD

It is not surprising that medieval logic—so metalogical in character, so clear about logical form and about the complementary nature of syncategorematic words and second intentions of the mind, so interested in the problem of universals—should have discussed the ultimate reference value of propositional expressions. Such discussions were salient in the fifteenth century. The state of researeh in this period (as on medieval logic generally) does not provide documentation of the discussion but, e.g. a text from Paul of Venice indicates the type of opinions current. He lists four: the significate of a true proposition is (1) a physical reality; (2) a psychical reality; (3) an objective meaning (the Stoic lekton); (4) a complex of the significates of its parts, there being nothing real corresponding to this total as such. The text is as follows:

> About the essence of the proposition ... there are many opinions.
>
> The first is that the significate of a true proposition is a circumstance (*modus*) of the thing and not the thing itself...
>
> The second opinion is that the significate of a true proposition is a composition of the mind (*mentis*) or of the intellect which compounds or divides...
>
> The third opinion, commonly received among the doctors of my (Augustinian) Order, in particular by Master Gregory of Rimini, is that the significate of a proposition is whatever in any way exists as a signifiable complex. And when it is asked whether such a signifiable is something or nothing, he answers

that the name 'something' and its synonyms 'thing' and 'being' can be understood in three ways. (1) First in the widest sense, according to which everything signifiable, with or without complexity, truly or falsely, is called 'thing' and 'something'... (2) In a second way these (names) are taken for whatever is signifiable, with or without complexity, but truly,... (3) In a third way the aforesaid names, are taken in such wise that they signify some existent essence or entity, and in this way, what does not exist is called 'nothing' ... So this opinion says that the significate of a proposition is something, if one takes the aforementioned terms in the first or second way ...

> The fourth opinion posits some theses. (1) The first is this: that no thing is the adequate or total significate of a mental proposition properly so called; since every such (proposition) signifies a variety of mutually distinct things, by reason of its parts to which it is equivalent in its signifying. And this is evident to everyone who examines the matter. Hence there is no total or adequate significate of such a proposition. (2) The second thesis: whatever is signified by a mental proposition properly so called according to its total signification is also signified by any of its parts... (3) Third thesis: no dictum corresponding to a mental proposition properly so called, e.g. an expression in the infinitive mood taken as significant, supposes for any thing. For instance, if the dictum, i.e. the expression in the infinitive mood, 'that man is an animal', corresponding to the proposition 'man is an animal', is taken materially it stands for some thing, namely for the proposition to which it corresponds; but if it be taken significatively, i.e. personally, then according to the fourth opinion it stands for no thing. This is evident, since such an expression, so taken, signifies a number of things, viz. all those signified by the corresponding proposition, and so there would be no reason for it to suppose for one of its significates rather than another; hence (it supposes) either for each or for none. But nobody would say for each, since the expression that man is an animal' would signify an ass or suppose for

> an ass. Therefore for none. And what is said of that instance, holds for any other. (*Logica Magna*, II II, 162ra-163rb)

The practice of the whole scholastic tradition sharply distinguished logic from ontology. For one school (represented, e.g. by Thomas Aquinas) it functioned as a science of second intentions; for a second school (represented, e.g. by John Buridan) it was a science of syncategorematic terms (logical constants) and its truths were formulated not in an object-language but in a metalanguage. Both schools regarded logic as being concerned with *discourse* about reality. The old theory of three kinds of discourse, written, spoken and mental had been revitalized by the Aristotelian doctrine that we become aware of things by receiving their forms into the soul; thought was portrayed as consisting of *propositions mentales* formed from natural signs in the soul. Some indeed—e.g. Pierrc D'Ailly (1350—1425)—conceived thought to have a grammar analogous to that of spoken and written sentences. As Bochenski notes:

> ... in the Middle Ages we find essentially only *one* logic. Exceptions only occur where epistemological or ontological problems exert an influence, as in the determination of the notion of logic itself, and in the assigning of denotations. Everywhere else we find a unified logic, developing organically. The very multiplicity of medieval views about extra-logical matters supports the thesis that formal logic is independent of any special philosophical position on the part of individual logicians. (*A History of Formal Logic,* p. 115)

In general, differences and divisions in philosophical opinions did not carry into the logic of the period. Thus no definite philosophy of logic was constructed. Yet, in the problem of universals, so widely and profoundly discussed in the Middle Ages, potential foundations were laid for investigating the nature of logical entities and the ultimate concern of logic itself. Further the nature of logical form was expressly explained as that which is determined by the syncategorematic terms. Thus a text of John Buridan says:

> When form and matter are here spoken of, by the matter of a proposition or consequence is understood merely the categorematic terms, i.e. the subject and predicate, to the exclusion of the syncategorematic ones attached to them, by which they are restricted, negated, or divided and given (*trahuntur*) a determinate kind of supposition. All else, we say, belongs to the form. Hence we say that the copula, both of the categorical and of the hypothetical proposition belongs to the form of the proposition, as also negations, signs, the number both of propositions and terms, as well as the mutual ordering of all the aforesaid, and the interconnections of relative terms and the ways of signifying (*modos significandi*) which relate to the quantity of the proposition, such as discreteness, universality, etc....
>
> E.g.... Since modals have subordinate copulas and so differ from assertoric propositions, these differ in form; and by reason of the negations and signs (*signa*) affirmatives are of another form than negatives, and universals than particulars; and by reason of the universality and discreteness of their terms singular propositions are of another form than indefinites... (*Tractatus cmsequentiarum magistri*, cap. 7)

Medieval Arabic logic was very western and while Latin logic owed many of its formal and metalogical ideas to it, Arabian logicians (in Spain and also in the Middle East) confined themselves to a retrieval and reconstruction of Greek logic.

IV. POST-RENAISSANCE LOGICIANS

We have already seen in surveys of the history of formal logic and metalogic that the period after the Middle Ages until the development of modern mathematical logic was not a creative one. As Kneale notes: 'From the 400 years between the middle of the fifteenth and the middle of the nineteenth century we have in consequence scores of textbooks but very few works that contain anything at once new and good.' (*The Development of Logic*, p. 298) Indeed there arose a distorted version of logic, the so-called 'classical' logic which in content was poor, logically, and confused metaphysical, psychological and logical ideas.

Leibniz was a remarkable exception in this period being one of the greatest formal logicians and metalogicians of all time. But he did not contribute to the philosophy of logic. He saw it as a calculus, a formal apparatus which would provide the syntax for his alphabet of symbols signifying the ultimate unanalysable notions, so that the correctness of all reasoning performed grammatically in the language would be made inevitable:

> If we had a body of signs that were right for the purpose of our talking about all our ideas as clearly and in as true and as detailed a way as numbers are talked about in Arithmetic or lines are talked about in the Geometry of Analysis, we would be able to do for every question, in so far as it is under the control of reasoning, all that one is able to do in Arithmetic and Geometry. All work in the sciences which is dependent on reasoning would be done by the changing and exchanging of signs and by a sort of Algebra; an effect of this is that the discovery of facts of great interest and attraction would become quite straightforward. It would not be necessary for our heads to be broken in hard work as much as they are now and we would certainly be able to get all the knowledge possible from the material given. In addition, we would have everyone in agreement about whatever would have been worked out, because it would be simple to have the working gone into by doing it again or by attempting tests like that of 'putting out nines' in Arithmetic. And if anyone had doubts of one of my statements I would say to him: let us do the question by using numbers, and in this way, taking pen and ink, we would quickly come to an answer. (*The Development of Mathematical Logic* by P. H. Nidditch. Published by Routledge and Kegan Paul, p. 20)

This vision, realized so greatly in modern logic and computerization, would indeed have made Leibniz the founder, historically, of mathematical logic if his writings had been published and they had become a force in time and place. The vision of logic, however, was not philosophical in character.

Since the time of Boole one can identify an historical mainstream of logical thought, in the form of mathematical logic. Outside it there were logicians who (like Hamilton) did or (like Whately and Mill) did not enlarge the common traditional logic; there were other logicians like J. N. Keynes and W. E. Johnson who had a logical style reflecting influence from both tradition and the new mathematical logicians. Their logical problems were not philosophical. The main one concerned whether they should be antimathematical, antitechnical: the tradition from Kant and Hegel was antimathematical (in combination with Kant's overestimate of Aristotle's logic).

John Stuart Mill is of special interest in that his *System of Logic* is in opposition to the whole traditional theory of formal logic, treating it as an empirical science. Following the extreme empiricist view—that only empirical statements can give any information about reality—he holds that the principle of non-contradiction must be seen to be a generalization from experience, and that the syllogism must be interpreted as representing inference from particulars to particulars if it is to escape the unanswerable objection of begging the question:

> It must be granted that in every syllogism, considered as an argument to prove the conclusion, there is a petitio principii. When we say. *All men are mortal, Socrates is a man, therefore Socrates is mortal*, it is unanswerably urged by the adversaries of the syllogistic theory, that the proposition, *Socrates is mortal*, is presupposed in the more general assumption. *All men are mortal...*
>
> All inference is from particulars to particulars. General propositions are merely registers of such inferences already made, and short formulae for making more. The major

premise of a syllogism, consequently, is a formula of this description; and the conclusion is not an inference drawn *from* the formula, but an inference drawn *according* to the formula; the real logical antecedent or premise being the particular facts from which the general proposition was collected by induction. Those facts and the individual instances which supplied them, may have been forgotten; but a record remains, not indeed descriptive of the facts themselves, but showing how these cases may be distinguished, respecting which, the facts, when known, were considered to warrant a given inference. According to the indications of this record we draw our conclusion; which is, to all intents and purposes, a conclusion from the forgotten facts. For this it is essential that we should read the record correctly; and the rules of the syllogism are a set of precautions to ensure our doing so. (*System of Logic,* Bk. II, iii. 2 and 4)

The main difficulty encountered in interpreting Mill's *System of Logic* is its inconsistency. The analysis of the syllogism in Book Two is that of an extreme empiricist for whom a universal proposition is really a number of particular propositions formulated in shorthand form, and for whom validity is a derivative of experience not of form. The analysis of induction in Book Three is, on the other hand, that of a utilitarian for whom a machinelike reality underlies experience, the business of an inductive logic being to provide rules and models to which if inductive arguments conform these arguments are conclusive and not otherwise'. Thus, paradoxically, there is a stronger basis for valid conclusions in applied logic than within formal logic itself.

It is clear from Mill's work that there is no room within a philosophy of extreme empiricism for logic as a study of form and a science of formal necessity. In treating logic as an empirical science one distances oneself from the historical achievements of formal logic.

V. THE PERIOD OF MODERN AND CONTEMPORARY MATHEMATICAL LOGIC

In discriminating between metalogic and philosophy of logic and conceiving the latter as the level of reflection in which one seeks ultimate clarifications about logic and logical entities and in which one must take cognizance of extra-logical, philosophical, ideas—one finds, naturally, that most modern logicians are formal logicians and metalogicians rather than philosophers of logic.

Charles Sanders Peirce (1839—1924) is a case in point. One of the great logicians of all time, with an unusual comprehension of ancient, medieval and modern logic, he was, above all else, a master of logical technique and an innovator whose works are full of original technical suggestions. But he did not devote himself at all to a philosophy of logic. There are logicians who are important through establishing historic theorems within formal logic, e.g. Kurt Gödel (b. 1906), Leopold Löwenhcim (b. 1878), Alonzo Church (b. 1903), Thoralf Skolem (1887—1963), Jacques Herbrand (1903—31). Others are famous for developing significant technical innovations, e.g. Gerhard Gentzen (1909—45), Stanislaw Jaskowski, Moses Schönfinkel, Haskell B. Curry (b. 1900), Willard Van Orman Quine (b. 1908).

As a group from a single nation, Polish logicians are uniquely great in modern history as formal logicians, metalogicians and philosophers of mathematics including, as they do, Kazimierz Twardowski, Jan Lukasiewicz, Stanislaw Lesniewski, Tadeusz Kotarbinski, Kazimierz Ajdukiewicz, Alfred Tarski, Mordchaj Wajsberg, Stanislaw Jaskowski, Leon Chwistek, Andrzej Mostowski, Czeslaw Lejewski and Boleslaw Sobocinski. But as Kotarbinski points out about the leading figure, Jan Lukasiewicz (1878—1956), Polish logic was conducted 'in a technological spirit independent of any general philosophical preconceptions'; indeed he comments on 'how wide was the range of the general philosophical attitudes of the various members of a group, who were still all agreed on the importance of mathematical logic as the only adequately scientific modern form of formal logic'. (*Polish Logic 1920—1939,* edited by Storrs McCall, Introduction, p. 12) Thus, in terms of the distinction we have drawn between philosophy of logic and metalogic, Polish logic focused on the latter and not on the former.

Unquestionably it is Wittgenstein who, among modern thinkers, has made the deepest and widest contribution to a philosophy of logic. His writings on the nature of logic, logical space, the proposition and logical operators are of fundamental importance, and the development of his thought which occurred between the time of the *Tractatus* and that of the *Investigations* gives basic guidance to any exploration of the relationship between logic and subjectivity. The influence of Frege, explicit in formal logic and metalogic, is of course implicitly great in philosophical reflection. *Mutatis mutandis* this is also truie of Bertrand Russell an important figure in both the history of logic and of philosophy who, however, formulated few positions in philosophy of logic (as it is specified here). A general implicit influence from metalogic roust be taken for granted and indeed be emphasized in respect of the Polish logicians. Some, like Caroap and Quine, contributed predominantly to metalogic but also to philosophy of logic.

The only philosophical question to be so extensively discussed over the last fifty years as to give rise to schools of thought is whether an ontological theory is built into logical language. In his paper 'Ontological commitment' Alonso Church snows how, in philosophical discussions, theses put forward can be at variance with an ontological model presupposed by the very language used. He concludes: 'No discussion of an ontological question, in particular of the issue between nominalism and realism, can be regarded as intelligible unless it obeys a definite criterion of ontological commitment.' I.e. one must work out the kind of features in our language (e.g. analytic propositions, quantifiers) which implicitly carry assertions about reality.

To what extent does modern logical language commit logic to an ontological theory? The language of propositional logic does not carry with it any commitment about one world more than any other possible one, for it expresses the logical connectivity of propositions irrespective of content. However, in the logic of monadic predicates and relations one uses individual constants, individual variables, proper names, predicate letters and quantifiers; if, in the pursuit of logical truth, logic uses such notation, does it not presuppose the reality of individuals, properties and relations? What, in this area of logic, is the minimum ontological commitment that must be made? What theory of logical language is implicit in this limited commitment? (Outside modern standard logic one has a logic devised by the Polish logician, Lesniewski, which makes no ontological presupposition.)

In his *A History of the Corruptions of Logic* Peter Geach notes:

> Aristotle's first logical ideas can be described with reasonable certainty. Aristotle's logic, from first to last, was mainly a theory of the subject-predicate relation; and the view of predication he began with was a development of one sketched by Plato in the *Sophist*. Plato there put forward the view that the simplest form of proposition is composed of two heterogeneous elements, a noun (*onoma*) and a verb (*rhema*); for example, 'Man walks', 'Theaetus flies'. A string of nouns, like 'man lion', or of verbs, like 'runs walks', is on the other hand not intelligible discourse at all... Unfortunately ... Aristotle lost the Platonic insight that any predicative proposition splits up into two logically heterogeneous par: instead, he treats predication as an attachment of one term (*horos*) to another term. Whereas the *rhema* was regarded as essentially predicative, 'always a sign of what is said of something else', it is impossible on the new doctrine for any term to be essentially predicative; on the contrary, any term that occurs in a proposition predicatively may be made into the subject-term of another predication. 1 shall call this 'Aristotle's thesis of interchangeability'; his adoption of it marks a

> transition from the original name-and-predicable theory to a *two-term* theory ... Aristotle's going over to the two term theory was a disaster...
>
> The restitution of genuine logic is due to two men above all: Bertrand Russell and Gottlob Frege. To Frege we owe it that modern logicians almost universally accept an absolute category-difference between names and predicables; this comes out graphically in the choice of letters from different founts of type for the schematic letters or variables answering to these two categories. Bartrand Russell re-emphasized this point: and he added a denial that significantly many-worded expressions can ever have the logical role of naming; Frege had still allowed many-worded names- (pp. 1. 4. I9)

As a result of a two-level semantics which excludes both subjective concepts and objective meanings, the relationships between names and reality, and between predicables and reality have been directly examined. This correlation has led, naturally, to various theories of representation, to Tarski's development of a theory of the truth of *sentences*, and also to problems of what exactly is real.

It is not controverted that individuals exist, that implicit in the use of names is a belief in the reality of individuals and that logic is consequently committed to this belief. The specific form of the belief is open. In *Individuals* Peter Strawson argues (on the side of Aristotle) that the basic objects of reference are spatio-temporal particulars of a pretty substantial sort—material bodies and persons, the latter being thought of as essentially, though not only, corporeal beings. Here Strawson opposes the classical British empiricism in which particular sense impressions are the basic particulars. Bertrand Russell's final view was as follows:

> I have maintained a principle, which still seems to me completely valid, to the effect that, if we can understand what a sentence means, it must be composed entirely of

words denoting things with which we are acquainted or definable in terms of such words... The subject in psychology, and the particle of matter in physics, if they are to be intelligible, must both be regarded either as bundles of experienced qualities and relations or as related to such bundles by relations known to experience. The fundamental apparatus out of which ordinary proper names are manufactured must, according to the above theory, be composed of what would ordinarily be regarded as qualities rather than substances—e.g. red and blue and hard and soft and pleasant and unpleasant... We may perhaps define the 'stuff of the world as what is designated by words which, when correctly used, occur as subjects of predicates or terms of relations. In that sense, I should say that the stuff of the world consists, of things like whiteness, rather than of objects having the property of being white ... The importance of the conclusion lies in the fact that it involves the rejection of minds and bits of matter as the stuff out of which the world is built...

This whole subject [the correlation of language and reality] is discussed in the last chapter of my *Inquiry into Meaning and Truth*. I have nothing to add to what 1 said there:'We have arrived in this chapter, at a result which has been, in a sense, the goal of all our discussions. The result I have in mind is this: that complete metaphysical agnosticism is not compatible with the maintanance of linguistic propositions Some modern philosophers hold that we know much about language, but nothing about anything else. This view forgets that language is an empirical phenomenon like another, and that a man who is metaphysical by agnostic must deny that he knows when he uses a word. For my part, I believe that, partly by means of the study of syntax, we can arrive at considerable knowledge concerning the structure of the world'(*My Philosophical Development*, pp. 169—71,3)

A really divisive problem concerns the predicate signs:

have they real reference,? A platonistic language is committed to an ontological model or universe containing not only individuals but classes of individuals; it determines the well-foundedness of predicate signs according to this model. The entities presupposed by a nominalistic language, on the other hand, are individuals: there are no classes. While every platonistic language contains a sub—language which is nominalistic, it also admits quantification over predicate signs whereas in the sub-language quantification extends univocally over a range of individuals only (predicate expressions are admissible only in so far as they are syncategorematic, i.e.in so far as they correspond in function to a name, being the sign of that which is true of individuals).There are, naturally, many problems and opinions concerning what precisely count as individuals or as abstract entities. Within mathematics, from which the designations 'platonism' and 'nominalism' have become widespread, a language of moderate platonism seems to be indispensable: as Guido Küng points out (*Ontology and the Logistic Analysis of Language*, p.154) a 'decisive drawback of nominalism seems to be that it can interpret mathematics only as an abacus'.

Is there a criterion for determining when language is explicitly assuming existence? Quine says:

> There are those who feel that our ability to understand general terms, and to see one concrete object as resembling another, would be inexplicable unless there were universals as objects of apprehension. And there are those who fail to detect, in such appeal to a realm of entities over and above the concrete objects in space and time, any explanatory value. Without settling that issue, it should still be possible to point to certain forms of discourse as *explicitly* presupposing entities of one or another given kind, say universals, and purporting to treat of them; and it should be possible to point to other forms of discourse as not explicitly presupposing these entities. Some criterion to this purpose, some standard and of ontological commi-

> tment, is needed if we are ever to say meaningfully that a given theory depends on or dispenses with the assumption of such and such objects...In general, *entities of a given sort are assumed by a theory if and only if some of them must be counted among the values of the variables in order that the statements affirmed in the theory be true. (From a Logical Point of View,* pp. 102—3)

Language, then, explicitly assumes the existence of any value that can be substituted for a variable in true statements. Quine's best-known formulation of this conclusion and the consequent criterion goes back to 1939:

> Here, then, are five ways of saying the same thing: 'There is such a thing as appendicitis'; 'The word "appendicitis" designates'; 'The word "appendicitis" is a name'; 'The word "appendicitis" is a substituent for a variable'; 'The disease "appendicitis" is a value of a variable.' The universe of entities is the range of values of variables. *To be is to be the value of a variable.* ('Designation and existence', *Journal of Philosophy*, 36. p. 708)

Thus by examining a language for the quantified variables in it we can determine the ontological model or univ-erse it is presupposing. Quine's criterion has been generally accepted, e.g. by Alonso Church, a platonist, and by Nelson Goodman, a nominalist. He himself takes the view that language should be as nominalist as possible but cannot be completely so: quantification over mathematical entities is indispensable for science, both formal and physical; accepting such quantification we must accept the existence of the mathematical entities

He emphasizes that the problem of ontological commitment concerns logical language rather than ordinary language

> The philosophical devotees of ordinary language are right in doubting the final adequacy of any criterion of the ontological presuppositions of ordinary any language, but

> they are wrong in supposing that there is no more to be said on the philosophical question of ontological presuppositions In a loose way we often can speak of ontological presuppositions at the level of ordinary language, but this makes sense just in so far as we have in mind some likeliest, most obvious way of schematizing the discourse in question along quantificational lines. And it is only in this spirit, in reference to one or another real or imagined logical schematization of one or another part or all of science, that we can with full propriety inquire into ontological presuppositions. (*From a Logical Point of View,* pp. 106—7)

Rudolf Carnap has always maintained that predicate notation represents something, and he has also been slow to accept abstract entities His final view which has gradually developed in the course of his work of the logistic formulation of scientific theories is as follows: language must have two levels, an observational one which is nominalistic and expresses the actual data of experience (*Tatbestand der Erfahrung*;). and a theoretical one which is platonistic and expresses a freely chosen form (*wahlbestimmte Form*), the latter represents a heuristic, subjective, pragmatic approach to the world and carries no commitment to an ontological mode' In 1934 Carnap had formulated his *thesis of extensionality*, which states that any system expressed in intensional language can always be translated into an extensional system, i.e that no statement can be ultimately resistant to translation into extensional language—on the presupposition that any two predicates which agree extensionally (i.e are true of the same objects) can be interchanged salwa *veritate* However, the thesis has not been established and even if it were that would not decide the relative merits of the ontological models presupposed by nominalistic and platonistic languages

VI. CONCLUSION

We have seen that in modern times the question, whether the

use of logical language carries with it an ontological commitment, has been very fully discussed and indeed has given rise to two schools of thought. Other philosophical questions have not the benefit, however, of such organized treatment and settled opinions.

The following chapters will offer a survey and definite philosophical viewpoint on the following topics: the definition of logic; the nature of logical space, of the proposition and of logical operators; logic and subjectivity; logic and the ideal rational life. In this way a philosophic treatment will be provided of what is intrinsic to the science of logic (its matter and form), of its origin and of a valuable perspective it brings to human rational living. In other words, the four causal aspects, which the Greeks required for a complete treatment of any topic, will be covered.

Chapter-2

The History of Formal Logic: A Survey of Creative Periods

Chapter-2

I. INTRODUCTION

Formal Logic begins with Aristotle (384—322 B.C.). At the end of an early work on argumentation he points out that his approach is distinctive and original: 'Of this inquiry ... it was not the case that part of the work had been thoroughly done before, while part had not. Nothing existed at all...on the subject of Rhetoric there exists much that has been said long ago, whereas on the subject of reasoning we had nothing else of in earlier date to speak of at all, but were kept at work for a long time in experimental researehes.' (*De Sophisticis Elenchis*: 183b, 35: 184b, 1) However, it was possible for Aristotle to found the science of Formal Logic mainly because the Greek people were excellent practitioners of logic, highly skilled in analysis, the organization of knowledge and the strategies of argumentation, and interested also in the syntax and semantics of language. Important also were the Platonic concept of universally necessary laws, the Platonic correspondence theory of truth and the demand, in Greek philosophy, for positive proof rather than negative dialectic.

'Since logic is not simply valid argument but the reflection upon principles of validity, it will arise naturally only when there is already a considerable body of inferential or argumentative material to hand. Not every type of discourse provokes logical inquiry. Pure story-telling or literary discourse, for example, does not provide a sufficient amount of argumentative material. It is those types of discourse or enquiry in which *proof* is sought or demanded that naturally give rise to logical investigation; for to prove a proposition is to infer it validly from true premisses. The conditions of *proof* are two: true premisses, or starting points, and valid arguments. It is not easy to tell how soon it was realized that the two conditions are independent, but this was perfectly clear to Aristotle when he drew the distinction between apodeictic and dialectical reasoning [reasoning respectively from what is known to be true and from what is not known to be true] in the *Topics* and again in the *Prior Analytics* (The *Development of logic,* by Kneale, p. 1)

II. ARISTOTELIAN LOGIC

Focusing inference as such rather than the varied values of the particular premisses used. Aristotle consciously looked for basic relationships of dependence that would guarantee the validity of conclusions and thus he originated the idea of a formal logic where truths are independent of subject-matter. Technically, through his use of variables and his sensitivity to logical syntax, he isolated many logical structures or forms and contributed important observations. He axiomatized his logical discoveries although he did not use the method of formalism or distinguish between laws and rules. No contribution to the science of Formal Logic is really comparable to Aristotle's.

His logical works, collectively called the *Organon (instrument or* science*)*, are the *Categories*, the *Toatcs* with its appendix *De Sophisticis Elenchis*, *De Interpretatione*, the *Prior Analytics* and the *Posterior Analytics*. The Organon covers Formal Logic, Metalogic and the logic of science; and in Formal Logic it contains not only Aristotle's major contribution but also a number of laws, rules and observations dealing with areas where development was later—the logic of classes, the theory of identity, the hypothetical syllogistic, the theory of relations, propositional logic and many-valued logic. There are very few questions completely untouched by him. However his major contributions in Formal Logic were to *Syllogistic Logic and Modal Logic*. With no more than a simple notation, consisting of a few Greek letters, he made direct, logical observations of methods of proof, classifying them as inductive and deductive; he formulated a complete axiomatized theory of the assertoric syllogism (having as its sub-structure a theory of the functioning of terms, the structure of predicative statements and the laws of opposition both between terms and between sentences—the latter presupposing his theory of quantification) and he made a major contribution to modal logic.

The explicit presentation of the Aristotelian system is to be found in the *De Interpretatione* (in which the formal study of opposition is central) and the *Prior Analytics* (whose theme is the syllogism). In this latter (and principal) work, logical technique makes an enormous advance with the appearance of term-variables (Aristotle simply uses letters as variables); indeed in one passage formulating what we know now as the principle of contraposition, Aristotle uses propositional variables: 'First then that it is not possible to draw a false conclusion from true premisses, is made clear by this consideration. If it is necessary that *B* should be when *A* is, it is necessary that *A* should not be when *B* is not. If then *A* is true, *B* must be true: otherwise it will turn out that the same thing both is and is not at the same time. But this is impossible.' (*Prior Analytics*, Book II, 2, 53^b 12; Oxford translation) The early work, the *Topics*, is also of great interest to the historian of Formal Logic although ostensibly it is simply a practical handbook on argumentation- For the theory of the predicables which gives unity to the treatise) is developed from distinctions between necessary and non-necessary predication and between convertible and non-convertible predication; these distinctions suggested many forms of valid argument to Aristotle in the *Topics* and. indeed, in approach and observation this work may be described as a rudimentary form of his system. Centuries later it contributed to the development of the medieval theory of *consequentiae*.

The remaining parts of the *Organon* are the *Categories* (a metaphysical treatise really: its inclusion by the compilers of the *Organon* was unfortunate for the history of formal logic), and the *Posterior Analytics* (a study, in applied logic, of scientific investigation and reasoning).

III. MEGARIAN-STOIC LOGIC

Aristotelian logic continued institutionally, as a school, but uncreatively. New work in logic begun by contemporaries of Aristotle in Megara and developed by the Stoics is the next creative contribution. Even the indirect and fragmen— tary knowledge we have of this pre-Christian Greek school shows how important it is in the history of all sections of logic. In Formal Logic, it developed propositional logic, making an explicit study of the functors—implication, disjunction, conjunction, equivalence (using not letters but ordinal numbers as propositional variables—an important help in identifying Stoic texts) It distinguished various types of implication and the Megarian, Philo, formally worked out the matrix (truth-table) for our material (their Philonian) implication, the idea of truth functional dependence being obviously quite clear to Philo. The logic of this school was worked out formalistically and was presented not as a body of laws but as a body of rules of inference schemata—a natural deduction system. The preference for this technique probably stems from the fact that the study of conditional propositions was central in this logic. While there is no complication in expressing a principle of syllogistic in the form of a conditional proposition: If *MaP* and if *SaM*, then *SaP* (this being a statement of what is so, a law), it is easier when dealing with material that is already conditional to list skeleton arguments (formats or schemata) and to say of each whether it is valid or not (this being a statement of what is permitted in one's system, a rule).

It is not possible to distinguish the contributions of the various members of this school (the Megarians. Eubulides, Diodorus Cronus, Philo; the Stoic, Chrysippus) But the Stoic. Chrysippus, seems to be the most important; indeed it was said 'If there were dialectic among the gods, it would be none other than that of Chrysippus.' He practised the *ars combinatoria* working at the number of complex propositions that could be constructed from simple ones. And he seems to have constructed a natural deduction system, with about five inference schemata as basic (indemonstrable) moods and a vast number of theorems. Details of the proofs of two of these theorems are given by Sextus Empiricus.

It is clear that this school developed very systematically the primary section of formal logic—propositional logic. In its work on Modal Logic it had a great advantage over Aristotle. Although in his analysis of modal statements, modal words modify the whole statement to which they are attached, he used his syllogistic as a basis for his investigation of modal reasoning The Megarian-Stoic school made this investigation from the correct basis of propositional logic, their logic of unanalysed propositions Unfortunately, only fragments of their work and discussions are extant.

It is quite possible that the hostility between this school and the Aristotelian school arose from claims that their logic was more fundamental than Aristotle's. Certainly, in ancient times the two logics were treated as alternatives, and their complementary character remained unappreciated.

Creative work in logic finished with the Stoic, Chrysippus of Soli (*c.*279—206 B.C.). From then until the fall of the Roman Empire the literature of logic consists of general handbooks and of commentaries on Aristotle. Galen (A.D.129-*c.* 199) is one of the best logicians of the period; Alexander of Aphrodisias (*c.* A.D.200), one of the best commentators on Aristotle, made explicit the distinction between form and matter. The last Roman logician, Boethius (*c.*480—524) is very important because his works were a primary source of Greek logic for the Middle Ages.

IV. MEDIEVAL LOGIC

Since the 1930s it is an accepted fact that in the strictest contemporary sense of *Formal Logic, Metalogic and Philosophy of Logic* the medieval period is most important and creative. The researeh that made this clear and established the shallowness of previous historical accounts of the period, however, confronted historians with a mass of unedited material from the twelfth and later centuries. Thus our survey must begin by noting, with Bochenski, that 'at the present time much less is known about the history of scholastic than of ancient logic ... the present state of research permits no general survey of the sources, growth and details of scholastic logic ... [even] with regard to the list of logicians we hardly ever know whether a logician was original or only a copyist.' *(A History of Formal Logic-*, pp. 148—9)

There is satisfactory evidence for the following general observations:

1. The period from 1150 to 1300 is a rich, creative one in logic; from then until the end of the Middle Ages may be described as a period of organisation and elaboration. Peter Abelard (1079—1142) exercised a major influence in the development of this period. Apart from transmitting familiar Aristotelian logic, he discussed and contributed in practically all the areas that were subsequently developed. It is only since the text of his *Dialectica* was printed in full, in 1956, that the magnitude and importance of his work was properly established. The following are some of the medieval logicians:

Albert the Great (1193—1280)
Robert Kilwardby (died 1279)
William of Shyreswood (died 1249)
Peter of Spain (died 1277) (The "best known Scholastic textbook in the later middle ages was his *Summulae Logicales*)
William of Occam (died 1349/50.)
John Buridan (died about 1358)
John of Crnubia' (Pseudo-Scotus) (wrote possibly during the first half of the fourteenth century)
Walter Burleigh (died about 1343) (His *De puritate artis logicae* is a very rich and pure example of metalogic)
Albert of Saxony (1316—1390)
Ralph Strode (wrote about 1370)

Paul of Venice (died about 1429) (His *Logica Magna*, a vast and systematic work, indicates the range of Scholastic discussions)
Peter Tartaret (wrote about 1480)
Stephanus de Monte

2. Scholastic logicians worked in the context of ordinary language. Characteristically, their work tends to be descriptive and metalogical. In the area of formal logic they have not an elaborate, artificial notation and their work has not the modern format of a simple *exhibition* of a system of laws or rules. And working, as they do, with vernacular language the content of the propositions they cite as examples often proves an unhelpful distraction, logically. However, their achievements in formal logic are very considerable indeed. They constructed a system of propositional logic that seems superior to the Megarian—Stoic one: since only fragments of Megarian—Stoic logic were available (transmitted) to them, this was done from the starting point of Aristotelian term-logic (their theory of consequences covered both propositional and term-logic consequences).

With regard to the assertoric syllogistic, the Aristotelian system was very completely formulated with the addition of mnemonics, a combinatorial technique for determining possible moods, and a formal development of indirect moods of the first figure (this was their way of treating the fourth figure, although the thirteenth century Jewish philosopher Albalag explicitly deals with it as a separate figure). With regard to the modal syllogistic there is a full formal development from the starting point of Aristotle's system on the basis of the distinction between propositions that are modal *de re* and those that are modal lie *de dicto*. For every Aristotelian mood Occam has four, according as both premisses are *de re* or both *dicto*, or that there is one of each. Including the assertoric proposition as a possible premiss, the total number of valid moods within his stipulations is about a thousand. Scholastics dealt also with 'oblique syllogisms' where indirect premisses are used (e.g. Every man is an animal, Socrates sees a man; therefore Socrates sees an animal). And Occam developed syllogisms with singular terms, equating singular terms with universal ones on the ground that they are names of classes, just like universal terms, only in this case unit classes. This was not a question of instantiation, substituting singulars for general values, but was a widening of the Aristotelian syllogistic.

'We do not know whether the Scholastics were acquainted with a more comprehensive logic of relations than Aristotle' (Bochenski, ibid., p. 231) but there is good evidence that they developed a number of logical theories outside the areas of propositional logic and syllogistic. For example, they dealt with the correctness of logical operations performed on propositions in the future and past tense, and on exponible propositions (i.e. propositions that are equivalent to a product or a sum of categoricals).

Thus working in the context of a living (Latin) language. Scholastic logicians achieved a formal knowledge of a wide variety of logical techniques, laws and rules. 'So even in the present incomplete state of knowledge, we can state with safety that in scholastic formal logic we are confronted with a very original and very fine variety of logic.' (Bochenski, ibid., p. 251)

V. From the End of the Middle Ages to the Development of Modern Mathematical Logic—A Period that is not Creative and in which a Distorted Version of Logic, the So-Called 'Classical' Logic, Developed

This (1450—1850) was a period of decline for logic: as part of the medieval tradition it was under attack; it survived only in an elementary form on the curriculum of most universities, and while many textbooks were current the best of them were summaries or commentaries on earlier work. Some of the text-books studied in this period were: Peter of Spain's *Summulae Logicales*; *Logica Hamburgensis* by Joachim Junge (1638); *Logica Fundamentis Suis a quibus hactenus collapsa fuerat*

Restituta by Arnold Geulincx (1662); *La Logique ou I'Art depenser by* Antoine Arnauld and pierre Nicole (1662)—it is often called the *Port Royal Logic*, its authors being leaders of the Port Royal movement: 'the eatstemological interest of the authors is shown by the division of the work into four parts which are said to treat respectively of conception, judgment, reasoning and method ... the general conception of logic which they expounded in this book was widely accepted and continued to dominate the treatment of logic by most philosophers for the next 200 years.' (Kneale's *Development of Logic,* pp. 316,320) John of St Thomas' *Ars Logica* is a very fine example of the commentaries on Aristotle and Aquinas written in this period.

Many reasons are given for the decline of logic. Renaissance scholars were repelled by its style and content; the new scientists did not look on logic as an instrument of discovery: indeed the study of formal necessity seemed singularly barren and in general writers such as Descartes and Bacon 'tended to make philosophers neglect formal logic in favour of the new study of heuristic methodology.' (Kneale: ibid., p. 310) Again the new mathematics which developed—algebra and analysis—were conceived as new reckoning procedures, not axiomatic systems governed by logical entailment (such as geometry); thus logic lost the close link with mathematics that was traditional to it and it was not until the nineteenth century, when mathematical methods achieved a high degree of formal abstraction, that mathematicians re-established the traditional association with logic. The result was the development of modern mathematical logic, including the recovery of the Formal Logic of Aristotle, the Stoics and the medievals.

The four hundred years from 1450—1850 saw not only the decline of formal logic but also the growth of a new, distorted logic, often called the 'classical' logic The *Port Royal Logic* (1662), J. N. Keynes *Formal Logic* (1906) and' Joseph's *Introduction to Logic* are representative- in the best possible sense of this classical logic. For in general, as Bochenski notes, it was 'poor in content, devoid of all deep problems, permeated with a whole lot of non-logical philo sophical ideas, psychologist in the worst sense'. (*A History of Formal Logic*, p 258) Although Kant expressed concern for the purity of logic, protesting agai-nst the presence of psychological, metaphysical and anthr-opological chapters in treatises on logic, it was his trans-cendentalism which 'began the production of the curious mixture of metaphysics and epistemology which was presented as logic by Hegel and the other Idealists of the nineteenth century' (Kneaie ibid , p 355)

However there were some mathematicians who concerned themselves with Logic during this period of its general decline—*Leibniz, Saccheri, Lambert, Ploucquet, Euler* (famous as popularizer of 'Leibniz's device of illustrating logical relations by geometrical analogies' [Kneale, p.349], *Gergonne* (who developed Euler's work on relations of extension), and *Sir William Hamilton* (who tried to work out a system for the quantification of predicates)

Of these it can be said that Leibniz is out of character with the period in being one of the greatest logicians of all time. This was only realized when the first really substantial catalogue of his writings was made in 1895, and it became clear that this philosopher, for whom Aristotle's syllogistic was 'one of the most beautiful discoveries of the human spirit', had visualized a basic science (neither mathematics nor logic as he knew them) which would be a general theory of structures and whose abstract formality would provide the possibility of various interpretations and isomorphic inferences Associated, in his mind, with this science, was a scientifically designed symbolism—a *characteristica universal is*—although he never produced any detailed plan of the new ideal language And a formalistic method must be included also, for he conceived 'the idea of an alphabet of human thought with which all possible thinkables, might be constructed by suitable combinations and by which reasoning might reduced to the quasi -mechanical operation of going through a list. His inspiration came from the *Ars Magna* of Raymond Lull and the *Computatio sive Logica* of Hobbes.

To the end of his life he thought of the theory of combinations as something more fundamental than ordinary logic' (Kneale, ibid, pp 325-6) In general indeed he conceived, as a possibility, formal technical procedures which, integrated into scientific investigation, would constitute a powerful logic of discovery.

He wrote in detail only two formal calculi—a geometrical calculus of similarity and congruence, and a calculus of identity and inclusion. Of the latter 'the most interesting feature is its abstract formality. What he produced was certainly much less than he hoped to produce . . . . [But] here for the first time there was an attempt to work out a piece of abstract mathematics, i.e. mathematics that is not specially concerned with space or numbers. The calculus covers in fact part of the field of logic, but it can be manipulated without regard to any interpretation ' (Kneale. ibid-, pp 344-5)

Finally, in this period, apart from philosophers in the Scholastic tradition (such as Cajetan and John of St Thomas) who wrote commentaries, *Bolzano* (1781-1848) interested himself in some of the logic of Leibniz, and John Stuart Mill (as we shall see in the history of metalogic) tried to expound logic as an empirical science, rejecting the whole of the traditional theory of formal logic.

VI. MODERN MATHEMATICAL LOGIC

A broader history will be given later. Here we are concerned, not with reflection on logic but simply with 'doing' logic.

Modern formal logic began with the calculus of classes of Boole: to this a similar calculus of relations was added by De Morgan. Hugh McColl seems to have been the first (1877) to construct a real propositional calculus. Two years later Frege's *Begriffsschrift* appeared and his full formalization has been developed and varied in many rigorous axiomatizations. especially by Russell. Lukasiewicz, Nicod, Wajsberg, Hilbert, Ackermann. Bernays, Meredith, Sobocinski, Jaskowski, Rasiowa. Tarski, Heyting. Many partial systems have been constructed—

notably that using equivalence as sole connective by Lesniewski.

The truth-table method is used informally by Frege in his *Begriffsschrift;*. in 1885 Peirce presented it as a general decision procedure. Through the work of Lukasiewicz and Post it has been used very extensively since the 1920s. Lukasiewicz was the first to introduce a three-valued propositional calculus. Independently of each other, he and Post generalized this to a many-valued propositional calculus and indeed Lukasiewicz introduced an infinitely many-valued one. Slupecki provided primitive bases for finitely many-valued propositional calculi.

Modern predicate logic began basically with the notion of proposiotional function and the use of quantifiers: these originated with Frege's *Begriffsschrift* (1879), although quantifiers were later introduced independently by C. S. peirce who was respondible for the terms 'quantifier' and 'quantification'. Early work on quantification was sone by Schröder, Peano and Russell. The axiomatic approach of Frege and Russell has not jbeen developed and varied here to the same extent as in propositional logic and nowadays natural deduction procedures are preferred. the Hilbert—Ackermann axiomatization (1928, modified in 1938) of first order predicate logic is, perhaps, the best known axiomatic system. Many important results, for predicate logic, were achieved by the work of Löwenheim and Skolem.

The development of a natural deduction approach stems from the work of Jaskowski and Gentzen whose pioneer articles were published in 1934. Modern modal logic owes its inception to the concern of C.I. Lewis that strict implication rather than material implication should be central in logic.

Although principally known for his metalogical proofs, Kurt Gödel has made many important contributions to formal logic as indeed (similarly) have Church, Quine, Carnap.

Chapter-3
Perspective on Metalogic

Chapter-3

I. INTRODUCTION

Broadly speaking, in formal logic one is 'doing' logic, in metalogic one is reflecting on what is already done: (1) making explicit concepts that are operational in formal logic and (2) establishing results or theorems about logical formulas and systems (these theorems being *metatheorems* since they are not reached *within* formal logic but are about it).

II. MAKING EXPLICIT CONCEPTS THAT ARE OPERATIONAL, IN FORMAL LOGIC

These concepts fall under two main categories when they are made explicit in metalogic: they are either syntactic or semantic. In classing and establishing expressions as being, e.g. *well-formed, derivable, proavle*, the formal logician works formalistically, i.e. without having to take into account the meaning of the expressions since his rules of operation refer solely to the material shape of symbols as in mathematics. Accordingly the concepts *well-formed, derivable. provable* are purely syntactic. On the other hand *consistency, entailment, logical* truth are conceptions which grow out of attention to the meaning of expressions and are called *semantic* notions. It is interesting to note that for finite sets of statements it can be proved that if *A* is syntactically derivable from it will also be semantically entailed by *S*; further that if *A* is logically true (being entailed by the null set of statements) it will have to be provable also since provable means being derivable from the null set of statements; and finally that the semantic notion of consistency (which is the possibility of an interpretation in which all the statements of a given set are true) has also a syntactic counterpart, syntactic consistency (predicated of a set of statements when no contradiction is derivable from it).

While a certain coincidence in range is expected of syntactic and semantic concepts, it is important to note that a theorem of Church (1936) showed that there can be no purely syntactic (i.e. mechanical, formalistic, automatic) way of determining, for all possible cases, whether the semantic properties of logical truth, entailment or consistency are present. Thus there is not and cannot be a syntactic procedure for the solution of all logical problems.

Modern formal logic operates at the syntactic level to a considerably greater extent 'had any other historical form of logic. A formalistic method predominates, it being a strict rule of mathematical logic that within the context of proof one must appeal to nothing but the forms of the symbols and the 'formal' rules of inference which apply to such rules. Of course formalism was not absent from earlier logics but mathematical logic is unique in laying it down as a general principle of logical method and in recognizing that its formalism consists essentially in the extension to logic of a method used for centuries in the language of numbers—calculation (so that sections of logic constructed purely syntactically are called calculi)

It has been humorously said that formalism puts us in the position of not knowing what one is saying nor whether what one is saying is true. But as Bochenski notes:

(1) The goal of formalism is always knowledge. A formalistic system only fulfils its task, therefore, if it is ultimately possible to interpret its results eidetically.

(2) The rules governing formalistic operations must make sense eidetically. They prescribe what we are to do and it must be possible to understand them, ultimately

(3) In practice, formalized systems are nearly always

developed by first establishing meaningful signs, then abstracting from their meaning and building up the system formalistically and finally giving a new inter pretation to the finished system. (This holds in particular for logic.)

(4) Although it would not be impossible to have a science whose system had no meaning except a syntactic one, this cannot be the case with logic. For logic has to provide rules of deduction for all indirect thinking and if its rules were not eidetically meaningful no deduction could be carried out. Accordingly most contemporary logicians hold that systems which do not permit any known eidetic interpretation are not really logic (*The Methods of Contemporary Thought*)

Formalism is a very useful method to use in conjunction with other methods, for the following reasons.

(a) in very complicated matters our eidetic understanding may break down and be helped on by formalistic processes:

(b) the use of formalism (which handles signs according to their written shape) help to exclude tacit presuppositions about objects;

(c) the process of formalistic deduction is suitable for delimiting and clarifying primitive concepts or terms;

(d) a system that is developed purely formalistically may permit of many interpretations and therefore of many uses.

Bochenski points out that the formalism of modern logic is connected with 'a deeper and more revolutionary innovation. All the other varieties of logic known to us make use of an *abstractive* method; the logical theorems are gained by abstraction from ordinary language. Mathematical logicians proceed in just the opposite way, *first constructing* purely formal systems, and later looking for an interpretation in everyday speech. This process is not indeed always purely applied; and it would not be impossible to find something corresponding to it elsewhere. But at least since Boole, the principle of such construction is consciously and openly laid down, and holds sway throughout the realm of mathematical logic.' (*A History of Formal Logic*, p. 266) Model Theory is the modern theory of interpretations of formal systems.

One can see how very important it is to distinguish, in modern times, between a *logic* and the *calculus* which it interprets and manipulates. 'A logic will always depend upon some intuitive techniques, while a calculus will be defined as an axiomatic system whose construction can be made entirely formal. Calculi as such are uninterrupted, but a calculus associated with a logic will always be chosen because it may receive interpretation (or interpretations) useful to the employment of the logic in solving its range of problems.' (Ackerman. *Introduction to Many-Valued Logics*, p. 3) It is of the essence of a logic to know what it is dealing with, taking account of the eidetic meaning of expressions and rules (i.e. what they refer to and express). A logic cannot be constructed like a calculus, purely syntactically, on the basis-of operational meaning only (i.e. knowing how to use symbols and how to operate syntactical rules).

III. ESTABLISHING METATHEOREMS

The metatheoretic part of reflection on formal logic establishes results or theorems about logical formulas and systems. It is precisely a theory of those sentences, constructed in logical language, which are used to express truths of logic. Thus it requires a special metalanguage which names and talks about the expressions used in formal logic. These expressions 'must be formulas of a *formal language*, i.e. a "language" that can be completely specified without any reference at all, direct or indirect, to the meaning of the formulas of the "language". It was by the insistence on this requirement that the metatheory of logic, after a long and interesting but desultory history of over two thousand years, came in this century to yield exact and new and deep results and to give promise of systematic growth.' (Geoffrey Hunter, *Metalogic: An Introduction to the Metatheory of Standard First-Order Logic*, p. 3)

However, it is important to note that one is using metalanguage when one gives even the simplest explanations, using words such as *term, variable proposition, predicate, rule, deduction, system, syntactic category, truth function*, which are all metalogical in character. Thus it is useful to distinguish a general (vernacular) discussion of concepts and principles that are operational in logic, from a technical, formalized presentation of metatheorems. Both use metalanguage whether by adapting English, e.g. or by inventing a special symbolism), both reach results (which may be called metatheorems) and both attempt to validate these results (giving proofs). But the mode of procedure and communication is so different that one can very profitably use the word *melalogic* for the whole section of logic and *metatheory* for its *highly* formalized study of properties of logical systems, in particular of their deductive apparatus. The metatheory of predicate logic is considerably more complex than that of sentential logic and, of course, beyond these sections of elementary logic there lie the highly technical fields of, e.g. higher-order predicate calculi and various non standard logics.

The most basic metatheoretic work is concerned with whether sections of logic are essentially consistent (not admitting of internal contradictions), complete (containing all the truths of their domain) and decidable (possessing a mechanical decision procedure for discriminating truth and falsity). Metatheoretic proofs involve reasoning that is not exemplified within formal logic itself, for while a proof *within* a formal system satisfies purely syntactic requirements a proof *about* a formal system must be a meaningful justification of a true statement about the system. Here Gödel's methods are the best known.

IV. PERSPECTIVE ON METALOGIC

'Logic from Aristotle to Gödel has had three ends in view. The first is to explicate in precise terms various intuitive notions of "logical truth". The second is to codify, with the aid of formal systems and other devices, those statements or formulas that are to count as logical truths. The third is to apply these systems and devices as a means of testing the formal validity of certain arguments and inferences in the sciences and in everyday life.

'Modern logic, since Frege, has sought to achieve these ends by exploiting a variety of mathematical methods and notions, in particular that of formal system. The creation of the formal disciplines of syntax and semantics by Carnap and Tarski added new tools and sharpened older ones. The syntactical notions—formal system, consistency, deducibility and theory—on which the original systematization of modern logic by Frege and Russell primarily relied have now been paired with their semantical counterparts; interpretation (simultaneous), satisfiability, consequence and validity. The combined use of syntactical and semantical characterizations has resulted in a clearer view of logic itself and of its role in formalizing mathematical and other types of theories.' (Albert Blumberg article on Modern Logic, *Encyclopedia of Philosophy*, vol. 5. p. 32)

This 'clearer view of logic' must be built up at two levels of reflection, that of metalogic and that of a philosophy of logic. ln the latter one seeks to form an ultimate definition of logic and to situate it precisely in the corpus of humon sciencc and wisdom. In the former one seeks the kind ol clarification that does not commit one to extralogical, philosophical positions and remains closer to the experience of actually doing logic. This experience brings logic into view as a system which is both syntactical and semantic in character, which pervades every other system of thought as inference roules and which has unique properties and problems In our treatment of metalogic we will be concerned to explicate the technical details of this experience, presenting (a) the main concepts and principles that are operational in formal logic, paying particular attention to its concepts of formal language, paradox, meaning, truth, derivability, system, class, predication and the logistic concept of mathematics; (b) the fundamental metatheorems which are concerned with consistency, completeness and decidability. These metatheorems are conveniently presented in an examination of the rigour and range of proof in elementary formal logic.

Our first concern, however, is to present the reader with a survey of the actual development, historically, of self-reflective logic. The position at present is that while there is reasonably exact and complete information on the deliberations, problems and conclusions of modern mathematical logicians, there is not comparable information with regard to the Greek or medieval logicians. We have already seen however that the formal logics of the modern and earlier periods correspond substantially and that the 'classical' logic current from 1500-1900 is alien not only to modern mathematical logic but equally to the logic of the earlier periods. It seems best then to make an historical survey by beginning with the perspective of modern mathematical logicians, then integrating our fragmentary knowledge of the earlier periods within the modern framework of metalogical ideas.

Chapter-4

An Historical Survey of Mathematical Logic

Chapter-4

MODERN MATHEMATICAL LOGIC IN PERSPECTIVE

The development of this logic and the endeavour to set it in perspective may be substantially presented through the work of Boole, Frege, Russell and Wittgenstein.

I. George Boole (1815-064). This English mathematician and logician made his contribution in *The Mathematical Analysis of Logic, being an Essay towards a Calculus of Deductive Reasoning* (1847). An article by him entitled 'The Calculus of Logic' appeared, the following year, in the *Cambridge and Dublin Mathematical Journal* and is valuable in being less technical and in underlining the human perspective of his work. His later book. *An Investigation of the Laws of Thought in which are founded the Mathematical Theories of Logic and Probability* (1859) is often described as the authoritative statement of his system: however while his treatment of probability is a new application of his system, there is no new development of its formal character.

Boole saw that the force of argument in any particular context derived partly from the particular concepts involved, but that it was also true that argument in all contexts subserved a common higher logic. His work was directed towards disengaging this logic, formalizing the principles of operation of the human mind, the subjective aspect of human rationality. He believed that these principles are as rigorously mathematical as are the laws which govern particular quantitative conceptions such as those of number and magnitude:

> It appeared to me that, although Logic might be viewed with reference to the idea of quantity, it had also another and a deeper system of relations. If it was lawful to regard it from *without*, as connecting itself through the medium of Number wild the intuitions of Space and Time, it was

lawful also to regard it from *within*, as based upon facts of another order which have their abode in the constitution of the Mind. (*The Mathematical Analysis of Logic*, Preface)

In one respect, the science of Logic differs from all others; the perfection of its method is chiefly valuable as an evidence of the speculative truth of its principles (Ibid.)

Boole perceived an analogy between the operations of logic and those of algebra. Using the symbolism of algebra he developed a formal system on the basis of laws which governed the combination of these symbols and not any content they might have. The argumentative processes of the system were disengaged from particular contexts and he showed how the system could be interpreted as a class logic, a propositional logic or a calculus of probábilities. He says:

They who are acquainted with the present state of the theory of Symbolical Algebra, are aware, that the validity of the process of analysis does not depend upon the interpretation of the symbols which are employed. but solely upon the laws of their combination. Every system of interpretation which does not affect the truth of the relations supposed, is equally admissible, and it is thus that the same process may, under one scheme of interpretation, represent the solution of a question on the properties of numbers, under another, that of a geometrical problem, and undir a third, that of a problem of dynamics or optics ... But the full recognition of the consequences of this important doctrine has been, in some measure, retarded by accidental circumstances .. The expression of magnitude, or of operations on magnitude, has been the express object for which the symbols of Analysis have been invented, and for which their laws have been investigated. Thus the abstractions of the modern Analysis, not less than the ostensive diagrams of the ancient Geometry, have encouraged the notion, that Mathematics are essentially, as well as actually, the Science of Magnitude ... That to the existing forms of Analysis a quantitative

> inter pretation is assigned, is the result of the circumstances by which these forms were determined, and is not to be construed into a universal condition of Analysis. It is upon the foundation of this general principle, that I propose to establish the Calculus of Logic and that 1 claim for it a place among the acknowledged forms of Mathematical Analysis, regardless that in its object and in its instruments it must at present stand alone . . The laws we have to examine are the laws of one of the most important of our mental faculties. The mathematics we have to construct are the mathematics of the human intellect. (Ibid, Introduction)

Thus the essence of his contribution was to conceive a method of deriving consequences which did not draw argumentative force from a context and to conceive a formal system, then, as being constructed, rather than abstracted from a context. In papers from his later life he speaks, of revising his book, *An investigation of the Laws of Thought* and in one paper distinguishes his Calculus of Logic from a higher logic which would be 'the Philosophy of *all* thought that is expressible in signs, whatever the object of that thought'. Kneale (*The Development of Logic*, p 407) says. 'he was on a wrong track when he began to look for the basis of logic in the constitution of the human intellect. .(indeed) it was Boole's work which showed clearly by example that logic could be studied profitably without any references to the processes of our mind He believed no doubt that he was dealing with laws of thought in some psychological sense of that ambiguous expression, but he was in fact dealing with some of the most general laws of thinkables.' However, 'thinkable' is a bipolar word and seems to include a reference to a subjective aspect of some kind. Boole's actual work, so original in fomalistic method, and his use of the words 'constitution of the human mind', provide strong support for the view that he is not psychologistic, that the subjective depth of his reference, left undefined, is below the level of phenomenal, psychic thinking.

II. Gettlob Frege (1848-1925). The most important date in the history of modern mathematical logic is 1879, when his *Begriffsschrift*—'concept writing' (Austin's translation), 'ideography' (Jourdain's translation)—was published. The book itself was neither widely read nor appreciated at the time and the ideas in it came to be known and understood only after many years and piecemeal through the writings of others. Bertrand Russell noted (*Introduction to Mathematical Philosophy*, 1919. p. 25): 'In spite of the great value of this work, I was, I believe, the first person who ever read it—more than twenty years after its publication.'

It was an influential work in philosophy generally, again very indirectly because, apart from Husserl. Russell and Wittgenstein, for most of this century philosophers simply have not been acquainted with Frege. But Frege made a very modern and important departure from Cartesian tradition- For him Philosophy does not begin with a theory of knowledge and with a methodic demolition of scepticism. It begins with logic. If we construct our logic properly, its language and rigour of proof will ramify, controlling and guaranteeing every other discipline.

Logic is something that is constructed. It begins in the Fregean sense when you say: I must construct a language able to signify, exclusively, the forms (simple, complex and systematic) of thought—where thought denotes not thinking (thought as a psychic vitality) but that which is signifie by, or contained in, thought. Frege rejected psychologism: logic is not concerned with the mental ideas and images which words may arouse in the mind of a speaker, hearer, writer or reader: it is nol concerned with the elements, organization or alteration of consciousness, and psychic realities should not enter basically into any precise and adequate theory of meaning. A logic-language will symbolize precisely what is gerimne to exact proof, to the inferential sequence as such; it will process conceptual content rather than formalize personal thinking.

Frege felt that meaning (e.g. of a remark or thought) is

best handled as an entity which ii neither psychic nor physical; similar to both in being factual it is different from both in being timeless. Sentences in many languages may have the same sense. 'And the sense is properly just that which matters to us. The sentence has a value for us through the sense which we apprehend in it, and which we recognize as the same in the translation too. This sense I call "thought" (*Gedanke*). What we prove is not the sentence but the thought. And it makes no difference what language we use for that purpose.' (*Uber Logik und Mathematik*, 1914) 'The thought belongs neither to my inner world as an idea nor yet to the outer world of material, perceptible things ... Thoughts are by no means unreal but their reality is of quite a different kind from that of things ... A property of a thought will be called inessential which consists in, or follows from the fact that, it is apprehended by a thinker.' (*The Thought: A Logical Inquiry*) Here we have meaning as something independent of any particular language and of any particular mind; it can be called thought not in the sense of that which is produced by this or that mind, but in the sense of that which can be understood by any mind and is the same for every mind—it may be named 'objective thought' and it is the *lekton* of Stoic doctrine.

Whatever we may feel about Frege's three-level semantic approach to language (in which there were three elements, the world we speak about, our language and objective meanings), it is quite clear that his conception of logic included a complete rejection of psychologism and implied that the most basic need of logic is a language of objective thought, able to symbolize all those things and only those things that are germane to exact proof. He devised a language consisting of a few primitives and a simple grammar and in his system demonstrated its expressive power, range and flexibility.

The symbolism was two-dimensional and would have the following appearance for the expression, *It is not the case that for every value of x, if fx then gx:*

The primitive symbols were:

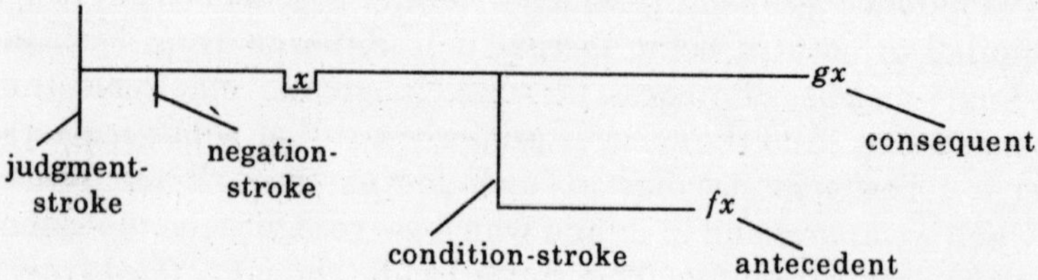

1. Symbols to designate objects. Roman letters in Roman and Gothic script were used.These symbols covered both individual constants and individual variables.

2. Symbols to express concepts, i.e. symbols that were a formalized expression of concepts. Greek letters were generally used.

3. A symbol expressing the concept of negation—the negation stroke.

4. Variable notation for expressing generality—i.e. quantifier-variable notation. The symbol was a concavity ⌐⌊x⌋⌐ containing the variable.

5. A symbol to express the antecedent—consequence sequence in proof. The symbol was the condition stroke.

6. A symbol to express the activity of asserting that the thought expressed is true. This is an element conveyed in language, a force it has as an utterance. It does not affect the truth-conditions of the sentence: it is something *done* with a sentence. We may use sentence otherwise, e.g. to give a definition, ask a question. Assertion is symbolized by the judgment stroke (definition by $\vdash$)

Frege's grammar is very simple. The formation of an expression is such that some symbols can be replaced by others. The 'part of the expression that shows itself invariant under such replacement is called the function, and the replaceable part, the argument of the function'. (*Bergriffsschrift*) The part of the expression that is the function may be e.g. a predicate or a relational expression and it may require one place or many places for arguments Each place or gap is marked by brackets and a variable or constant appears within the brackets to complete a sentence. With the quantifying symbolism attached to it this function-argument grammar is very powerful and flexible for formalizing propositions

At this point three observations may be made :

1. Frege's wort in constructing a language for logic created in him a basic distract of natural vernacular language. He saw that power and flexibility of expression did not involve (as was commonly supposed) the kind of complexity that vernacular languages have Further, where logicians before him had failed to solve the problem of expressing generality by studying the devices of everyday language, he had succeeded by freeing himself from such guidance. Thus the fact that in everyday language one could form a proper name without a reference, or utter a well-formed expression that was neither true nor false— this was not for him a logical problem: it indicated how basic are the defects of everyday language

2. Frege's next step was to apply his technique of expressing propositions and his method of proof and systematization to the important area of numerical reasoning in Mathematics (From some basic postulates he had already derived and organized a large number of logical principles) In doing this he became convinced that there are no basic notions or axioms peculiar to arithmetic— concepts and principles within logic are sufficient to generate it Subsequently, his main works were devoted to giving an account of this logistic view both without the use of his symbolic language (in *Die Grundlagen der Arithmetik*, 1884) and through the construction of a strict formal system (in *Die Grundgesetze der Arithmetik:* vol 1, 1893. vol 2, 1903) The preface to this latter work is a very precise statement of Frege's logic Its second volume was published in 1903, ten years after the first. While it was in the press, Frege received a letter from Russell informing him of contradiction in his system. Frege modified an axiom as an *ad hoc* device without being satisfied with his system In 1923, two years

before, his death, he was quite convinced that his logistic approach had been a mistake, that he and others had been over influenced and misled by the theory of classes He conceived the possibility that geometry was fundamental in mathematics.

3 Frege's formula language gave rise to some very interesting and fundamental problems In the course of dealing with them he developed important metalogical theories:

(a) His theory of object (the correlate of proper name) and concept (the correlate of the functional feature of an expression). This will be discussed in the treatment of predication.

(b) His theory of the meaning of words: 'it is only in the context of a sentence that a word has meaning'. (*Grundlagen*) This appears in Wittgenstein as the principle that it is only in the utterance of a sentence that we make 'a move in the language-game'. The meaning of a word consists in its contribution to this linguistic act, to determining the truth-conditions of the sentence.

(c) His theory of sense and reference which plays an important role in modern semantics and in contemporary logical and philosophical discussion of intension and extension. A remarkable feature of this theory, which focuses what an expression designates and what it expresses, is that it identifies the reference of a *sentence* with its truth-value. The theory will be discussed in the chapter on the nature of a proposition.

(d) His theory of assertion as the force carried by an utterance.

All the essentials of modern metalogic are in Frege. His basic contribution was the theory and practice of concept-writing, the idea and the model of primary logical language and of exact logical proof. The best measure of this contribution is the logistic use of it in *Die Grundlagen der Arithmelik* and *Die Grundgesetze der Arithmetik,* and in the *Principia Mathematica* of Russell and Whitehcead.

III. Bertrand Russell (1872-1970). In his autobiography

Russell describes how about 1898 1 was beginning to emerge from the bath of German idealism in which I had been plunged by McTaggart and Stout [at Cambridge]. I was very much assisted in this process by Moore, of whom at that time I saw a great deal. It was an intense excitement, after having supposed the sensible world unreal, to be able to believe again that there really were such things as tables and chairs. But the most interesting aspect to me was the logical aspect. I was glad of think that relations are real, and I was interested to discover the dire effect upon metaphysics of the belief that all propositions are of the subject-predicate form.' (*Autobiography*, vol. I, pp. 134-5) Ever afterwards he was strongly realist: it is the business of philosophy to deal with the world of fact, to say what there is in the world, what it is like. There are direct relations of the knowing subject to objects, providing basic knowledge by acquaintance. With regard to Russell's logic, Gödel observes: 'What strikes me as surprising in this field is Russell's pronouncedly realistic attitude, which manifests itself in many passages of his writings. "Logic is concerned with the real world just as truly as Zoology, though with its more abstract and general features," he says in his *Introduction to Mathematical Philosophy* (edition of 1920, p.169). It is true, however,, that this attitude has been gradually decreasing in the course of time and also that it always was stronger in theory than in practice.'

We have seen Frege's objective of inventing a primary language processing, precisely, objective thought- Both he and Frege believed that a logical calculus constructed from such a language would do for theoretical mathematics what the decimal system of numbers had done for numerical computation. Their belief echoed the expectations of Leibniz, he says he had developed his calculus of reasoning to a large extent and that in time a few select scientists would be able to so develop it that 'humanity would have a new kind of an instrument increasing the powers of reason far more than any optical instrument has ever aided the power of vision'. Frege indeed uses the same metaphor: 'I believe that I can best make the relation of my ideography to ordinary language clear if I compare it to that which the microscope has to the eye. Because of the range of its possible uses and the versatility with which it can adapt to the most diverse circumstances, the eye is far superior to the microscope. But, as soon as scientific goals demand great sharpness of resolution, the eye proves to be insufficient. The microscope, on the other hand, is perfectly suited to precisely such goals, but that is just why it is useless for all others.' (Preface to *Begriffsschrift*) We have seen Frege *use* his language to express, prove and systematize the propositions of two basic sciences—logic and mathematics.

Russell was with Frege in departing from the abstractive tradition of logic: the best logic would be a constructed logic. Both Russell and the early Wittgenstem have been criticized as being preoccupied with the theory of a perfect language. It is certainly true that a great deal of attention was devoted by both to problems of a primary language and to a philosophy of it (variously called 'philosophical grammar', 'clarification of language') Russell's seareh for the perfect and minimal language followed from his constructionist method. The kind of Russellian analysis called reduction aims at reducing the number of terms in scientific philosophizing to a minimum. Only those things with which we have immediate experience (by sense or introspection) are to be named by primitive terms. And we should not be trying to systematically infer the existence of entities not directly experienced; instead we should construct classes of the genuinely primitive entities and develop a system accordingly. 'The supreme maxim in scientific philosophizing,' he said (1918), 'is this-whenever possible logical constructions are to be substituted for inferred entities' In constructional systems 'he language has to be carefully and logically structured so that its primitive and class levels are clearly distinguished and that all sentences can be translated into primitive symbolism.

Thus in various areas in which Russell makes contributions

in philosophy, logic and mathematics you tend to get not ordinary argumentation but *carefully built up language systems*—'constructional systems'—which are em pineal also in that their basic terms refer only to immediately experienced entities. This empirical data is provided by careful analytical procedures. His objective always is to construct a system toased on a union, at the level of basic, atomic propositions between empirical data and logical form, the development thereafter of the system is extremely logical.

With regard to his own primary language, the problems he worked on and his philosophical grammar:

1. Russell is clear on the fact that constructing a language involves one in *ontological commitments*. These are presented in presuppositions we have to make about the word and in our criteria for an ideal language For him the most important requirement for an ideal language is an empirical one, formulated, in 'the principle of acquaintance': Every proposition which we can understand must be composed wholly of constituents with which we are acquainted. Nothing is said or spoken in his language by any expression which cannot be reduced or brought back to such a proposition.

2. For Russell, Logic is essentially concerned with *implication*, the objective involvement of evidence and conclusion which justifies inference: 'Where we validly infer one proposition from another we do so in virtue of a relation which holds between the two propositions whether we perceive it or not: the mind, in fact, is as purely receptive in inference as common sense supposes it to be in perception of sensible objects.' (*Principles of Mathematics,* 1903) Implication and the correlates of other primitive symbols in logic are indefinable. The discussion of these indefinables is the chief part of philosophical logic, this discussion being 'the endeavour to see clearly and to make others see clearly, the entities concerned, in order that the mind may have that kind of acquaintance with them which it has with redness or the taste of a pineapple'. (*Principles of Mathematics*) Later he preferred to-become acquainted with

implication through defining it as 'Either not *p* or *q*' or, like Sheffer and Nicod, in terms of the stroke functor.

3. In summary his logical grammar is: Sentences are built up (a) through functors that form sentences from names—*fa.* Here *f* is formative; *a*, the individual constant, is logically structureless: its function is to pick out an individual, that is all; (b) through functors that form sentences from verbs—quantifiers: $(x)fx$; (c) through functors that form sentences from sentences— $.p \supset q$; $(x)\ fx \supset \sim(EX)\sim fx$....... There can be indefinite development of sentences from functors that already form sentences.

4. Quantification is the logical beginning of the number series. Quantifiers are functors of functors-that-form-sentences-out-of-names, and numbers are implicit components of such functors. For $\sim(Ex)$ (*x* is a man) we could write 'For no x is *x* a man': (*Ox*) (*x* is a man). And we can continue the series. 'At least one *x* is a man' | (*Ex*) (*x* is a man) | combined with 'At most one *x* is a man' (For .some *x*: for any *y*, if *y* is human, *y* is identical with *x* translates into 'Exactly one thing is a man': (*Ix*) (*x* is a man). Similarly, 'At least two things are men' (For some *x* and for some y, x is a man, *y* is a man and *x* is not identical with *y*) combined with 'At most two things are men' (For some *x* and for some *y*, for any *z* if *z* is a man *z* is either identical with x or identical with y) translates into (*2x*) (*x* is a man)—for exactly 2-*x's*, *x* is a man, exactly two things are men. This is a very natural translation and analysis of the number series. Unfortunately before he deals with arithmetic in his system, Russell has added to his primary language a secondary 'class-language' of devices used in common speech. This language obscures the basic naturalness of his analysis of number. Gödel notes that the concept of class needs to be made very much clearer in mathematical logic; Frege came to regret its dominant position in modern logic.

5. We have seen that Russell had to be concerned with the indefinable', of his system. In his language there is no way of constructing *names* precisely because, logically, they are

structureless. A genuine proper name (Russell usually takes the demonstrative 'this' as an example) contributes nothing to the meaning of a sentence except the identification of some individual as subject. It picks out an individual; it does not contribute to what is being said: it is logically structureless. But in natural language we seem to construct proper names out of concept words in descriptive phrases like 'the golden mountain'. 'the present King of France' (which have no reference value), and 'the author of *Waverly*'. Russell's theory of descriptions makes the point that when translated into primary language such phrases are seen not to be proper names at all. The sentences with such phrases have not any subject: they are statements not about individuals but about functions. Thus the golden mountain does not exist' translates into 'For all values of x, the propositional function "x is golden and a mountain" is false.' 'Scott is the author of *Waverly'* translates into 'For all values of x. the propositional function "x wrote *Waverly*" is equivalent to the propositional function "x is Scott".'

6. Russell's theory of types was designed to explain paradoxes as being rooted in the permissiveness of natural language grammar, and to prevent, in his language system, the possibility of well-formed expressions being logically meaningless (neither true nor false). Gödel notes that the reason given by Russell 'is very similar to Frege's, who, in his system, already had assumed the theory of simple types for functions, but failed to avoid the paradoxes, because he operated with classes (or rather functions in extension) without any restriction. This reason is that (owing to the variable it contains) a propositional function is something ambiguous (or, as Frege says, something unsaturated, wanting supplementation) and therefore can occur in a meaningful proposition only in such a way that this ambiguity is eliminated (e.g. by substituting a constant for the variable or applying quantification to it). The consequences are that a function cannot replace an individual in a proposition, because the latter has no ambiguity to be removed, and that functions with different kinds of arguments (i.e. different ambiguities) cannot replace each other; which is the essence of the theory

of simple types.' The same point is made from a more nominalistic: viewpoint in the second edition of *Principia Malhematica* and in *Meaning and Truth*: propositional functions are presented as constructed out of sentences by leaving one or more constituents undetermined. They can be combined in forming propositions 'only if they "fit together", i.e if they are of appropriate types'.

Russell's isomorphism (theory of a picture relationship between sentence and fact got a classic presentation and complete analysis in Wittgenstein's *Tractatus*.

In the historic *Principia Marhematica* he effected, more satisfactorily than Frege, the reduction of mathematics to logic. With the help of A. N. Whitehead in Cambridge he worked on this book over a period of about ten years. His Theory of Descriptions (1905) and Theory of Types (1906) were important moments of progress in dealing with baffling difficulties. 'I worked at ... [the mechanical job of writing the book out from ten to twelve hours a day for about eight months in the year, from 1907 to 1910. The manuscript became more and more vast, and every time that I went out for a walk I used to be afraid that the house would catch fire and the manuscript get burnt up. It was not, of course, the sort of manuscript that could be typed or even copied ... The strain of unhappiness combined with very severe intellectual work, in the years from 1902 till 1910, was very great ... In the end the work was finished but my intellect never quite recovered from the strain. I have been ever since definitely less capable of dealing with difficult abstractions than I was before' (*Autobiography*, pp. 152-3) The development and powerful use of primary logical language in the *Principia* is such that Russell must be ranked with Frege as a founder of modern mathematical logic.

Russell describes his philosophical development as 'a gradual retreat from Pythagoras', from the world of mathematical truth which has sustained him in fervor, exultation and peace for much of his early life. Turning more and more to the world of human problems he carried everywhere, however, his realist, constructionist and primary language approach. His thought moved powerfully, utilizing logical technique and syntax, always seeking answers that had the quality of science. He was a humane representative of our scientific and computer culture which owes so much to the development of mathematical logic.

IV. Ludwig Wittgenstein (1889-1951). Russell said of him- 'His thought had an almost incredible degree of passionately intense penetration, to which I gave whole hearted admiration.' Bearing in mind this unique quality of his thought, it is no small thing to say (yet it is perfectly true), that the core of his life's work—both scientific and positivist in spirit—was to study what exactly is given in language and in thought. A remark in the early part of his life (*Notebooks* 1914-1916) is apt 'My whole task consists in explaining the nature of sentences—how is it that a combination of words succeeds in *saying* something, in *telling someone something;* what is *'saying*, what exactly is *said?'*

Only his *Tractatus Logico-Philosophicus* (80 pages long) (1921) and a short paper 'Some remarks on Logical Form' were published his lifetime. Although so much of his philosophical and logical work was done at Cambridge, only two collections of lecture notes, the one in a blue folder, the other in a brown (published accordingly as *The Blue and Brown Books*), are without a German original. The main work of his later life is *Philosophical Investigations.*

The development from the logic of the *Tractatus* to the logic of the *Philosophical Investigations* involves a distinct change in the direction and climate of his thinking. One might say in summary that with the later Wittgenstein the whole development of mathematical logic is seen, philo- sophically and humanly, in perspective.

The following is a systematic presentation, first of his early work, then of the development of his later thought:

1.1 WITTGENSTEIN'S EARLY WORK (THE TRACTATUS):

1.11: The logic of speech

1.111: In investigating and understanding the logic of speech one is also investigating and understanding the logic of the world and of thought. All three occupy the same logical space, are governed by the same logical conditions and possibilities. 'The limits of my language mean the limits of my world.' (*Tractatus*, 5.61) It is logically meaningless to question the correspondence between language, thought and the world: we can never get into a position outside logical space from which to ask if all three have the same logical space.

Thus the logical structure of language provides the complete set of possibilities for the world: what actually occurs in the world is given only in experience of course. Logical possibilities together with everything that is the case and everything that is not the case set boundaries to the real world. Linguistically, therefore, the logical operator, *negation*, and the predicate, *true*, play a large part in showing boundaries. 'The comparison of language and reality is like that of a retinal image and visual image: to the blind spot nothing in the visual image seems to correspond, and thereby the boundaries of the blind spot determine the visual image—just as true negations of atomic propositions determine reality.' (*Notebooks*, p. 95)

1.112: Wittgenstein is concerned with what is *given* in *language*; accordingly he presents the world as made up not of elements and things but of facts. A fact is what is the case. i.e. that which verifies or falsifies a proposition. There must be something in the world in terms of which a given proposition is either true or false—this is 'fact' for him, and the world as it enters into this philosophy is factual reality and not the substantialist world of traditional philosophy. Each fact is the occurrence or non-occurrence of a state of affairs. The latter is the primary datum of language: it is a combination of objects but, in factual reality, objects never occur except as constituents of states of affairs. Similarly a name occurs meaningfully only in a sentence construct.: which is the simplest linguistic act.

1. 113: A sentence is a picture: it shows its sense. A true sentence shows how things are: what the picture elements stand for are related in the same way as those elements: they have *form* in common since the sentence is a true picture. All sentences—true or false—have logical form and show the form of reality, that which the pian of reality allows.

Not everything can be pictured, not everything therefore can be- said. It would be necessary to gel to a view point outside language in order to discuss, e.g. the model character of language or its logical form.

The cardinal problem in philosophy is finding out what can be said in propositions—i.e. in language—and what cannot be said but can only be shown. Thus the agreement of a statement with reality is not logically demonstrable; it is seen, it manifests itself. 'A proposition *shows* its sense. A proposition *shows* how things stand *if* it is true. And it says *that* they do so stand.' (*Tractatus*, 4.022)

1.1.14: Reality is mirrored, depicted, most clearly in logically formed language. It is the business of logic to provide the rules by which what can be said is said clearly. What is given in everyday language is actual situations; these are very complicated and the everyday use of words is impure, so very often the real situation seems opaque or is not properly seen. What is given in logical language is not the factual occurrence of a situation but the possibilities of a situation actually occurring. While the variable signs in logical notation represent things and facts, logical constants have no referential meaning; their meaning is logical consisting in their possibilities of being true and false, truth-tables being an appropriate technique for their definition. Logical truths do not share in the uncertainties of reality and do not give us an experience of, or information about, the actual and thus contingent states of affairs. Again, every deduction proceeds by logical rule unaffected by real situations. Thus while logical language achieves clarification, the formal systems it builds up represent possible rather than actual reality. 'Logic must look after itself.' (*Tractatus*, 5.473)

There are no logical rules for verifying statements about actual states of affairs. There are only practical directions and the verified statements fall within natural science. If a verifying test cannot *in principle* be carried out, there are no truth possibilities and the statement accordingly is void of sense.

1.115. In determining the *limits* of what can be thought or said, in defining what can be 'given' in thought or speech, one indicates or shows what cannot be said. He uses the word *mystical* for that which manifests itself in and through the logical exposure that nothing can be said about it.

The mystical is not something in addition to other things but the bounded nature of thought and language which gives the limits also of what cannot be thought or said. Thus it becomes apparent in clear thinking and meaningful language without falling within the bounds of either.

The mystical is a solution to the riddle of life in a unique sense of the word *solution*. Neither question nor answer about the meaning of life and of the universe can be genuine since they cannot occur within the bounds of language and thought. The mystical is not given within these hounds either to raise an intelligible problem or to clarify or prove something factual. But it shows itself, is manifested through the logical awareness that nothing can be said about it.

When we view the world as a whole, we reach beyond its bounded nature, but we cannot move logically or linguistically. Logical thought and mystic vision can never form one perspective.

1.116: Philosophy is an activity not a system of doctrine. It is a clarification of language with a view to determining what can be said (the tautologies of logic and mathematics, combined with the verified statements of natural science) and what cannot be said. 'What we cannot speak about we must pass over in silence.' (*Tractatus*, 7)—his metaphysics consists of a silent pointing towards what cannot be said.

1.2: HIS LATER WORK (FROM 1929 WHEN HE RETURNED TO CAMBRIDGE)

1.21: He no longer conceives language as being always descriptive (specifically a reflection of things), or measures it in terms of a logical model, or believes that there is a uniform structure in every language. He came to appreciate more and more the many ways in which language serves human life and the limitations of logical language which lacks points of contact and friction with actual situations. To use language in only one way is to let our minds become held and set in one position. 'Philosophy is a battle against the bewitchment of our intelligence by means of language.' (*Philosophical Investigation*, §109) It is 'to show the fly the way out of the fly-bottle'. (Ibid.) He came to see how absolute and extreme has been his confidence in the notation and rules of logic for understanding language and determining meaning.

1.22: Holding now that the viewpoint of logic is only one viewpoint from which to study language, he proposes to teach not a theory but a skill in probing the depth grammar of language uses. His treatment of language-games constitutes a critique of his earlier logical period. He explains his use of the word language-game for any particular language-system or language-usage: 'Here the term "language *game*" is meant to bring into prominence the fact that the *speaking* of language is part of an activity, or of a form of life ... It is interesting to compare the multiplicity of kinds of word and sentence, with what logicians have said about the structure of language. (Including the author of the *Tractatus Logico-Philosophicus*)' (*Philosophical Investigation*,#23) He presents the following basic insights:

1.23: Language *does* something. The action of ordinary language effects more contact with reality than the mirroring of logical language. With his gift of speech man involves himself with the world, acts on it and creates pathways through social life.

1.24: Words are a boxful of tools with a great diversity of possible uses in real life. The meaning of words is precisely the use we make of them: words have meaning only in the context of their use, and the rules governing a context are public. Every meaning has a background of social convention and is acquired by practising the language game. Wittgenstein rejects the vrew that meaning is naming, and also the view that it consists of thoughts or feelings. An entire social convention provides both the meanings of the words and the depth grammar of each language game

I 25: It is the business of philosophy to analyse and clarify all forms of language not to solve problems but to give a clear view in language, of them. Since he now. conceives language to be so flexible and diverse, the distinction between what can be said and what cannot be said is no longer sharp—although it is still present.

1.26. What is the relation between language and reality? He no longer conceives language as being real because, like a mirror, it reflects what is real; but as a form of living with the real. In this interaction it both corresponds to the experienced world and transforms it. The correspondence is clear because it functions in, and belongs to, a real situation and so cannot be arbitrary. Transformation is there also, for reality is plastic: it is affected by the manner in which it is measured and approached and can be remoulded by language and thought Thus any use of language expresses a decision to take a certain path in life, to interact with reality through the concepts and proofs of a particular language-game; our vision, experience and life is reorganized, given new dimensions, new directions. Wittgenstein says more than once 'The limit of the empirical is concept-formation.' (*Foundations of Mathematics*)

Thus behind our languages and thought today, and expressed in them, lies the history of the forms of life of our people.

1.27: We are hack full-circle to the question that constitutes the core of Wittgenstein's life-work: what is *given in* language? The answer is not now: a picture of things, ideally clear if the language is logical. The new answer is: what is brought into view by probing is human vitality. 'What has to be accepted, the given, is—so one could say—forms of life.' (*Philosophical Investigations)*

One can distil from the immensely technical work of Wittgenstein the human point that primary logical language is only one usage of language, that mathematical logic channels the vitality of formalization and clarification, and that in helping to provide our times with the formal efficiency of a computer-culture it must also endeavour to point the way towards maintaining flexibility, variety and human proportion in life. With Wittgenstein modern mathematical logic was seen, from within, in human and philosophic perspective.

A broad survey of metalogical problems and interests in antiquity, the middle ages and in modern and contemporary times

I. Introduction. Any second-order discussion of an operation, structure, system, theory or calculus occurring in formal logic belongs to Metalogic. When such a discussion is completely formalized a special metalogical language is devised the signs of which refer to *terms* of the system under examination and any metalogical theory developed, therefore, systematizes the names of expressions, not their content.

II. Aristotle. Some fundamentals of a metalogical system are in Aristotle and many metalogical observations. He formally classified methods of proof into induction and the syllogism, and he described his syllogistic metalogically, i.e. he explained its mechanism in terms of general rules. Basic to his syllogistic were theories concerning the functioning of terms, the structure of predicative statements and quantification. With regard to predication he does not seem alive to the complexity of general statements: 'In order to justify Aristotle's doctrine as a whole it is necessary to suppose that he assumed application for all the general terms with which he dealt. To a modern logician this seems a rather curious restriction of the scope of logic.' (Kneale, *The Development of Logic*, p. 60) But he is keenly alert about a distinction between the logical phenomenon of predication and the grammatical, and about the need to free predication from its association with a verb of existence. Indeed in the *Prior Analytics* four forms are used interchangeably to express predication: *A* is *predicated* of *B*, *A belongs* to *B*, *B* is *A*, *B* is in *A* as in a whole. Finally, the outlines of axiomatics are clear in Aristotle; he initiated the study of necessity, impossibility, compatibility, opposition; and his study of 'there will be a sea-battle tomorrow' opened up the topic of bivalency in logic.

III. Megarian-Stoic logic. Metalogic made an important advance with this school which maintained that formal logic has a unique subject—the *lecta* of expressions, i.e it deals neither with words nor with psychic ideas but with what is objectively meant by words—*conceptus objectives* (to anticipate Scholastic language), their *sense* (to anticipate Frege). *Lecta* are divided into deficient and complete; deficient are the lecta of subjects and predicates; complete are the lecta of assertions, questions, enquiries, commands, oaths, prayers, suppositions and addresses. It is lecta that are properly true or false, complete lecta of course.

Another major contribution of this school was an explicit discussion of implication—its nature and types. It seemed to equate the truth and force of implication with the truth and force of a conditional statement. (This outlook was transmitted to the Middle Ages by Boethius in his treatment of *consequentia*.)

Technically, this school advanced Aristotle's conception of system, being very formalistic and clear on the distinction between law and rule. And the interest of the Megarians in paradox produced *The Liar*('A man says that he is lying Is what he says true or false?') and demonstrated the strange results that follow when one interprets a statement as saying something about its own truth or falsity.

In the period before the fall of the Roman Empire, two interesting metalogical contributions were made by Alexander Aphrodisias: he was the first, it seems, to make the explicit distinction between form and matter, and came close to an explicit definition of variable.

IV. Medieval logic. Medieval logic has a rich metalogical content: 'in the later period there is nothing but metalogic, i e. formulae are not exhibited but described, so that in many works, e.g. in the *De puritate artis logicae* of Burleigh not a single variable if the object language is to be found'. (Bochenski, *A History of Formal* Logic, p 152)

Working in the context of the Latin language they built it up a very general semantics and syntax In their doctrine of the properties of terms they very carefully examined the manifold functions of vernacular words and phrases when they are terms of propositions Before the time of Occam it was held that basic in every term was its *signification*, its function of convering a form: based on this was *suppositio* (the function of 'standing for', 'referring to'. 'representing' things), *appelatio* (the function of naming) and *ampliatio* (the function of extending the supposition of the subject term which certain terms exercise, e.g 'possibly', 'can', adjectives, verbs in the past, present or future tense) Occam however rejected *significatio*, making supposition basic there is nothing else real nothing else in the world to signify, than individual things For him a general term is shorthand for a list of proper names. This conception of language as nomenclature was to get its classical presentation and analysis in Wittgenstein's *Tractatus*.

In general the medieval doctrine of properties of terms, had the limitation of covering topics as diverse as meaning and reference on the one hand and inference based on quantification on the other hand; it was also bound up with peculiarities of the Latin language (e.g. its lack of an indefinite article). Thus it could never be incorporated as such into modern logic whose strength lies very much in the careful discriminations made by exact symbolization.

The peculiar problems associated with a proposition about the future were widely discussed in the context of divine foreknowledge, as was also the timeless quality of truth. Some accepted Aristotles view in the *De Interpretatione* that a proposition about, e.g. a sea-battle tomorrow is neither determinately true nor determinately false even though the disjunction of that proposition and its contradictory is true. But the discussions did not lead to anyone conceiving a three-valued logic.

Antinomies or *insolubilia* (to use the medieval term) were very extensively treated. Paul of Venice lists fifteen solutions, the- modern distinction of language and meta-language being used in some of them. He defines an *insolublie* as a 'propositio habens super se reflexionem suae falsitatis aut se non esse veram totaliter vel partialiter illativa', focusing self-reference as a defining feature.

Scholasticism has a very clear doctrine of logical constants (*syncategoremata*) as being the formative elements in expressions. Some logicians indeed were content to say that these words were the subject matter of logic. Others pointed out that words express thought so that it is the *lekta (sense)* of these words which are absolutely and basically formative. In this second view logical form is defined as having its being primarily, basically, in thought although, as with the Stoics, it is nothing psychical but something objective. These two views (locating the subject matter of logic in 'syncategoremata' or in 'second intentions' of the mind) were not regarded as conflicting but as complementary and within both the practice of logic was the same.

Scholastic logicians analysed the structure and sense of propositions very well, their analysis of predication being particularly penetrating. They achieved a quite modern analysis of the quantifiers,'every' and 'some', and in this context used propositional logic as the basis of termlogic. They also analysed the community of reference in analogous terms and the significance of this for inference by analogy, this being the first known formulation of the notion of *isomorphy*.

Finally, the Scholastic theory of consequences is a major contribution covering, in area, both propositional and term logic. Technically excellent, it describes a wide variety of argument structures metalogically with their rules. The modern paradoxes of material implication were exhibited and analysed, and a distinction between a material truth-functional connection and a strict formal connection in meaning was drawn. The meaning of entailment was explored (the Pscedo-Scotus gives three definitions: Paul of Venice gives ten different interpretations) and it is clear that some logicians were concerned to root the validity of an argument in propositional contents rather than in the correlations of propositional truth-values.

The following text from Albert of Saxony is an example of the formal excellence of Scholastic description:

> Eighth rule: every consequence of this kind is formal: 'Socrates exists, and Socrates does not exist, therefore a stick stands in the corner'. Proof: By formal consequence it follows: 'Socrates exists and Socrates does not exist, therefore Socrates exists', from a complete copulative proposition to one of its parts. Further it follows: 'Socrates exists and Socrates does not exist, therefore Socrates does not exist' by the same rule. And it further follows: 'Socrates exists, therefore either Socrates exists or a stick stands in the corner'. The consequence holds, since from every categorical proposition a disjunctive proposition is deducible (*infert*) of which it is a part. And then again: 'Socrates exists and Socrates does not exist; therefore (by the second part of this copulative proposition): Socrates does not exist; therefore a stick stands in the corner'. The consequence holds since the consequence is formal from a disjunctive with the denial (*destructio*) of one of its parts to the other. And so every proposition similar in form to this would be

a valid consequence if it were formed. This rule is usually expressed in the following words: 'from every copulative consisting of contradictorily opposed parts there follows any other (proposition by) formal consequence'. (*Logica Albertucii Perutilis Logica:* : IV, 2, 24 vb—25 ra)

V. From the end of the middle ages to the development of modern mathematical logic. In our survey of the history of formal logic we have seen that this period (of about 400 years) was not a creative one and that a distorted version of logic, the so-called 'classical' logic (permeated with non-logical topics, problems and ideas) developed. In general, apart from the work of Leibniz. logical writings were mainly summary textbooks and commentaries, and contributed nothing new to metatogic. As we saw, Leibniz conceived the kind of development that has actually taken place with modern mathematical logic. Thus his work, mainly descriptive and visionary in character, is in effect a primary draft covering some very fundamental elements of modern metatogic. It would be impossible to overestimate this as a personal achievement. Within the Scholastic tradition, commentaries such as those by Cajetan and John of St Thomas have the importance of transmitting a good deal of medieval metalogic.

At the level of detail, two interesting points may be noted. Firstly, for Leibniz every true statement has on ultimate analysis, a subject-predicate structure—ascribes an attribute to a subject. Thus 'to prove a proposition is to show that its predicate concept is contained in its subject concept, and for this purpose we must analyse the two concepts far enough to make their relations clear . . . Discovery consists in the marshalling of chains of definitions, or, at a more fundamental level, in the survey of possible combinations of predicates. This account of demonstration is unsatisfactory because it is based on the assumption that in every affirmative truth *predicatum inest subjecto*. As always Leibniz is thinking of complexity as arising solely from the conjunction of attributes.' (Kneale, op.cit.,pp. 332-3) It is interesting to see the philosophers,

Bolzano and Mill, also assuming that ultimately all propositions have a subject-predicate structure.

A second interesting detail is the growing interest in relations of extension. It is exemplified in the work of Euler and Gergonne and in the attempt by Hamilton to enlarge Aristotle's syllogistic by including provision for the quantification of predicates. This interest undoubtedly influenced and facilitated the work of Boole.

VI. Modern and contemporary metalogical problems and interests presented as a function of the development of mathematical logic. In this history Boole and Frege are central; Leibniz and Peirce are individualistic. Frege is the dominating figure: both in its ideas and in its deductive system his *Begriffsschrift* (1879) contains all the essentials of modern formil logic, metalogic and philosophy of logic.

6.1: *Boole*: The essence of his contribution was to conceive a method of deriving consequences in completely abstract fashion, i.e. without regard to interpretation. He thought of a formal system as being constructed rather than abstracted, and going to Mathematics for a model to imitate in the construction of a logical system, he wrote the classical description of calculation as formalism and he presented algebra as an abstract calculus capable of various interpretations.

6.2: *Frege*: The essence of his contribution was a comprehension of the structure and divisions of the science of logic; a freeing of loigic from undue attachment to the grammar of ordinary language and to the psychology of personal thinking; the construction of a formalized language which processed conceptual content exclusively and was characterized, technically, by the use of quantifiers which made it superior to symbolism of the algebraic type used by Boole and by the central position of function: a sharpening of Euclidean and Aristotelian concepts of axiomatic system, and also of Boolean and contemporary concepts of formal rigour in proof; an excellent presentation of logic as a system, displaying the great variety of thought-forms it accommodates and providing an exact and explicit system of proof for theorems: a philosophy of logic in which it was conceived as the most general of all sciences about reailty, the *doctrina formarum* of Leibniz.

6.3: The place of Frege in the history of mathematical logic is such that this history can be conveniently mapped in relation to his work:

6.31: *Developments after Frege in the area of logical symbolism*: Improvements and extensions in symbolism: problems of symbolism and their solutions; theories of language, meaning and logical necessity:

(a) *Triumph of linear symbolism* (Peano, Russell, Lukasiewicz).

(b) *Refinements of notation*, e.g. for expression and for designation (Russell's theory of description); notation for class and function abstractors; Schönfinkel's elimination of variables (combinatory logic); many sorted quantification (where variables of mixed types are used)

(c) *Intenstional and extensional language*:: An extension is either an individual, a class or a truth value, an intension is either a concept, a propositional function or a proposition A language is said to be intensional when ii is able to designate intensions and so can be a medium for discussing intensions. The Thesis of Extensionality says that every intensional utterance can be translated without loss into extensional language. The second edition (1925) *of Principia Mathematica* accepts this; also Carnap in his *Logical Syntax of Language* (1934) It is generally easier to work technically with extension rather than intension, e.g. Frege found it easier to deal with the range of values of a function rather than with the function itself, and notation for the former was an important innovation in his later work.

(d) *Paradoxes:* Logical, mathematical and semantical Russell's theory of types as a solution for the logical, mathematical ones, Tarski's doctrine of meta-language as a solution foe semantical ones.

(e) *The development of a two-level semantics* which excluded subjective psychological concepts and the objective meaning of words and focused the direct relationship between signs and what they stand for. As a result the relation of representation was studied in general, and in particular the relation of representation of predicate signs (giving the traditional problem of universals a new dimension). Important contributions were made by Russell, Wittgenstein, Tarski, Carnap. Lesniewski Quine and Goodman .

(f) *Meaning:* the meaning of words and of sentences; of variables and of operators, naming and propositioning. The distinction of two modes of meaning, characteristic respectively of subject and predicate terms, as part of logical tradition. Theories of meaning *de facto* and *de jure types*

(g) *The nature of logical operators:* The work of symbolizing logical operators, representing them and formalizing them with technical precision, is the *way* we isolate phenomena we study in logic. The more technically precise is our symbolization, the more presentable are our phenomena, the *lekta* of the Stoics. In his syllogistic Aristotle showed that reason is bound by operators in a wholly objective way. Logical operators are not psychic processes or psychic facts. For Wittgenstein one gets a better grasp of them by seeing how they govern and exhaust logical space (the relevant sphere of possibilities). The nature of the predicative operator is intimately connected with the nature of the proposition as such.

(h) *Logical necessity and language*: Since the time of the *Tractatus* a conventionalist theory of necessity has been adopted by many philosophers (cf. the view of Tarski, the thinking of Quine)

6.32: *Developments after Frege in the area of formalization:* These developments were threefold (a) improvements and developments of Boole's and Frege's formar systems, development of other formal systems both standard and non-standard; (b) studies of the process of formalization and of the nature of formal system as such; (c) the development of techniques and theorems related to many problems that were raised about formal systems.

(a) With the development, after the *Principia Mathematica*, of many systems in the various areas of standard logic, and with the work of Hilbert and Bernays in the theory of proof or metamathematics, *a great deal of study has been devoted to axiomatized systems generally*, to methods of proving consistency, independence and completeness of axioms, to the nature and form of exact proof, to the distinction between theorems and rules of inference, to a comparison between the formalized concept of the consequence relation and the ordinary sense of this relation, to the notions of truth and provability, to the problem of priority as between meaning and extension, etc. The Polish School, especially Tarski, has been strongly associated with the study of deductive theory.

(b) Up to 1918 mathematical logicians used only one notion of implication, the Philonian or material one. Thus logic was exclusively assertoric, a logic without modalities, a two-value logic. (The only exception was the system of McColl). For Lewis, *strict entailment* was the heart of logic. He used modalities to formalize it. With Lukasiewicz, Post and Wajsberg there was the development of *many-valued logic*, with the attendant metalogicai question what is the meaning of value here and is many-valued logic simply the application of a calculus—mathematics rather than logic?

(c) The development, through Gentzen and Jaskowski, of *natural deduction systems* was an important contribution to the theory of proof and to the comparative study of axioms and rules in logic. It also raises the question of the relationship between deducibility and implication.

(d) After the time of Boole efforts were made to work out *a logic of relations in an algebraic form* similar to the logic of classes. (De Morgan and Peirce were pioneers here). Some logicians now doubt the value of presenting the theory of relations as an algebra. (Today the term 'algebra of logic' frequently denotes that part of logic which can be presented without the use of quantifiers).

(e) A proof of completeness for a system of general logic was first published by Gödel in 1930. This is *Gödel's completeness theorem*: every valid formula in the predicate calculus of first order is provable. In 1931 .he theorem relating to formally undecidable propositions and generally known as *Gödel's Theorem* was published—in any formal system adequate for number theory there is an undecidable proposition, that is, a proposition such that neither the proposition itself nor its negation is provable in the system. Gödel's results by showing that mathematics cannot be completely and consistently formalized in one system raised questions about the value of formalization in mathematics and generally. They also brought general logic and mathematics into contrast.

(f) The impossibility of a *universal decision procedure* for general logic and for many formal systems has been established through the work of Church, Tarski. Mostowski and Robinson. Thus there is not and cannot be a method for the solution of all mathematical or all logical problems. To many (e g Wittgenstein) it was a normal expectancy that the truisms of logic would be certifiable as such by some simple procedure.

6.33: *Developments after Frege concerning the question of the boundaries of logic, situating it in the corpus of the sciences*:

(a) *Logic's connection with inference*: In the corpus of logical tradition everything has a connection with the enterprise of classifying and articulating the principles of formally valid inference. Some (e.g. Lewis) would like to see strict entailment, that which governs and guarantees inference, central in logic. Contemporary developments such as many-valued logic seem to move logic in a different direction.

(b) *Logic's connection with language and grammar*: there is great contemporary interest in the relationship of logical language to ordinary language, and in the question whether *a priori* truth and logical necessity are determined by language.

(c) *Logic's connection with mathematics*: The development of formalism and formal systems gave rise to the controversy in this area: can all mathematical terms be defined by logical ones and all mathematical theorems be deduced from logical axioms (*the logistic position*—Frege, Russell)? Do mathematics and logic constitute a single system of symbols (*the position of formalism*— Hilbert)? In contrast to logic has mathematics empirical roots, in the intuition of time, so that it does not presuppose a system of logic (indeed the technique of formalization is to be distrusted), logic being a study of regularities abstracted from mathematical systems (*the position of intuitionism*—Brouwer and Heyting)?

(d) *Logic's connection with technology*: Can a formal system be always used as a computer device? What is the significance of an affirmative answer?

VII. Conclusion. It is clear that basic studies in metalogic have been concerned with language, meaning, truth, proof, generality, classal thought, paradox, the nature of logical principles and logic's connection with mathematics. These topics will be treated in the following chapters.

Chapter-5

On Mathematical or Intuitive and Logical or Discursive Synthesis *a priori*

Chapter-5

1 We have said in the preceding chapter that Hume had *taken for granted* the analytic nature of mathematical reasoning. This is no arbitrary assertion, on the one hand, for there exists no proof nor hint in his writings of his having particularly proposed the question as a subject of any distinct enquiry; and on the other hand the omission is not to be wondered at, as it was an error which he had in common with all the logicians and analysts of the human mind in his own age and at least a century preceding. Add to which that the occasion of the error is obvious, and has been already mentioned. I refer to the confusion of the common condition with the particular ground, as explained page [1540-ff]. The proper ground of analytic judgments being the condition, though not the proper and sufficing ground, of synthetic judgments, as the latter could not be true except under the condition of their congruity with the so-called principle of contradiction and identity, these principles were considered as the positive grounds of their actual truth. The condition, I say, under which alone the truth of any judgment is possible, was mistaken for the ground of the actual truth of these particular judgments. Accordingly this is one among the many instances that might be brought to confirm the remark of the celebrated Paley, and which we may apply to logical, with no less reason than he to moral, enquiries, that in the majority of cases the solution is easy in proportion to the insight into the difficulty of the problem[1] 'For supposing the problem. (or question proposed) clearly and distinctly comprehended, "Is mathematical reasoning merely analytic or not rather synthetic", is the B introduced by the "then" or "therefore" of the demonstrator actually included in the preceding A, from which it is deduced? We need only refer to our explanation of the term" analytic judgments, p[p 174-7], and then simply to ask ourselves whether by any exertion of

our reflecting powers on the terms contained in the first proposition of Euclid, without adding any one form or relation not actually thought of by us in the act of representing the former to our minds, in the same manner as we are certain that in thinking of a circle we actually must have thought of the centre and circumference, or have used the word without meaning anything by it at all; we need only ask ourselves whether in this way we could ever have arrived at the properties of the cycloid or the proportion of the area of the curve to the area of the generating circle. In short, we have only to attempt raising our minds to a comprehension of the mighty pile and fabric of truth, which (faith in God and the moral law alone excepted) is the proudest honour and glory of the human intellect, that in which above all others it finds the clearest sense of its own permanency and at the same time the most infallible evidence of its progressiveness, its still organised and ever organising growth, to find the supposition monstrous, too monstrous to have ever been distinctly believed, though, however, the phantom or substitute of belief is rendered possible by the confusion of terms through the imperfection and unsteady flitting of the attention and memory.

Such is the rise of forms
Sequestered far from sense and every spot
Peculiar in the realms of space and time;
Such is the throne which man for truth amid
The paths of mutability hath built,
Secure, unshaken still; and whence he views
In matter's mouldering structures, the pure forms
Of triangle or circle, cube or cone,
Impassive all; whose attributes nor force
Nor fate can alter. There he first conceives
True being, and the intellectual world
The same this hour and ever. Thence he deems
Of his own lot; above the painted shapes
That fleeting move o'er this terrestrial scene
Looks up; beyond the adamantine gates
Of death expatiates; as his birthright claims
Inheritance of all the works of God;

Prepares for endless time his plan of life,
And counts the universe itself his home.[2]

2 But if the assertion were not that each successive turn of the geometrician is analytically contained in the preceding, but that each and all the terms are perfectly independent affirmations, that mathematical reasoning is no interlinked chain, but a rope of sand, or if, in the poetic tone inspired by the recent quotation from Akenside, we may venture to elevate the subject by recurring to our former metaphor, when the vast complex of mathematic truth was represented as a magnificent palace—if, I say, this whole pile be, in all its apparent orders, dependencies, insertions, but a phantom in the desert, when on the contingence of some I know not what whirl blast

the desert sands rise up
And shape themselves:from Earth to Heaven they stand,
As though they were the pillars of a temple,
Built by Omnipotence in its own honour!'
But the blast pauses, and their shaping spirit
Is fled the mighty columns were but sand,
And sophist snakes trail o'er the level ruins![3]

—if, in short, mathematical reasoning be no reasoning at all, if gometical demonstration be *monstratio de nihilo*,[4] and the consequents [are] not only not contained and understood in the antecedent, but having no true or necessary connection therewith—to such an assertion, 1 say, no answer can be given. And were it not so, no answer ought to be given but that of requesting the assertor to make or renew his acquaintance with the elements of geometry or with any one proposition. For either the assertor, supposing him to understand what he asserts, speaks that which he himself knows to be false, or we must condole with his case as an anomaly no less strange than that of the two men who had the misfortune, the one of losing his shadow, and the other his reflection in the looking-glass, and who were both perfectly persuaded, the one that what the rest of mankind called their shadows, and the other that what they took for their own image, were unconnected, independent, and self-grounded verities.[5]

3 An easy experiment will convince us, that is, occasion us to be conscious, that even the simplest processes of common arithmetic suppose a synthetic judgment, and that the supposition of their being analytic only arises from the original facility of the operation, but still more the facility acquired by habit, and our incapability of remembering the time when it was not already habitual. Under this impression it might be supposed that the position or judgment "7+5=12" is a mere analytic judgment that follows out of the conception of a sum composed of 7 and 5 according to the principle of identity and *de non sibi contradicendo.*[6] But if we examine the matter more closely we find that the conception of a sum of 7 and 5 really in the first instance, and previously to the arithmetical operation, contained no more than the union of both numbers in some single number without its being any actual part of this conception what this single number must be The conception "12" is by no means thought of necessity at the time that I first put the question to myself, " What is the sum of 7 and 5 ? " Even what we have shown in a former chapter concerning the nature of a question will prove this, for there we saw that every question consisted in an expression of knowledge and an expression of ignorance and that the latter, that viz of which we are ignorant, is expressed by the interrogation and in cases like the present by the interrogative pronoun[7] Now here the knowledge already possessed, and which is contained in the conception, is simply, there is a sum of 7 and 5, or the union of 7 and 5 constitutes a sum. Our ignorance is expressed and acknowledged in the word[s] "What is it" In order to convert this ignorance into knowledge—in order to perfect the position—we must call in the help of the imagination (*intuitio, vis intuitiva*).[8] The scholar will perhaps, if he begins with 7, take his five fingers, or as in some of our popular ciphering books five points,[9] and add them one by one to the original number, giving at each step to the number thus constituted its

proper name But if any doubts remained they may be removed at once by taking very much larger sums as the component factors, as, for instance, 35,942,768,412+57,843,647, and we shall be convinced at once that we might dwell for centuries on the two sums without discovering what the product of both would be,[10] if we did not proceed to a third, and perfectly distinct, act of the intellect, the synthetic act, or that of putting the numbers together according to the laws derived from the inherent forms of the sense or intuitive faculty so that they must produce or, in the language of the mathematicians, generate a third intuition contained in neither of the former, and which could not have existed for the mind otherwise than by the synthesis or copula of the two, any more than water could have been known to the senses by the mere consideration of oxygen and of hydrogen gas separately, without the act of their combination by means [of], and in proportions agreeable to, the laws of chemical nature. Thus too with pure geometry there is [not] even a single axiom or fundamental principle that is properly analytic—that a straight line between two points is the shortest: for the conception "straight" is in no respect a conception of quantity and of itself determines nothing respecting degrees of quantity, but expresses a particular quality only. The conception "shortest" is added to it or put in connection therewith, συντιθεται, by an act or, if I may so say, an experiment of the intuitive or imaginative power. We *find* that it is so, and we *find* too that we *cannot* imagine it otherwise, and this not from any defect or deficiency of the power in us, but by the nature of the intuition itself, involving the impossibility of the contrary Now this is what we mean by αποδειξις, or "apodictic", and its Latin correspondent *demonstratio* or demonstrative reasoning [11] Where I affirm that [a] tree grows on a given spot, and that it is an oak, and my companion being doubtful of the fact, 1 take him to the spot and show him the object, this is δειξις, *monstratio*, an evidence of the senses, but it involves no proof that the contrary was impossible, it is not *apodictic*, not demonstrative. It does not even amount to a positive proof that the showing did not depend on some individuality, or peculiar state of my companion's senses, or of the medium through which they were thus affected. The evidence here is rather moral than logical, and rests on the senselessness of supposing the contrary on the ground of a mere possibility, without any reason for asserting its reality in the particular instance. It is true that certain assumptions or principles presupposed by the geometrician are actually analytic, and rest on the principle of contradiction, but these serve only as identical positions, as when we say "A being A", or " +A not being –A", as links of method, ways of recalling and enlivening the attention and memory of the demonstrator, not as principles out of which there flows any increase of evidence. Such, for instance, are "A=A", "the whole is equal to itself", or "the whole is greater than its parts". And yet even these, though valid as mere conceptions and logically coercive, are admitted in mathematics on this account only, that they can likewise be presented to the sense, and have an intuitive evidence because we not only understand, but likewise see, that so it is.[12]

4. I have said, and I now repeat, that the distinction between analytic and synthetic, once admitted and fully understood, its [non-]application to the different classes of positions or judgments can be accounted for only by some confusion or rather entanglement of thought; and in minds acute and highly cultivated, [such] as that of the Scottish philosopher,[13] the occasion of this perplexity is to be found in an obscure sense (and, might I say, a dim half-consciousness, a felt anticipation) of a truth that has its source and derivation from powers higher than the understanding considered as the discursive faculty of truth, that can be duly contemplated only from a higher point of view than that on which the logician can make a firm footing, truths that have more than subjective reality. The condition of the error is the confusion of philosophy with logic, but the efficient cause of it is the dissatisfaction connected with confused recognition, for which we have no other than the popular term, the "feeling" of the difference between them. For while the naturalist seeks to remove as far as possible all

mixture of subjective form and influences, and the logician with the same solicitude excludes all that is objective, the philosopher seeks to raise himself into a sphere in which both are one, and where of course the opposition ceases and the antithesis no longer has any meaning. In the same sphere, the antithesis of analytic and synthetic disappears likewise and loses all import; for it rises out of the forms of the understanding and of the sense, that are instruments for the knowledge of true relations, of *relative*, not *absolute*, truth, which latter appertains to a higher principle, which may enlighten the understanding that receives it as its base and centre, but which can neither be deduced by the understanding [n]or from the objects that properly fall under its cognisance The Epicurean, whether sceptic or dogmatist, will admit nothing but the understanding, yet demands of the understanding what by its constituent forms it is incapable of realising, and makes this the pretext of denying it absolutely and altogether. *Non est ibi; ergo, nullibi est*[14] He cannot find it where he expected it to have been found It did not exist there, and therefore it does not exist at all. Thus, παντων ςητουντες λογον αναιρονσι[15] which equally to the purposes of truth, though not with equal fidelity, we may paraphrase either thus.

5 Seeking a reason *for all* things, they take away reason itself—and all the truths *of* reason, *for* which no reason can without absurdity be required, because they *are* reason. Logically speaking, they *constitute* the reason, but in the language of the philosopher, the reason affirms itself in them. Or, "seeking the understanding of all things, they render the understanding itself baseless and unsubstantial "To which we may add, as a corollary, that logic by itself, except where logic itself (that is, the forms of the understanding and the rules grounded on the same) is the subject, is but a cabinet of many drawers and pigeonholes, all empty. But are we, therefore, to procure no cabinets, and content ourselves with lumber-rooms and slut-corners? And who are these that are most forward and frequent in depreciating the science and discipline of logic,

whether its technical rules or the knowledge which the understanding acquires by reflection on its own processes? Those who will profess that the mere words "transcendental" and "aesthetic" are *quite enough* for *them*—the wax of Ulysses[16] not more potent? Why, the very men who, with keenest contempt and most confident self-complacency, reject and ridicule the supposition of any higher source of truth than that of the senses, or any higher form of knowledge than that which results from these very processes of the understanding, and from the mechanism and inherent constitution of the faculty, which it is the express object of transcendental research to discover and explain'! Men who make a merit of not knowing the meaning of the terms which they ridicule, professors (but of no *Socratic* character) of the science of nescience, who measure their sense by their ignorance—the genuine successors of Mr Pope's "Coxcombs that vanquish'd Berkeley with a grin" [17] We, however, will endeavour neither to overrate nor to undervalue the science, but to take logic as it is, and use it accordingly. And consistently with this profession, we readily acknowledge that the distinction between analytic and synthetic judgments, on which, and its historic occasion, we have discoursed so largely, is of small importance except in the investigations of transcendental logic, that its utility and application is confined with few exceptions to enquiries, the subject of which is not the knowledge real or supposed, but the faculty by which, either as the source or instrument, such knowledge is rendered possible But is this nothing or of small value? Does it form no part of that knowledge that ought most to interest us, if our great moral poet have truly said that" "The proper study of mankind is man"?[18] Is it not included in the heaven-descended precept γνωπι σεαυτον?[19] As the critical inquisition into the constitution of the intellectual faculties is the proper sphere in which this finds its use and validity, it cannot surprise us that it is scarcely noticed by logicians and metaphysicians previously to the appearance of the *Critique on the Pure Reason* which in fact would have been open to fewer objections, had it been proposed by the author under the more appropriate name of "Transcendental Logic". For considered as *logic* it is irrefragable; as philosophy it will be exempt from opposition and cease to be questionable only when the soul of Aristotle shall have become one with the soul of Plato, when the men of *talent* shall have all passed into men of *genius*, or the men of *genius* have all sunk into men of talent. That is, *Graecis calendis*, or when two Fridays meet.

6 The ignorance, however, of this distinction is not only to be inferred by the absence of all reference to it in the writings of the metaphysicians, metaphysical divines of the dogmatic philosophy, but by the effects of this ignorance. For had the distinction between synthetic and analytic judgments been present to their minds, they could not have thought of deducing the principle of the sufficient cause from the principle of contradiction and identity, on which alone the truths of the common logic rest, as both their ground and their condition They must have seen that the principle of contradiction is the adequate ground of analytic judgments only, or identical propositions, as they are more commonly named by our English metaphysicians, but that a cause implies a synthetic judgment or a position resulting from the conjunction of two subjects.' Yet on this mistake rest all the pretended scientific demonstrations of the Divine Existence and all other fundamental truths of religion and of morality; an attempt and an assumption that has been injurious in more ways than one. For first it has given a wrong direction to the mind of the enquired by directing it to expect and demand a *kind* rather than a *degree* of evidence in moral and religious truths, which they could not possess without ceasing to be moral and religious, inasmuch as it would exclude all participation of the will, which constitutes the moral, without counteracting its own end, by sacrificing the life and freedom of faith to a worthless, because compulsory, acquiescence. Secondly, it is injurious to other truths differing from these supposed demonstrable ones, chiefly by their being less calculated to permit the same delusion, or because they stand in a more particular connection with the

conscience and the experience of the moral state of mankind These truths, though their grounds and justifications are essentially the same with those of the former, are henceforward contradistinguished from them as mysteries, the subjects of ridicule to those who will believe nothing but by virtue of some legitimate conclusion from premises cognisable by the understanding, and who profess that their belief is commensurate with their logic, and consequently therefore confined either to the objects of their senses or to the mere forms of the understanding itself as notions formed by reflection, or a pretext of pretending (without any insight at all) to believe in the truth of words of which they confess they do not know the meaning—a pretext equally favourable to the ambitious fanatic and serviceable to the designing hypocrite. And thirdly, these dreams of demonstration have this inevitable consequence, that the negative may be proved on premises equally undeniable by the understanding, and by deductions equally logical as the affirmative; and atheism, pantheism, fatalism, the nonexistence of a responsible will, and the absurdity of the orthodox faith in all its leading points, have had their demonstrations, which, if we could, as in speculative reasoning and on a question of demonstration we ought to, free ourselves from all influence of our moral feelings and associations, will be found as logically legitimate as those given in proof of the contrary. Or if there were any difference, I fear that in point of strict consequence, Clarke and Wolff would yield the palm to Benedict Spinoza,[20] and the dogmatic idealism, spiritualism, of Berkeley be found less acceptable to the majority than the dogmatic materialism of Hobbes. Such are the results of resolving a synthetic judgment into an analytic, and thus of confining the character of truth and rational convictions to identical propositions, which, however long the series may be, are in reality so many repetitions of A is A, and what is cannot be affirmed not to be. Thus it appears that one of the great uses of logic is, first, that of circumscribing its own application and, secondly, of determining the conditions and circumstances under which it can be productively applied even within this sphere; and in like manner, that one of the most substantial services which transcendental logic performs for philosophy is that it confines the plenipotentiary power, the conclusive evidence of common logic, to truths that can be made evident without any other aid than that given in the principle of identity: that is, to every subject there belongs a predicate that is identical with it, or the principle of contradiction, which expresses the converse, viz. to no subject can a predicate belong that is in contradiction with it. Now these principles taken together constitute the highest and most general principles of the forms of discourse. They are, I say, the two universal principles of the understanding in the formal exercise of its functions; but they can prove nothing more than the legitimacy of the form. They enable us to ascertain whether the understanding has contradicted itself or no, whether it has affirmed something respecting the predicate which it had already denied in the subject (e.g., that a circle has three angles), but by no means can it prove that our assertion is consistent with facts of experience, or with substantial truths, whencesoever derived. We may be certain that whatever is incompatible with these two principles must be false, but we cannot infer that what is compatible with them is therefore true. Whatever is more than this must be either true by its own evidence, truths, I mean, in the sense of realities—truths as distinguished from mere general principles, if such there exist, which is a question of *metaphysics, not of logic*[—]or facts learnt from experience, or the necessary products of a combination which the mind is enabled to make by virtue of its own constituent forms, whether the forms of sense or the forms of the understanding; in other words, whether intuitions or conceptions, truths immediately or mediately acquired. The first of the three does not belong to logic at all, not even the determination whether it is entitled to presuppose them affirmatively (that is, otherwise than problematically) in the premise or major of its syllogism. The second and third are synthetic judgments, the former, synthetic judgments *a posteriori*, the latter, synthetic judgments *a priori*, and the materials of which a "they consist; and that in the latter case synthetic judgments mean and might be called conjoint propositions or propositions by union or conjunction, as opposed to identical propositions or judgments simply analytic, which neither have nor require any other ground than that of the two above mentioned.

7 It is indeed a singular fact that the distinction between these two judgments should have remained so generally unnoticed that the only exception is to be found in Locke's *Essay*, and even here in one passage only, viz. the third chapter of the fourth book.[21] In this chapter, however, our great essayist expressly distinguishes two sources of the mind's judgments, and two sorts of knowledge as resulting therefrom—the first being the agreement or disagreement of the idea with itself, that is, analytic judgments, and the other the combination of two ideas into one subject, that is, synthetic judgments. And he adds that with regard to the latter the power of the mind, acting on its own resources, is very limited—but without particularising what the limits are, or what the knowledges contained within them. Had he proceeded to this enquiry, he must have been led to the transcendental logic, that is, a true analysis of the understanding and not a mere classification of the ideas; and would thus have rescued the truth, which he actually meant, from the attacks of Berkeley and others, to which it was exposed by the impropriety of the expression consequent on the want of distinctness and adequacy in the conception of it. We need not therefore find it wonderful that the distinction had escaped Mr Hume[22] even when the nature of the question started by him and the direction which his enquiries took seemed to have placed it within his arms, if I may borrow a metaphor from a game not altogether dissimilar from that of metaphysics, the game of blind[man's]-buff, or that with his collateral views and hostility to all superstition it should have rather led him on a false scent. With this great advantage, however, that what he caught was so worthless and so intenable that it induced a more patient and dispassionate

huntsman to seek the scent again at the point from which his predecessor had flown off and, having again once more caught it on the breeze, he follows it undeterred by the steep and difficult uplands whither it leads him, and

> Along the mountain's breast
> Stretches secure, and leaves the scattered crowd
> To puzzle in the distant vale below.[23]

Footnotes:

1. William Paley (1743—1805) *The Principles of moral and Political Philosophy* (2nd ed 1786) viii: "in discoursing to young minds upon topics of morality, it required much more pains to make them perceive the difficulty, than to understand the solution. . ."

2. Mark Akenside (1721—70) The 131—49 (var): Poems (1772) 156—7. *Pleasures of Imagination* bk II lines.

3. Cs *The Night-Scene* lines 77-83 (var);*PW* (EHC) 1 423. An earlier version appears in the fragment *The Triumph of Loyalty: PW (EHC) II 1072.*

4. "A showing from nothing".

5. C may be referring to Erasmus Spikher and Peter Schlemihl; see E.T.A. Hoffmann "Die Gesellschaftim Keller" and "Die Geschichte vom verlornen-Spiegelbilde" in "Die Abentheuer der Silvester-Nacht" in *Fantasiestücke in Callot's Manier...* (1814-15). If so, he has altered the case by making their condition subjective. There is a copy fo the 2nd ed (Bamberg 1819) annotated by C in BM.

6. "Of not contradicting oneself".

7. Ch IV

8. "Intuition, intuitive power".

9. Kant, from whom C is quoting here, attributes the term to Segner. *C d r V 15* (53) and *Prolegomena* § 2 (1783) 29. J. A. Segner *Elementa arithmeticae et geometriae. . .* (Göttingen 1739).

10. From p 201 line 6 to this piont C is translating *C d r V* 15-16 (53—4). Cf *Prolegomena* § 2 (1783) 28-9.

11. From line 12 to this point C is translating, with variations, from *C d r V* 16-17 (53-4). Cf. *Prolegomena* 2 (1783) 29.

12. From p 202 line 35 to this point C is tranlating from *C dr* V 16—17 (54). Cf *Prolegomena* § 2 (1783) 29.

13. Hume.

14. "It is not there; therefore it is nowhere."

15. Theophrastus *Metaphysics* 8.26 (var). Used as an epigraph in *Friend (CC)* 464. C appears to have found it in Hooker Of *the Laws of Ecclesiastical Politie* I 8: *Works* (1682) 80. Cf *CN* III 3574.

16. The wax used to prevent his men from hearing the Sirens. Homer *Odyssey* 12.173-80.

17. John Brown (1715-66) *An Essay on Satire, Occasioned by the Death of Mr. Pope* line 224 (2nd ed 1749) 17. The peom was published in Warburton's ed of Pope's *Works* (9 vols 1751) III XV and in later collections, hence, presumably, C's misattribution. Cf *BL* ch 8 (1907) I 93n and *CN* III 4397.

18. Pope *Eassy on Man* ep II line 2.

19. Juvenal *Satires* 11.27. See above p 116 n 3.

20. See above, p. 150

21. *Essay on Human Understanding* bk iv ch 3 §§ 22ff.

22. Paragraph 7 up to this point is based on Kant *Prolegomena* § 3 (1783)31.

23. Untraced. The passage bears an interesting resemblance to WW *An Evening Walk* lines 179-88, 196-205; *WPW* 1 22, 23.

Chapter-6

On Mathematical Evidence

Chapter-6

1 We have seen that mathematical reasoning or all truths respecting measure, number, and motion, susceptible of strict demonstration from self-evident premises, consist of synthetic judgments *a priori*. We have now briefly to show by what means this is effected, and how it is possible. Observe, not *whether* it be possible; for we have proved that mathematical truths are synthetic *a priori*, and of the existence of mathematics we are quite certain, and it were idle to offer any further proof of the possibility of a thing than is contained in its reality. We have not, I say, here as in the instance of metaphysics to enquire *whether* such a science be possible, which implies that its existence hitherto may be questioned, but *how* are synthetic judgments *a priori* possible. And in the first place, how are those in particular [possible] which belong to the mathematical sciences? Here we have a most assured knowledge which, vast even to astonishment in its present extent, promises to enlarge itself without limit in the future—a science of which it may with severest truth be said that it, "Hath made Earth's reasoning animal her lord", hath enabled man to behold the ends of the earth, and to survey what is beneath the heavens! He measureth the sea, and appointeth the laws to the flowing thereof, he unravelleth the maze of the moon. He foretelleth the courses of the stars, yea, he weigheth them out and doth compass them as with a line. And this too a science, in the pure and most perfect sense, that carries with it, throughout, demonstrative certainty, an absolute *necessity* of truth, resting therefore on no grounds of experience, which could at best only give us the knowledge that it is so, not the clear insight and irresistible sense that so it must be, which consequently must be a pure product of the intellect acting by its own powers on its own wealth, and

this science, moreover, wholly and in all its parts synthetic. It is the work of reason, for where, except in the reason, can necessity and universality be found? But by what means and instruments doth the human reason bring it to pass? Is it by means of the universal principles of which the reason itself is the immediate source, and which are therefore rightly named principles of reason, and distinguished from *material* truths from the same source (supposing such to exist) by being merely *formal?* But we know of no other *principles*, that is, universal *forms*, of reason but those of identity and self-contradiction, the congruity with which is indeed a necessary *condition of all* judgments but the immediate ground of the analytic only. They supply the sufficient ground of *logical* certainty alone and therefore not the ground of mathematic evidence, which is altogether synthetic. But if not wholly or chiefly by its *formal* principles, so neither does the reason effect it by its *material* truths, by IDEAS (*sensu Platonico*) or supersensual realities, the very existence of which is not of universal admission but which if allowed to exist might constitute a *mathematical* certainty and give birth to a series of synthetic judgments *a priori*, the sum of which would constitute the science of *metaphysics*; but not to those that constitute the *mathematics*, which instead of being supersensual is the very purity and perfection of *sense. A priori* therefore (and all means and materials *a posteriori* are excluded from the problem) there remain only the constitutive *forms*, or constitutional acts and functions, of the SENSE and of the *understanding*, with the several products of these, as far as they are producible *a priori* : viz. the pure intuitions of the one and the self-derived notions and conceptions of the other. By which then, or if by means of both, in what characteristic relation and proportion of the one to the other, does the speculative reason bring about this its most magnificent work?

2 A few references to what we have already learnt will

narrow still more the sphere within which the answer must be found We have already seen that the right application of the mind to realities, and in order to the true knowledge of what really is, constitutes philosophy, which, according to the difference of the object, receives a different name, as natural, political, or moral, physical, or metaphysical philosophy, that the knowledge ol the constitution of the mental faculties forms the science of transcendental analysis, and lastly that the rules and methods of conclusive discourse resulting from the constitution of the discursive faculty of the mind (that is, the understanding), under the universal principles of reason in reference to the *form* of the reasoning, constitute the science of common logic We have seen too that the transcendental analysis consists of two parts, viz the transcendental aesthetic and the transcendental logic. Now we shall [?attain] to the point in view if we assume, and in the first instance hypothetically only, and as a possible case, that the transcendental aesthetic is subdivided into two parts, of such disproportionate magnitude and extent, the one too circumscribed and perfectible, the other indefinite and illimitably progressive, yet ever travelling in the same fullness of light and leaving the light steady and undiminished along the whole of the vast line over which it had passed—not like the glowworm or firefly bearing the light along with it, but like a living fire that engenders a permanent light at every point of its progression It would follow of itself that this latter form a science of itself especially if it should be found that in this instance as in that of common logic the evidence is complete in itself and in no way dependent on an insight into the grounds of its possibility This insight therefore, and the investigations necessary thereunto, would alone belong to the transcendental aesthetic, or analysis of the pure sense On the other hand, we will suppose that the second branch in our primary division, viz the transcendental logic or analysis of the pure understanding, is in its nature so circumscribed that not only its inherent forms or its several functional powers are capable of being enumerated and defined, which is the case likewise with the transcendental aesthetic, but that the pure products and the connections of these products as far as they are produced and connected *a priori* are likewise predeterminable, having their *ne plus ultra* in an assignable boundary. In this case, where both the producing powers and the possible products are presentable in our [?panoptic] and may be harmoniously combined in the same panorama, there would be no adequate motive for disjoining them as in the former case into separate sciences The same science, that is, transcendental logic, would comprise both. Not only would the same science comprise both, but even the pure aesthetic shrunken in its dimensions by the contrary circumstance, that is, by the separation of its more important part, and too small for practical insulation, may more conveniently sink into a subdivision and be contained under the name of its more comprehensive co-factor. The analysis both of the pure sense and that of the pure understanding would stand under the common head, and be distinguished only as the several chapter of transcendental logic We have only further to assume that the science separated from the transcendental aesthetic by its own magnitude and the independency of its evidence is that of mathematics, and in order to discover whether our assumption is well grounded we have only to compare it with the fact, that is, whether the acts of the pure sense under the universal form[s] of space and time, and the immediate products in and by which these acts are made manifest and which are indeed one with the acts, form the subject-matter and determine the proper character of the mathematical sciences. For this comparison is in no other way possible but by reflecting on the way in which the mind proceeds and the means it adopts in mathematical reasoning, but the statement of the way and means in and by which they are accomplished contains the full answer [to the question] "How are mathematical judgments as one class to synthetic judgments *a priori* possible?" Nor can this be done without at the same time answering in part—that is, as far as the negative characteristics are concerned—and in part preparing for the answer of the other question which then alone will remain, viz. "How are logical judgments possible, that is, synthetic judgments *a priori* that are not mathematical?"

Chapter-7

Mathematical Abstraction

Chapter-7

1. GEOMETRY AND AXIOMATICS

For the Greeks the most important part of mathematics was geometry, and in Euclid's *Elements* vii-x we find even theorems of pure arithmetic, e.g. about prime numbers, presented as propositions about the commensurability or incommensurability of lines. It has been suggested that the comparative neglect of other branches of mathematics by the Greeks was due to the deficiency of their system of numeration; but it seems more likely that geometry was developed first because the effort of abstraction which it requires is not so great as that needed for algebra and analysis. We shall see presently that even mathematicians of a much later age have had difficulty in freeing themselves from excessive reliance on spatial intuition. However that may be, for many centuries Euclid's *Elements* set the standard of rigour in all demonstration, and we must begin by considering the pattern of his work, although our main concern in this chapter will be with later developments.

Obviously Euclid did not discover all the theorems which he presents in the *Elements*. There were treatises on geometry before the beginning of the third century B.C. when he worked, and we know, for example, that the beautiful theory of proportion which he uses in book v comes from Eudoxus, a younger contemporary of Plato. But he achieved fame by his masterly attempt to derive all previous discoveries from a relatively small number of common notions (*κοιναο εννοιαι*) and postulates (*αιτημαπα*). The common notions are propositions said to be fundamental in all sciences, e.g. that the whole is greater than the part; and the postulates are five propositions, peculiar to geometry, which we are asked to concede at the beginning. In later times the two sets of primitive propositions were sometimes put together under the name of axioms. It must be admitted that in various places Euclid assumes geometrical propositions which are neither included among his axioms nor proved to follow from these, as when, for example, he takes it for granted in the proof of the first proposition of book i that circles drawn about the two ends of a straight line with radii equal in length to that line must intersect in two points. But there can scarcely be any doubt that he intended to put all his extra-logical assumptions at the beginning and then to derive the theorems from them by logic alone. For anything else would be a compromise inconsistent with that desire for rigour which is obvious throughout his work. The use of a figure may help us to concentrate our attention when we are following a proof, and for psychological reasons it may even be necessary in the process of discovery; but if we accept propositions merely because they seem evident to us when we consider a figure, we are in effect adding to our axioms without due notice, and this is contrary to the whole spirit of Greek geometry.

Euclid and all his successors until last century assumed that his postulates were universal and necessary truths about physical space. But there is one among them which has always seemed more complicated than the rest. This is the famous parallels postulate: 'If a straight line falling on two straight lines makes the interior angles on the same side less than two right angles, the two straight lines, when produced indefinitely, meet on that side on which are the angles less than two right angles.' In antiquity Ptolemy and Proclus both tried to show that this proposition should not appear as a postulate because it could be demonstrated as a theorem, and many similar attempts to improve on Euclid's work were made by later geometers.[1] One of the most interesting was that of Saccheri in his book of 1733 called *Euclides ab Omni Naevo Vindicatus*. This is based, as he himself says,[2] on the principle of the *consequentia mirabilis* which he used in his *Logica Demonstrativa*; and although it does not succeed, as he thought, in establishing the necessary truth of the parallels postulate, it deserves fame as the first work containing theorems of non-Euclidean geometry.

Most of the earlier geometers who claimed that they had proved the parallels postulate assumed as an explicit or implicit premiss some other proposition with the same deductive force as that they were trying to prove. John Wallis, for example, assumed that for any given figure it is possible that there should exist a similar figure of any size whatsoever. Saccheri's enterprise was much bolder: he wished to show that the parallels postulate was a necessary truth because it followed even from its own negation. In order to get this negation into a convenient form he considered not Euclid's statement of the postulate but an equivalent suggested by a figure in Clavius's edition of Euclid. From the ends of a straight line AB two perpendiculars of equal length, AC and BD, are erected on the same side, and the points C and D are then connected by a straight line. In the resulting quadrilateral the angles at C and D must be equal, and it can be shown that Euclid's parallels postulate is equivalent to the assumption that they are both right angles. Saccheri therefore examines the two other conceivable hypotheses, namely, (i) that the angles are obtuse and (ii) that they are acute. These correspond respectively to the two forms of non-Euclidean geometry later distinguished as elliptic and hyperbolic; and in the course of his investigation he proves some characteristic theorems of those geometries. He shows, for example, in proposition ix that on the hypothesis of the obtuse angle the internal angles of a triangle are always together greater than two right angles, and that on the hypothesis of the acute angle they are always less. But his attempt to prove the parallels postulate from consideration of the two distinguishable alternatives covered by its negation is not so happy. For the first case he seems to achieve the desired result easily by showing in proposition xii that the hypothesis of the obtuse angle entails the parallels' postulate (and is therefore self-contradictory, since the parallels postulate itself entails the hypothesis of the right angle). But he does so only by assuming tacitly that a straight line can be produced to any desired length. This assumption is in fact inconsistent with the hypothesis he is considering, since in elliptic geometry there must be a maximum length for a straight line. The other hypothesis gives him much more trouble, and although he speaks later as though he had relied throughout on the *consequentia mirabilis*, he does not even try to show that this alternative entails the parallels postulate. But he claims to prove in proposition xxiii that it involves a self-contradictory consequence. If his proof were satisfactory, it would, of course, suffice with proposition xii to establish the truth of the parallels postulate; but there is a flaw in his reasoning.

It is not known for certain whether Saccheri's work had any influence on the mathematicians who developed non-Euclidean geometry in the nineteenth century, but the book found its way into a number of libraries and was noticed in some works of reference such as Montucla's *Histoire des mathematiques* of 1758 and Klügel's *Conatuum Praecipuorum Theoriam Parallelarum Demonstrandi Recensio* of 1763.[3] In this way it may have come to the attention of Gauss (1777-1855), who was the first to recognize the possibility of developing non-Euclidean geometry in a consistent fashion and regarded it as a question to be settled by observation whether the interior angles of a triangle in physical space are or are not equal to two right angles. But in this field of mathematical research, as in many others in which he made brilliant discoveries, Gauss published nothing. The first printed work to develop a form of non-Euclidean geometry for its own sake was a paper of Lobachevsky published in 1826. This dealt with the hypothesis of the acute angle (that is to say, with hyperbolic geometry in which there are two lines through a given point parallel to a given straight line). The development of the hypothesis of the obtuse angle (that is to say, of elliptic geometry in which there are no lines through a given point parallel to a given straight line and every straight line returns on itself when produced) had to wait for Riemann.Indeed it was not until the posthumous publication in 1867 of Riemann's inaugural lecture of 1854 *Uber die Hypothesen welche der Geometrie zu Grunde liegen* that non-Euclidean geometry was taken seriously by pure mathematicians; and even after that the speculations of Riemann and his disciple Clifford about the possibility of using non-Euclidean geometry in physics went unregarded for more than a generation.

These advances in geometry are important to the logician chiefly because of the attention which they drew to axiomatics, or the theory of postulate sets. If it had been shown that a contradiction was introduced by the negating of Euclid's parallels postulate in a system which retained all his other axioms, it would have been proved by *reductio ad absurdum* that the parallels postulate followed from those other axioms. On the other hand, mere failure to discover a contradiction does not suffice by itself to prove the consistency of a non-Euclidean geometry. For that it would be necessary to establish that no contradiction could ever be derived. This is a very large requirement, and, as we shall sec later, by no means easy to satisfy. But without going so far, we may do something to establish the respectability of a non-Euclidean geometry by showing that it cannot be inconsistent unless Euclideani geometry is also inconsistent; and this result was in fact achieved in the last century by the discovery of ways of representing non-Euclidean geometry within Euclid's system. In the best known of these we suppose that when a phrase from the left in the following list occurs in elliptic geometry it is to have the same sense as the corresponding phrase on the right has in Euclidean geometry:

plane	surface of a sphere
straight line	arc of a great circle
angle between two straight lines	angle between the planes of two great circles.

If the other phrases used in elliptic geometry of two dimensions are allowed to retain thc mcanings customary for such phrases in Euclidean geometry, the system as a whole is then transformed into the geometry of the surface of a Euclidean sphere,a study familiar to navigators, and all the peculiar propositions of elliptic geometry of two dimensions are found to hold true in the new interpretation. Through a given point no line can be drawn parallel to a given straight line;there is a maximum length for a straight line; and the interior angles of any triangle are together greater than two right angles. From this it follows that if Euclid's geometry is consistent so too is elliptic geometry of two dimensions.'[4] By suitable interpretations of a rather more complicated kind Felix Klein and others have shown that both elliptic and hyperbolic geometry of three dimensions can be represented within Euclidean geometry. This does not mean that non-Euclidean geometrie are identical with parts of Euclidean geometry,but only that they can be *mapped* within Euclidean geometry in a sense somewhat like that in which the surface of France may be mapped on part of the surface of England.

What are we to say then of the status of Euclid's parallels postulate? If Euclid's geometry is consistent, there is clearly no *logical* contradiction involved in the denial of this postulate nor yet in the conjunction of its negation with the other axioms of Euclid, which is as much as to say that it is logically independent of those other axioms. If anyone wishes to insist that the postulate is true of straight lines in physical space, he may perhaps do so; but the pure mathematician need not concern himself with this question. For the development of non-Euclidean geometries has inevitably produced a change of attitude among mathematicians towards all geometry, including that of Euclid. Since there are alternatives, all worthy of study,it cannot be the business of the mathematician to assert the axioms which make any one of the alternatives what it is. His task is to say what follows *logically* from a given set of axioms. Consideration of traditional geometry in this fashion has naturally led to the demand for an explicit formulation of all its presuppositions, that is, for the rigorous carrying out of the programme we have attributed to Euclid; and the results can be seen in modern presentations of Euclid's geometry, e.g. in Hilbert's *Grundlagen der Geometrie* of 1899. But this way of looking at geometry has also led to a kind of abstraction which is far removed from the interests of Euclid.

When one proposition follows logically from another, it should be possible to formulate the two propositions in such a way that their relation can be seen to depend on their form alone, that is to say, on their logical structure as opposed to their special subject-matter. Now this can be done for the propositions of geometry. In the customary presentations of Euclidean geometry the form of the axioms is not easy to grasp because we use a number of special signs such as 'point', 'line', 'plane', 'lies on', 'between', 'parallel', and 'congruent', but we can write all the axioms we need for ordinary Euclidean geometry without using any special signs except the word 'point' and the phrase 'A is at the same distance from B as C is from D', which expresses congruence as a four-termed relation between points. Thus instead of 'C is collinear (lies on the same straight line) with A and B' we may say 'If P and Q are any two points such that A is at the same distance from P as A is from Q and B is at the same distance from P as B is from Q, then C also is at the same distance from P as C is from Q'. And instead of 'C is between A and B' we may say 'C is collinear with A and B and there are three points P, Q, and R such that (i) P is collinear with A and B, (ii) P is at the same distance from A as P is from B, (iii) Q is at the same distance from P as P is from A, (iv) R is at the same distance from P as P is from A, (v) C is collinear with Q and R, and (vi) C is at the same distance from Q as C is from R'. And instead of 'The line AB is parallel with the line CD' we may say 'The class of points collinear with A and B and the class of points collinear with C and D have no member in common'. Even the word 'point' need not be used; for we may safely leave it to be understood that the things or elements to which we refer by single letters are those things, whatever they may be, which are suitable in nature to be terms of the four-termed relation mentioned in the axioms. It is obviously tedious to write in this style a set of axiom formulae sufficent for ordinary Euclidean geometry, but when the task has been done, it is clear that apart from the expression 'A is at the same distance from B as C is from D' the only words used are those we reserve for expressing form, e.g. 'and', 'or', 'not', 'if, 'any', 'there is', and letters serving as variables. And since the theorems can also be expressed in this notation, it is possible to establish beyond doubt that the entailment of the theorems by the axioms does not depend on the meaning which the phrase 'A'is at the same distance from B as C is from D'has in application to the things we perceive.

Having come so far, we may go a step farther and say that for pure geometry the ordinary meaning of the phrase is quite irrelevant. If there were any other phrase with four gaps which could be substituted for it consistently in all the axiom formulae, then the same phrase could be substituted for it also in the theorem formulae without change in the relations of the latter to the former. What the geometer asserts is the highly abstract proposition that any four-termed relation which satisfies .ill the logical conditions prescribed in the axiom formulae must also satisfy each of the logical conditions formulated in the several theorem formulae; and he may if he likes make this clear by using a letter in place of the phrase given above,much as Aristotle used letters in formulating his principles of syllogistic. The conditions expressed in the various formulae of geometry by the other signs are of a complexity not considered by Aristotle, but for all that they are purely logical.

Sometimes it is said that the axiom formulae of a system of geometry together amount to an *implicit definition* of the special geometrical signs which they contain. This way of speaking, which was introduced by J. D. Gergonne as early as 1818,[5] is useful, but it can lead to misunderstandings. The axiom formulae of a geometrical system define an extra-logical expression which they contain only in the sense of delimiting the logical range within which the meaning of that expression must lie. For they impose only formal conditions; and although a geometer using the phrase 'A is at the same distance from B as C is from D' in his professional work need not concern himself with anything but the formal conditions satisfied by this relation of congruence, in ordinary usage the phrase has a meaning which is not exhausted by those conditions. If this were not so, there would be no sense in speaking of the application of geometry to the world we perceive. For such application depends on the finding of a perceptible relation which satisfies a set of formal conditions without being exhausted by them. In short, a pure intelligence with no perception of things in physical space might conceivably study geometry in abstract fashion, but its knowledge of geometry would not be a substitute for the perception which it lacked. When this point has been made clear, it can be seen that the development of non-Euclidean geometry does not, as some philosophers have supposed, disprove the old view of Euclid and Kant according to which the parallels postulate is a necessary truth about perceptual space. For it is at least arguable that the logical conditions prescribed by the axioms of Euclidean geometry hold necessarily of the perceptible relation of congruence. If, however, they do so hold, the statement that they hold is not a truth of formal logic, and so not a truth of geometry in the sense in which the word 'geometry' is now used by pure mathematicians. For the purposes of mathematics it is sufficient that the conditions prescribed by the axioms of a non-Euclidean geometry are consistent, i.e. do not lead to a self-contradiction, and the procedure of representation or mapping has shown that there cannot be an inconsistency in the axioms of either elliptic or hyperbolic geometry unless there is also an inconsistency in the axioms of Euclidean geometry.

When 'space' and words of similar origin occur in pure mathematics, they refer to abstract patterns of ordering which may conceivably be exemplified by widely differing systems of objects. Geometrical studies began, of course, with thought about relations in physical space, but they have progressed to the consideration of patterns which cannot be visualized. This tendency to abstraction can be detected already in the non-Euclidean geometries which have been mentioned, but it is even more obvious in geometries of many dimensions. Such geometries can be constructed in the 'synthetic' fashion of Euclid, but the easiest approach is by extension of the notions involved in Descartes's 'analytic' geometry. When we draw graphs, we think of each point on our squared paper as determined by two numbers, one a value for the variable x and the other a value for the variable y, and we say that a line on the paper corresponds to a certain functional relationship between these variables. Thus a straight line is the graph of some equation of the form y -= ax+b, because each point on that line is associated by the frame of reference with a couple of numbers which satisfy such an equation. Here we have an interpretation for Euclidean geometry of two dimensions according to which points are number couples and relations between points are relations of the kind studied in algebra. Such an interpretation can easily be applied also to Euclidean geometry of three dimensions. And we need not stop there. Applying the analogy in the opposite direction, we may, if we wish, use the language of geometry to describe a system in which the related entities are sets of values for four or more variables. Thus if (x_1, y_1, z_1, w_1) and (x_2, y_2, z_2, w_2) represent two sets of values for the four variables x, y, z, and w, we may perhaps find it convenient to use the word 'distance' for the quantity represented by

$$\sqrt{[(x_1-x_2)^2 + (y_1-y_2)^2 + (z_1-z_2)^2 + (w_1-w_2)^2]}.$$

Whether or not they approach multi-dimensional geometry by the route which Descartes opened, mathematicians rely on a numerical interpretation of axiom formulae for the proof of the consistency of any geometry they construct in axiomatic fashion. Admittedly elliptic and hyperbolic geometry of three dimensions can be shown to be consistent on the assumption that Euclidean geometry of three dimensions is consistent, and it may be thought an excess of caution to ask for a proof of the consistency of this latter. But it is by no means obvious that physical space is Euclidean in the sense of satisfying all Euclids axioms. We can scarcely maintain, for example, that we perceive either an out-ward infinity of points beyond points for ever or an inward infinity of points between points for ever; and if we say that physical space is nevertheless Euclidean in the fullest sense, we must claim to know this as a necessary truth revealed in spatial intuition. During the nineteenth century such claims became suspect, and attempts were therefore made to free geometry from the last traces of dependence on sense experience. For the mathematician proofs of the consistency of axiom sets by means of numerical interpretations have the great merit of remaining entirely within the mathematical domain.

Consistency is the prime requisite of any axiom set. For a conjunction of inconsistent propositions entails any proposition whatsoever, as the writers on *consequentiae* remarked in the Middle Ages, and there is nothing to be learnt from study of a system in which the negation of every theorem is also a theorem. Mutual independence of axioms is not essential in the same way. That is to say, a deductive system is not shown to be worthless when it is discovered that one axiom can be derived from the others. But it is obviously inelegant to introduce as an axiom something which can be proved as a theorem; and apart from that, proofs of independence are required for a proper understanding of the structure of any system under investigation. Both points are illustrated clearly by the history of the parallels postulate. Now to prove that an axiom is independent of the other axioms of a set it is sufficient to show that its negation is consistent with those other axioms, and for this purpose the geometer relies once more on the method of numerical interpretation.

If two different interpretations of any kind for the extra-logical signs in a set of axiom formulae both yield truths and the systems of things described by the formulae in these interpretations are so related that for every item in the one there is a single corresponding item in the other, the two interpretations are said to be isomorphic.If, further, *all* the results of possible interpretations (or models, as they are sometimes called) for a certain set of axiom formulac are isomorphic one to another, the set of axioms is said to be categorical or monomorphic. This notion was familiar to Dedekind in 1887,[6] but the name 'categorical' was introduced by Veblen in 1904 on the suggestion of the logician Dewey.[7] Probably Veblen and Dewey had in mind a contrast between categorical and disjunctive propositions; but in origin 'categorical' means 'predicative', rather than 'non-disjunctive', and apart from that the word has the disadvantage of being much over-worked in other contexts. It therefore seems better to follow Carnap in talking instead about a contrast between monomorphic and polymorphic sets of axioms.[8]

A monomorphic set of axioms can be said to carry out completely the programme of implicit definition. For although the formulae in which it is presented may admit many different interpretations, these latter must all have the same logical structure and so be indistinguishable by purely formal criteria. If a set of axioms is monomorphic, it is useless to attempt further specification of the meanings of the extra-logical signs in its formulae by addition of any more axiom formulae in the same symbolism. For whatever formula we choose, either it or its negation is already a consequence of the axiom formulae in the sense of being true for every interpretation they admit. This is not to say, however, that a monomorphic set of axioms can never be usefully enlarged in any way. Monomorphism is always relative to a certain apparatus of primitive concepts, as may be seen most clearly in consideration of another geometrical example.

During the nineteenth century geometry developed not only by consideration of alternatives to Euclid's parallels postulate and by removal of his restriction to three dimensions, but also by distinction of different levels of geometrical properties. It had been known for a long time that there were some properties of figures which survived even when the figures were subjected to transformations of certain kinds. Thus Pascal (using methods suggested by Desargues, in particular the assumption of points at infinity) proved in the seventeenth century that if a hexagon is inscribed in a conic section the three points in which its opposite sides intersect must lie in a straight line. Since the theorem holds not only of a hexagon inscribed in a circle but also of any hexagon obtained by projection of that figure on a plane from a point, it is clear that we have to do here with a projective as opposed to a metrical property; that is to say, the theorem belongs to a level of geometry in which we consider relative positions without regard to measurements. There are other properties of figures which survive transformations even more drastic than projection. If, for example, we draw a square within a circle on a sheet of rubber and then stretch the rubber in any way we please, the figure which was originally inside remains inside, although it may cease to square or even to be rectilinear. Here we have to do with a property belonging to the yet deeper level of topology, where not only distance but even the difference between a straight line and a curve may be ignored. In the definition of a geometry of given level it is convenient to use the language of Klein and say that the geometry studies all properties which are invariant under the operations of a certain group. By 'operations' we mean here transformations such as displacements and rotations in space, projections, whether parallel or central, and the distortions described above; and by 'group' we mean a set of operations such that (*a*) the result of the successive applications of any two operations of the set is itself an operation of the set and (*b*) the inverse of any operation of the set is also an operation of the set. Incidentally, this notion of a group, first conceived by Galois (1811-32), is one of those high abstractions which now find application in many different fields of mathematics.'[9]

For our present purpose the important point is that the

axiom set of a geometry of lower level may be monomorphic although it certainly does not entail all the theorems belonging to geometries of higher level. We have seen that the propositions of ordinary Euclidean metrical geometry can all be formulated by use of a single special sign for the four-termed relation of congruence. In the paper in which he introduced the word 'categorical' to describe certain axiom sets, Veblen showed that all the prepositions of a deeper system called descriptive geometry could be formulated by use of a single special sign for the three-termed relation of betweenness or serial order. Since betweenness can be defined in terms of congruence and metrical geometry contains theorems which do not occur in descriptive geometry, it may be thought that a set of axioms for the latter must inevitably be polymorphic. But this is not so. Veblen's set of axioms for descriptive geometry is monomorphic *with respect to betweenness*. If his axioms were all rephrased by use of the definition for between-ness mentioned above, the resulting set would indeed be polymorphic but *with respect to congruence.*

Since for the purpose of specification a monomorphic set of axioms cannot be usefully enlarged by means of new axioms expressed in the same symbolism, it is in a sense complete. But there is a stronger sense of the word 'complete' in which a deductive system with a monomorphic set of axioms may still be incomplete. In order to understand this we must think of completeness as defined by reference to proof and related to the principle of excluded middle in much the same way as consistency is related to the principle of non-contradiction. Let us choose any proposition which requires for its expression no primitive extra-logical signs but those of a given axiom set. Then if the axiom set is to be consistent, it must not allow both the proof of that proposition and also for the proof of its negation. And if it is to be complete in the strong sense we are now considering, it must provide either for the proof of the proposition or for the proof of its negation. At first sight this requirement for completeness looks like a requirement for monomorphism which we mentioned above, namely that the axioms should have either the proposition or its negation as a consequence, but it is really more stringent. For there may perhaps be a proposition expressible in the symbolism of a monomorphic axiom set which is a consequence of the axioms and yet not provable by deduction from them because the derivation would have to be infinitely long and therefore not a proof. We shall see later that this is in fact the situation in some very important parts of mathematics.

2. NUMBERS AND FUNCTIONS

We have seen that for proofs of consistency geometers commonly use numerical interpretations of their axiom sets. In doing so they hope to free their science from all extra-mathematical assumptions. But what is the basis of the part of mathematics that deals with number? In order to give a satisfactory numerical interpretation of any system of geometry which involves the notion of continuity we must make use of numbers such as $\sqrt{2}$ and π., and these gave rise to perplexity already in antiquity.

By some argument which is not now clear to us the Pythagoreans convinced themselves that they had found the key to the understanding of the universe in the notion of ratio, i.e. in the concept of a relation between two natural numbers. No doubt they were impressed by the importance of ratio in music, and they may perhaps have been influenced by the fact that λογος, the Greek word for a ratio, is also the common word for reason or explanation. Alternatively they may have been the first to use λογος in a mathematical sense. But whatever the ground of their metaphysical claims may have been, they were greatly disturbed by the discovery of the incommensurability of the diagonal with the side of a square. For here in a very simple case it was shown that talk of the ratio between the lengths of two lines led to contradiction, although common sense seemed to support philosophy in insisting that there must be some determinate relation:

obviously the diagonal was more than a third bigger than the side, but not so much as a half bigger. Eudoxus saved the situation by providing a general account of proportion which was sufficient for geometry, and his theory (preserved in book v of Euclid's *Elements*) is a remarkable piece of work on the philosophy of mathematics. The essence of it is a new definition of the equality of ratios between magnitudes:

'The first of four magnitudes is said to have the same ratio to the second that the third has to the fourth, when any equimultiples whatever of the first and the third being taken, and any equimultiples whatever of the second and the fourth, if the multiple of the first be less than that of the second, the multiple of the third is also less than that of the fourth, and if the multiple of the first be equal to that of the second, the multiple of the third is also equal to that of the fourth, and if the multiple of the first be greater than that of the second, the multiple of the third is also greater than that of the fourth.'

This means in effect that where we cannot speak of a ratio in the strict Pythagorean sense (i.e. of a certain relation between natural numbers) we may nevertheless speak of a ratio in an extended sense, if it can be shown that every ratio in the strict Pythagorean sense is either too small or too large. In other words, the existence of a ratio in the extended sense is identified with the possibility of distributing all Pythagorean ratios between the mutually exclusive classes of the too small and the too large. We shall see presently that this suggestion is still used in mathematical analysis, i.e. the branch of mathematics which deals with continuously varying magnitudes; but in order to get the subject into proper perspective we must first consider the development of the number concept since Greek times.

The earliest numerals were probably adjectives like 'one', 'two', 'three'. In Greek and many other languages such words, or at any rate some of them, are declined like ordinary adjectives,but it is obvious that they cannot qualify nouns in the same way as other adjectives do. For although a man who says that he has two large dogs intends to convey that each of the dogs is large, he certainly does not mean that each of them is two. This is slightly puzzling, but it is even more curious that in some languages, including English, the same sounds or marks are often used as proper names. We say, for example, 'Two is the smallest prime'. This usage belongs to talk of numbers as objects distinct both from the sets of things we count and also from the numerals we use in counting them; for what is true of the number two cannot even be denied sensibly of a pair of dogs or of a word. And there can scarcely have been any such talk before the development of arithmetic as a calculus. We have, indeed, some evidence to show that it did not come easily to Greeks of Plato's time. In the *Theologumena Arithmeticae*, formerly attributed to Iamblichus, there is a quotation from Plato's pupil Speusippus which shows a remarkable uncertainty of language.[10] The passage is about the Pythagorean doctrine of the perfection of the number ten, and within a few paragraphs it contains no less than four different designations for the number ten, namely, τα δεκα, ο τωνδεκα αριθμος, ο δεκα, and δεκα. The first means literally 'the ten [things]', the second 'the number of the ten [things]', the third 'the [number] ten', and the fourth just 'ten'. Furthermore, when Speusippus wishes to say that four is a multiple of two, he produces a strange sentence in which the symbol for four is treated as neuter plural and the symbol for two as masculine singular.

Apart from adjectives like 'one', 'two', 'three', even the most primitive languages have numerical terms such as 'a half, 'a third', 'a quarter'; but the usage whereby signs such as—I, 3/2, √2, and √—I are said to stand for numbers is a product of the last few centuries. Like the use of numerals as proper names, this development is connected with the elaboration of mathematical calculi. It has been inspired in particular by Descartes's application of algebraic symbolism to geometry.

Let us suppose first that consideration of some problem has led us to formulate the equation $x+3=2$. It may be, for example, that we want to know how much money a man had in the bank before he brought his balance to £2 by paying in £3. Clearly the equation cannot be solved at all in terms of natural numbers, but if we allow ourselves to talk of negative numbers, we may write x = – I. And we can represent such numbers conveniently by placing marks on a line at equal intervals to the left of a point labelled 0:

–3 –2 –1 0 1 2 3

Secondly, numbers such as 3/2 must be recognized if we are to talk of solving equations like $2x–3 = 0$. With these we have an enormous addition to the numbers which can be represented by points on a line. For between any two fractions it is always possible to find another; and this is as much as to say that there is an infinity of fractions in any finite interval such as that between the numbers o and I. We must not assume, however, that with this enlargement we have recognized numbers corresponding to all the points on a line: if we construct a square whose side is one unit in length and then lay off its diagonal along the line from the origin, the end point is not one among those to which we have so far assigned numbers. But this gap and infinitely many others are closed by a third enlargement of the number concept to cover algebraic irrationals such as $\sqrt{2}$ and transcendental (or non-algebraic) irrationals such as π. With the former we are entitled to talk of solving algebraic equations like $x^2–2 = o$, and with the latter we can complete the linear continuum. Finally a fourth enlargement commits us to recognizing the 'imaginary' number $\sqrt{–I}$, as a proper root of the equation $x^2–I = o$. Here the impulse to enlargement seems to have come entirely from formal algebra. There is no point on the straight line corresponding to$\sqrt{–I}$, and tlie mathematicians of the eighteenth century who used imaginaries did so only in order to make their calculations simpler and more general. But so long as imaginaries were admitted for this reason alone, their status was thought to be very mysterious. If a pupil asked for a justification of their use, there was little his teacher could say except that faith comes with works. This appearance of mystery was dissipated when Wessel in 1797 and Argand in 1806 showed a way of connecting imaginaries with motion in a plane. In Descartes's analytical geometry numbers are correlated with points according to the *distance* of these latter from certain co-ordinates; but it is possible also to think of a number as a vector or measure of the *displacement* through which a particle must go to reach a point, and within this scheme multiplication of a vector by $\sqrt{-I}$ obviously represents reversal of the direction of motion. What could be more natural and satisfactory than to say that multiplication of a vector by ,$\sqrt{-I}$ represents rotation through a right angle, i.e. an operation whose repetition produces complete reversal? So at least most students of mathematics have thought from that day to this, and the fact that we can still derive pleasure from this interpretation gives some indication of the discomfort mathematicians must have felt when there was yet no known way of connecting the symbol with spatial intuition.

When we speak of successive enlargements of the number concept, we are inclined to think that the history can be summarized in a scheme of the following kind, where the names printed in italics stand for new kinds of numbers added to our original store:

Obviously integers are so called in opposition to fractions, rational numbers in opposition to irrational, and real numbers in opposition to imaginary; and the system of naming naturally suggests a classification of species within a genus. But this way of describing the development is mistaken. We should speak rather of an hierarehy of five different types of numbers in which each higher type contains a subset corresponding to each lower type. In the following scheme each type is represented by a horizontal line, and correspondences are indicated by dotted vertical lines:

Natural } Integral
Negative }

Integral } Rational
Fractional }

Rational } Real
Irrational }

Real } Numbers
Imaginary }

Complex numbers
Real numbers
Rational numbers
Signed integers
Natural numbers

The positive integer+2 is not the same as the natural number 2, and our custom of writing the symbol 2 instead of the symbol +2 is justified only by the fact that our rules for calculating with positive integers correspond exactly to our rules for calculating with natural numbers. Similarly the rational number +2/+1 must be distinguished in strict theory from the positive integer +2 and from the natural number 2, although we shall not fall into mistakes if we ignore the difference when we calculate. In the equation:

$$1+\frac{1}{2}+\frac{1}{4}+\frac{1}{8}+\ldots\ldots=2$$

we use the same sign 2 in yet another way, namely for a real number. And in certain contexts we may also make it serve as an abbreviation for the longer sign $2+0\sqrt{-1}$, that is for the symbol of a complex number in which the imaginary part is nil.

At each higher level in our diagram the whole of the type represented by a horizontal line is radically new-, though mathematicians, failing to recognize this, have sometimes devised a new name only for that part of the type which is represented by the projecting portion of the line. And, except in one respect, the order of the development is fixed, that is to say, we could not have a calculus of complex numbers before we had a calculus of real numbers or a calculus of real numbers before we had a calculus of rational numbers. The exception concerns signed numbers: we could, if we wished, delay the distinction of positive and negative numbers until after the introduction of rational numbers or even until after the introduction of real numbers. And it seems that men had in fact a special notation for fractions before they spoke of negative numbers. But the scheme suggested above is the simplest because it makes the order of the appearance of negative, fractional, and irrational numbers correspond to the customary order of the inverse operations with which they are historically connected, i.e. subtraction, division, and extraction of roots.

The field of natural numbers is closed under the operations of addition, multiplication, and exponentiation, that is to say, except for certain special cases involving o, we always get a natural number as result if we add one natural number to another, or multiply one by another or raise one -to the power of another. But this field is not closed under the operation of subtraction. The field of signed integers, on the other hand, is closed under all four of the operations mentioned so far, but not under the operation of division. For a field in which it is always possible to carry out that operation we must go on to consider rational numbers. But in this field we cannot always carry out the operation of extracting a root. And so we are led on to consider the field of real numbers, in which all positive numbers have roots of all desired degrees, and finally that of complex numbers, in which all the operations we have mentioned can be carried on without restriction. Apart from these there are other operations (such as that of taking the limit of a convergent infinite sequence) which may be applied already in the field of real numbers, but the field of complex numbers is especially interesting in the development of the theory of *functions*.

In mathematical language the word 'function' is used to indicate an operation which when applied to some entity called its argument (or to an ordered set of entities, if it is a function of more than one argument) yields some entity described (rather curiously) as the value of the function for that argument. Or if the word 'operation' suggests too strongly the intervention of men, we may say that mathematical talk of a function is equivalent to talk of a relationship in which an entity (normally unique) called a value of the function may stand to an entity called an argument of the function. Very often the relationship is expressed by a functional equation of the form $y = f(x\}$: in which the letter x is the independent variable, taking as its values the arguments of the function, and the letters the dependent variable, taking as its values the values of the function for the various possible arguments. Sometimes also a function is said to be *from* a certain class which is the range of possible arguments of the function *to* a certain class which is the range of possible values of the function.

This modern definition is so drawn that it can be applied already within the field of natural numbers. We may say, for example, that the function expressed by n^2 takes the value 4 for, the argument 2. But the terminology is derived from mechanics and associated historically with thought of continuous variation. Originally the word 'variable', now used to refer to letters occurring in certain ways in mathematical texts, was applied to physical magnitudes which varied with time, e.g. the distance of one particle from another or the pressure of a gas, and in formulae of the kind $y = f(x)$ the letters x and y were regarded as abbreviations for phrases such as 'the time elapsed' and 'the distance traversed'. When pure mathematicians began to talk of variables and functions, they did so because they were interested in the mathematical patterns exhibited by some physical laws; but they could no longer say that the letters they used were abbreviations for phrases like those just mentioned, and the usages which they then adopted, in particular the custom of calling the letters themselves variables, have given rise to a great deal of confusion and perplexity.

Sometimes it has been said that the letters called variables denote variable numbers, and at other times it has been said that they denote variably and ambiguously all the numbers which are their values. Neither explanation makes good sense. For numbers do not vary, and such variations as there may be in the denotation of signs are of no interest to mathematicians. Again it has been said: 'One variable y is a function of another variabley x if for every determinate value of x, or at least for every determinate value within some range, there is at least one value of y correlated with it according to a rule.' This explanation might have been satisfactory when the word 'variable' was used to refer to a physical magnitude; but it is very unsatisfactory when the word is used to refer to a letter, since it suggests that a function is a letter, or at any rate a symbol of some sort, although it is quite clear that the mathematicians who write about the theory of functions are not engaged in a branch of philology. Probably no mathematician engaged in his ordinary concerns has ever been seriously misled by remarks such as these, and in any case it is too late to think of abandoning the old terminology which gives rise to the trouble. But the point seems worth noticing, because the use of the word 'function' has been extended still farther in modern logic and has undoubtedly led to some serious misunderstandings there.

For the same reason it is worth remarking that there are at least two different ways in which a functional expression may occur with a variable in a mathematical text. When a mathematician\writes

$$\tan x = \frac{\sin x}{\cos x},$$

the letter x is part of a symbolism of universality by means of which he makes a statement about all numbers. The symbolism is extremely useful for its purpose, because it *suggests* what is in fact the case, namely, that replacement of the letter x throughout the equation by any numeral will yield another true statement. Moreover, we can safely reason with the equation in most contexts as *though* x were itself a numeral.

When, however, a mathematician says in his letter—press 'We shall now discuss the function tan x', the letter x does not express universality, and it is not clear what grammatical role we should assign to the whole complex symbol tan x. If, as is sometimes said, the letter x serves here merely to mark a gap, the expression tan x can scarcely be the name of a function, any more than 'father of—' is the name of a relationship in ordinary English. But we can speak sensibly of the function *expressed by* the complex symbol tan x just as we can speak of the relationship expressed by 'father of—', and the common mathematical phrase quoted above may perhaps be regarded as an abbreviation for this way of talking. We shall see later that failure to appreciate this point has sometimes caused bewilderment among logicians who have adopted the language of functions for their own purposes.

Obviously we cannot use number expressions of higher types in the same way as we use ordinary numerals: it makes no sense to say there $5+3\sqrt{-1}$ men in the room. Why then do we continue to talk of *numbers* throughout this development ? It seems that our enlargement of the number concept is really an extension of the usage of the word 'number' to cover entities of various types, and that this is justified only by the possibility of calculating with symbols for these various entities according to the same basic rules of algebra, i.e. the commutative rules:

$$x + y = y + x \text{ and } xy = yx,$$

the associative rules:

$$(x + y) + z = x + (y + z) \text{ and } (xy)z = x(yz)$$

and the distributive rule

$$x(y + z) = xy+xy$$

A system of numbers in the extended sense is indeed just a set of entities for which all these laws hold *with suitable definitions of addition and multiplication*. The last point is important, since the notions of addition and multiplication appropriate in the calculus of natural numbers cannot be applied in a calculus of numbers of another type. If, for example, we wish to speak of multiplication of signed integers, we must first explain how we use the word 'multiplication' in this context, i.e. according to the rules:

$$(+a)\ (+b) = +ab,\ (+a)\ (-b) = -ab,\ (-a)\ (-b) = +ab$$

This is as much as to say that the basic rules of algebra are systematically ambiguous, or better, that they give in abstract fashion certain logical conditions to be satisfied by the operations of any calculus which we call a calculus with numbers.

Up to and including the introduction of complex numbers the development was unconscious in the sense that mathematicians extended their use of the word 'number' without realizing exactly what they were doing. They were guided, no doubt, by respect for what G. Peacock in 1833 called 'the principle of the permanence of equivalent forms,[11] that is to say by a desire to retain the general rules of algebra stated above; but they thought of each successive novelty as something they were forced to adopt in order to solve problems posed at the previous stage, and they did not consider algebra in abstraction from its exemplifications or try to invent new calculi for the sake of carrying development as far as it could go. In the nineteenth century the situation changed. In the first place, a number of distinguished mathematicians began to think of algebra in an abstract fashion. Peacock has been mentioned already, but there were others. D. F. Gregory, for example, wrote a paper 'On the Real Nature of Symbolical Algebra' in 1838,[12] and De Morgan published a series of four papers about 'The Foundations of Algebra' between 1839 and 1844-'[13] Secondly, there were attempts to invent new calculi. H. Grassmann, for example, produced in 1844 a book on *Ausdehnungslehre* which carries out Leibniz's project of a geometrical calculus. And from 1844, when he published his first paper on quaternions, Sir William Rowan Hamilton of Dublin devoted a great deal of energy to perfecting a new algebra of hyper-complex numbers. It is interesting, however, to notice that Hamilton did not work entirely in the void. His efforts were all inspired by a desire to elaborate a calculus which would do for motion in three-dimensional space what the theory of complex numbers seemed to do very satisfactorily for motion in a plane. As complex numbers are expressible in the form $x+yi$ where the letter i is an abbreviation for $\sqrt{-1}$, so his quaternions are expressible in the form $x+yi+zj+wk$ where the letters i, j, and k represent rotations in three mutually perpendicular planes. But, unlike the theory of complex numbers, his system does not satisfy all the basic rules of algebra. In order to retain the other rules he had to abandon the commutative law for multiplication and declare $ij = -ji$. For this reason quaternions are not universally recognized as numbers. And the same can be said of other suggestions, e.g. matrices, which may perhaps be thought to provide an extension of the number concept beyond the domain of complex numbers. For it is now known that there can be no such extension without sacrifice of some one of the rules which determine the meaning of the word 'number' as that has been used hitherto in mathematics. This is not to say that it is foolish to talk of hyper-complex numbers, but that if we do so our usage is justified only by a partial analogy.

What did the mathematicians think of this progress from natural to complex numbers while it was taking place? At first each step produced a feeling of uneasiness, and then after a while each seemed inevitable. So far at least as real numbers, the progress was guided by spatial considerations; and even imaginary numbers, which had been introduced originally to preserve the generality of certain patterns of calculation, were accepted as fully respectable subjects of mathematical discourse only after they had been incorporated into a theory of complex numbers with a spatial interpretation. But very soon after the main development had been completed doubts began to arise about the reliability of spatial intuition as a basis for assertions about the continuum of real numbers. These doubts were not due to any difficulties in the application of mathematics, nor yet to the influence of non-Euclidean geometry, but arose rather from discoveries within matematical analysis itself. It was shown, for example, by Bolzano in 1830, and later also by Weierstrass, that some continuous functions are not differentiable.[14] In geometrical language this seems to mean that there may be continuous curves without tangents. And paradoxes even more surprising were to follow. One of the most striking is concerned with the density of the rational points in a line. Let us suppose that the numbers o and 1 have been assigned to two points on a line, and that we decide to place a little canopy over each of the intervening points which have thus been made to correspond to rational numbers:

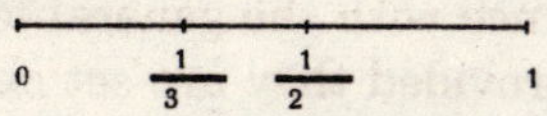

Since there are infinitely many fractions between any two fractions we may select, it seems natural to assume that every canopy will overlap with others and that the sum of their lengths will inevitably exceed one unit, however small the individual canopies may be. But this is not so. For if we consider the fractions between O and I in the order

$$\frac{1}{2}, \frac{1}{3}, \frac{2}{3}, \frac{1}{4}, \frac{3}{4}, \frac{1}{5}, \frac{2}{5}, \frac{3}{5}, \ldots\ldots$$

and then a sign to the first a canopy of length equal to 1/10, of unit to the second a canopy of length equal to 1/10 of a unit, to the third a canopy of length equal to 1/10 of a unit, and so on, the sum of the lengths of all the canopies will be only.

$$\frac{1}{10} + \frac{1}{10^2} + \frac{1}{103} + \ldots = \frac{1}{9}.$$

Admittedly we cannot draw all the canopies with a pencil, but it is evident that our rule of procedure assigns a determinate length of canopy to each distinguishable fraction, since each such fraction has a place in our order.

When once doubt had been thrown on the reliability of spatial intuition as a source of mathematical knowledge, it became necessary to re-examine all the currently accepted proofs, and the result was a radical reconstruction of mathematics by such men as Cauchy (1789-1857) and Weierstrass (1815-97). It has been said, indeed, that nothing was satisfactorily proved in analysis before the nineteenth century. Now in analysis, just as in geometry, rigour requires the explicit formulation of everything essential to a demonstration; and so we find attention directed in the nineteenth century to the formulae which provide implicit definitions of the various types of numerical expressions. Whether these formulae are regarded as special rules of calculation or as axioms from which theorems are to be derived in accordance with the general laws of logic is of no great importance, provided they are set out fully and recognized to be fundamental. But it is natural to ask why we should have just these formulae. Is there some inherent necessity in the course of development which has led us to adopt them? Or are they conventions of our own making, suggested indeed by an interest in the description of nature or by a desire for abstract generality in mathematics itself, but incapable of proof precisely because they are just conventions? These questions were raised in the nineteenth century and are still debated in our own day. Perhaps the proper way of dealing with the problem is to show that the antithesis of discovery and invention has been wrongly conceived. For it is certain that mathematicians may construct calculi to serve their special interests, and it is equally certain that they are not entirely free in their choice of conventions. We can say, if we like, that Hamilton invented quaternions, but we must allow that neither he nor anyone else could make a system of hyper-complex numbers which satisfies all the laws of algebra valid for complex numbers. However that may be, the first step towards the clarification of the issue was the exact formulation of the rules of the various calculi which had already won recognition, and this was taken in the nineteenth century.

At each stage in the enlargement of the number concept we have to do with entities of a new type defined implicitly by the rules of operation of a new calculus. But in some contexts where we commonly speak of signed integers or of rational numbers it is possible to say all we want to say without talk about numbers of a new type. Thus instead of the equation $3—5 = —2$ we can write $3+2 = 5$, and instead of $5/3=10/6$we can write $5 \times 6 = 10\times3$. And even when we find it convenient to reckon with signed integers or rational numbers we may regard these as ordered pairs of numbers selected from the next lower type and subjected to special rules of operation. The calculus of signed integers, for example, can be developed from rules such as:

$$(a, b) = (c, d) \text{ if and only if } a + d = b + c,$$
$$(a, b) + (c, d) = (a+c, b+d),$$
and $$(a, b) (c, d) \ (ac+bd, ad+bc)$$

At first sight this seems unfamiliar, but in order to obtain the usual method of representation we need only write +a and — a as abbreviations for the two standard forms (a, o) and (o, a) to which our new numerical expressions are reducible in accordance with our special rules of equality. The special rules of the calculus of rational numbers are different, of course, but no more complicated. Nor is this the end of the possibilities of explanation by means of ordered pairs; for in 1835 Hamilton showed that the calculus of complex numbers could be presented as a calculus of ordered pairs of real numbers with suitably devised rules of equality, addition, multiplication, &c. If it could be shown that talk about real numbers was related in somewhat similar fashion to talk about rational numbers, the chain wouid be complete and we should be able to say in the terminology of Lord Russell that all numbers of higher types were logical constructions from natural numbers. That is to say, it would no longer be necessary to introduce numbers of higher types as new entities discovered by intuition of spatial or temporal continuity, since talk about them would be equivalent in principle to rather complicated talk about natural numbers and their properties. This programme, which has provided the inspiration for much later philosophy, is called the arithmetization of analysis.

Unfortunately real numbers have proved as troublesome to modern mathematicians as they were to the school of Pythagoras. The reason is that the calculus of real numbers cannot be presented as a calculus with any *finite* sets of rational numbers. As soon as we begin to reckon with real numbers, we commit ourselves to talk about infinity with all the difficulties that entails. This may be seen clearly from consideration of two theories of real numbers which were formulated last century.

The first was suggested by Weierstrass and developed by Cantor. In effect it amounts to identifying a real number with an infinite sequence of rational numbers which are commonly said to be successive approximations to it. In elementary arithmetic we have, for example, a procedure for extracting square roots, and by continued application of this we can work out the value of√2 to as many places of decimals as we desire. Since √2 is irrational, the procedure never leads to a conclusion, that is to a decimal expression which is completed by noughts or by a recurring period of digits, though our use of the phrase 'working out the value of√2' may tempt us to think that there is some complete decimal expression, i.e. that √2 is of the same nature as the number we call our approximations. According to Cantor the real number -√2 maybe identified with the sequence 1·4, 1·41, 1·414, 1·4142, &c., through which we proceed when we work first to one place of decimals, then to two, then to three, then to four, and so on. The sequence is potentially infinite, but we are able to lay down rules for reckoning with it as a number because the succession of its terms is fixed by a law.

The second theory of real numbers, which was put forward by Dedekind in his *Stetigkeit und irrationale Zahlen* of 1872, is a modern version of Eudoxus's theory of proportions. Although we cannot find any rational number whose square is equal to 2, we can divide the rational, numbers exhaustively into those which are and those which are not positive numbers with squares greater than 2. According to Dedekind √2 is just the cut by which the rational numbers are divided in this way. If this sounds too paradoxical, we may say that √2 is the infinite set of rational numbers satisfying the second condition; for the place of the cut is uniquely determined by the constitution of the lower set, and this formulation has the advantage of making it easier to compare the definition with other definitions of numbers of higher types. For as signed integers, rational numbers, and complex numbers are all defined as sets of numbers of the next lower type, so too are real numbers in this theory; but here, as in the scheme of Cantor, the set used for definition of a real number must be infinite. The two theories of real numbers are equivalent in the sense that a calculus of infinite sequences constructed to the prescription of Cantor has the same structure as a calculus of cuts constructed to the prescription of Dedekind. And this is not surprising, for a convergent infinite sequence is the appropriate instrument for locating a Dedekindian cut.

The definition of real numbers by means of infinite sets of rational numbers seems satisfactory in the sense that it gives us what we expect in the calculus of real numbers and relates this to the calculus of rational numbers which precedes. But it does not allow for the arithmetization of analysis, if we mean by that phrase, as apparently Kronecker did, the reduction of all mathematical statements to statements about natural numbers. For a statement which refers to an *infinite* set of rational numbers cannot be reduced in the strict sense, as a statement which refers only to a finite set of particular rational numbers may be. And if we give up the programme of complete reduction, we have still to face the difficulty of proving the consistency of the special rules we adopt for our calculus of real numbers. How is this to be done without begging the question at issue, namely the existence of the numbers which the rules are supposed to define ? Although these criticisms were not worked out in detail during the nineteenth century, they were sufficiently well understood to produce misgivings in the minds of some mathematicians. Frege, for example, like Kronecker, was never completely satisfied by the theories of real numbers current in his time. In later chapters we shall have occasion to consider some of the difficulties in more detail.

3. BOOLE AND THE ALGEBRA OF LOGIC

Geometry and algebra have contributed in different ways to the development of mathematical logic. Geometry, as we saw in the first section of this chapter, has provided a field for the working out of the notions of axiomatics, while algebra has furnished a model for imitation in the making of a logical calculus. Leibniz realized already in the seventeenth century that there is some resemblance between disjunction and conjunction of concepts on the one hand and addition and multiplication of numbers on the other, but he did not find it easy to formulate the resemblance precisely and then to use it as the basis of a calculus of logic. It was this that George Boole (1815-64) achieved in his *Mathematical Analysis of Logic*.[15] The idea that algebraic formulae might be used to express logical relations occurred to him first when he was still in his teens, working as an usher in a private school at Lincoln and educating himself by extensive reading. But the renewed interest in logic which led him to write this little book in 1847 was due to the appearance in periodicals of letters on the once famous controversy in which Sir William Hamilton of Edinburgh claimed priority in adoption of the doctrine of the quantification of predicates, charged Augustus De Morgan with plagiarism, and made foolish remarks against mathematics as an element in education. Before publishing his work Boole wrote to De Morgan, whose interests he shared, but the latter was finishing his *Formal Logic* at the time and suggested that they should both publish before consulting on their results. The two books appeared at about the same time; according to one story they reached the shops on the same day.

Although Boole's interest in mathematical logic was stimulated by an ephemeral dispute, it was surely no accident that there had been considerable discussion of the nature of algebra shortly before he wrote. We can safely assume that he had read some of the papers of Peacock, Gregory, De Morgan, and Sir William Rowan Hamilton which were mentioned in the last section. Gregory, the editor of the *Cambridge Mathematical Journal*, was a personal friend who had given him confidence in his powers as a mathematician. And apart from that Boole's aesthetic interest in mathematics led him to value very highly all attempts to achieve abstract generality. His reputation had been established by an essay of 1844 on *A General Method in Analysis*, in which- he contributed to the generalization of algebraic reasoning by making free use of the calculus of operators, or separation of symbols, as it was then called.

From works which had already been published it was possible for Boole to collect two important discoveries: (i) that there could be an algebra of entities which were not numbers in any ordinary sense, and (ii) that the laws which hold for types of numbers up to and including complex numbers need not all be retained together in an algebraic system not applicable to such numbers. With his genius for generalization he saw that an algebra could be developed as an abstract calculus capable of various interpretations. The view of logic which he derived from this insight is clearly stated in the opening section of his *Mathematical Analysis of Logic*:

'They who are acquainted with the present state of the theory of Symbolical Algebra, are aware that the validity of the processes of analysis does not depend upon the interpretation of the symbols which are employed, but solely upon the laws of their combination. Every system of interpretation which does not affect the truth of the relations supposed, is equally admissible, and it is thus that the same processes may, under one scheme of interpretation, represent the solution of a question on the properties of numbers, under another, that of a geometrical problem, and under a third, that of a problem of dynamics or optics.... We might justly assign it as the definitive character of a true Calculus, that it is a method resting upon the employment of Symbols, whose laws of combination are known and general, and whose results admit of a consistent interpretation. That to the existing forms of Analysis a quantitative interpretation is assigned, is the result of circumstances by which those forms were determined, and is not to be construed into a universal condition of Analysis. It is upon the foundation of this general principle, that I purpose to establish the Calculus of Logic, and that I claim for it a place among the acknowledged forms of Mathematical Analysis, regardless that in its objects and in its instruments it must at present stand alone.'

Specimens of the first edition of Boole's pamphlet are now scarce, and it cannot be supposed that many were sold. In the following year, however, he published a short account of his Calculus of Logic in the *Cambridge and Dublin Mathematical Journal*, and this may have been more widely read among mathematicians. It adds nothing to the theory of the pamphlet, but it is somewhat easier to follow, and it ends with a paragraph which summarizes Boole's position very clearly:

'The view which these enquiries present of the nature of language is a very interesting one. They exhibit it not as a mere collection of signs, but as a system of expressions, the elements of which are subject to the laws of the thought which they represent. That these laws are as rigorously mathcmatical as the laws which govern the purely quantitative conceptions of space and time, of number and magnitude, is a conclusion which I do not hesitate to submit to the exactest scrutiny.'

In 1849 Boole was appointed to the chair of mathematics in Queen's College Cork, then newly founded, and immediately began the preparation of a larger book about his logical theory. Of this period of his life he said that mental science was his study and mathematics his recreation. This does not mean that he was unproductive in mathematics (he composed notes on quaternions at this time), but that he spent a great deal of energy in familiarizing himself with what had been written by philosophers about the foundations of logic. The result of his labour was *An Investigation of the Laws of Thought on which are founded The Mathematical Theories of Logic and Probabilities*. This work, which was published in 1854 at the expense of Boole and a friend, did not sell very well, but it was read by many who had not seen the *Mathematical Analysis of Logic*, and it is often regarded as Boole's masterpiece. The chief novelty of the book is its application of his ideas to the calculus of probabilities. This is well done; but for the rest, the book is not very original. There is no important change on the formal side, and it cannot be said that the main ideas are presented more lucidly than in the earlier work. There are, however, some elaborate examples and some metaphysical passages which are interesting, if only for the light they throw on Boole's reading.

Towards the end of his life Boole said that he was dissatisfied with the exposition and arrangement of his *Laws of Thought* and wished he had spent twice as long in working out the ideas first presented in his *Mathematical Analysis of Logic*. In the year before his death he told Jevons in a letter that he was kept busy by the preparations for a new edition of his book on differential equations, but hoped to write again on logic as soon as he was free and therefore proposed to defer reading Jevons's work in order that there might be no possibility of misunderstanding about the origin of any views he later expressed. It is interesting to speculate on the changes he might have made in a revision of the *Laws of Thought*, but the selections which have been published from his drafts of the last few years suggest that what he had in mind was a development of his epistemological views rather than any alteration of the formal side of his work. In these papers he mentions in particular a distinction between the Logic of Clalls (i.e. his calculus of logic) and a higher, more comprehensive, logic that cannot be reduced to a calculus but may be said to be 'the Philosophy of *all* thought which is expressible in signs, whatever the object of that thought'.[16] It seems unlikely therefore that he would have produced a better book by working longer. For he wall on a wrong track when he began to look for the basis of logic in the constitution of the human intellect. It is indeed one of his chief titles to fame that he freed logic from the dominion of epistemology and so brought about its revival all an independent science. The first break with the confused tradition of the seventeenth and eighteen centuries had been made by Bolzano, himself a philosopher-mathematician, but it wall Boole's work which showed clearly by example that logic could be studied profitably without any reference to the processes of our minds. He believed no doubt that he was dealing with laws of thought in some psychological sense of that ambiguous expression, but he wall in fact dealing with some of the most general laws of thinkables.

In the exposition of Boole's system it will be convenient to begin with that interpretation from which, in all probability, he obtained his conception of a calculus of logic. Let us suppose that letters such as x and y stand for classes and that the use of the symbol = between two class symbols indicates that the classes concerned have the same members. Then the intersection or overlap of two classes, that is to say, the class consisting of all the things which belong to both these classes, may be represented by a complex symbol such as xy. This convention is suggested by the way in which we string adjectives together when we are trying to specify some narrowly defined class. We may speak, for example, of the class of large, red, square things. Boole, indeed, does not distinguish very sharply between adjectives and class symbols; sometimes he calls the letters *x,y, z, &c., elective symbols,* thinking of them as symbols which elect (i.e. select) certain things for attention.

Among all distinguishable classes there are, however, two limiting cases for which it is convenient to have special symbols. These are the *universe* class, or the class of which everything is a member, and the *null* class, or the class of which nothing is a member. In Boole's symbolism they are represented respectively by the symbols i and o. This usage may have been suggested to him by the conventions for the measure of probabilities, but it had the great merit of according well with his desire to retain as much as possible of the normal algebraic formalism in his new calculus of logic. For the two equations $ix = x$ and $ox = o$ are as valid in the class interpretation which has just been explained as they are in the ordinary numerical interpretation. But the appropriateness of this notation should not blind us to the fact that the introduction of the notions of the universe class and the null class involves an interesting novelty. Aristotle, as we have seen, confined his attention to general terms which were neither universal in the sense of applying to everything nor yet null in the sense of applying to nothing. When Boole wrote of the universe class and the null class, he made an important extension of the ordinary use of the word 'class'. If he had developed his new usage consistently, he would have been led farther away from the Aristotelian scheme than he ever wished to go. And since his time it has been discovered that the unrestricted use of the notion of the universe class can lead to serious paradoxes. In practice Boole takes his sign I to signify what De Morgan called the *universe of discourse*, that is to say, not the totality of all conceivable objects of any kind whatsoever, but rather the whole of some definite category of things which are under discussion. Thus in a context where the terms 'Briton' and 'alien' are supposed to determine complementary classes, the universe of discourse is mankind.[17]

Since there are obvious resemblances between Bocle's symbolism for the intersection of classes and the long-established symbolism for the multiplication of numbers, it has become customary to describe the intersection of two classes as their logical product. There is a very important peculiarity, however, in the rules of the symbolism for intersection, which is not to be found in the rules for numerical multiplication. If x denotes a class, the intersection of that class with itself is the same class, i.e. we have $xx = x$ as a basic equation. In his

Mathematical Analysis of Logic Boole often expresses this truth by the formula $x^n = x$, saying that it is the distinguishing feature of his calculus. We shall meet it again presently in another shape.

Division appears in numerical algebra as the inverse of multiplication, but Boole does not in general allow an operation analogous to division when he is talking of classes. He points out that if the letters *xy*, and *z* denote classes we cannot argue from the equation $xz=yz$ to the equation $x=y$. The class of bachelor archdeacons may perhaps be coextensive with the class of red-haired archdeacons, but it does not follow from this that all bachelors are red-haired. It should be remembered, however, that even in numerical algebra there are limits to the proper use of the operation of division. We cannot argue from the equation $2\times0=3\times0$ to the equation $2=3$. So far, then, it may be possible after all to find some analogue of division in the theory of classes, and Boole himself has suggested that the analogue may be abstraction (which Leibniz at one time represented by subtraction). Let us suppose that x,y, and z denote classes related in the way indicated by the equation $x=yz$. The suggestion is that we should write $x/y=z$: as an expression for the fact that *z* denotes a class we reach by abstracting from the membership of the class called *x* the restriction of being included in the class called *y*. Thus we might perhaps say that, as the class of men is the logical product of the class of rational beings and the class of animals, so in this new notation

$$\frac{\text{the class of men}}{\text{the class of rational beings}} = \text{the class of animals.}$$

But it is important to notice two limits to this convention. First the expression x/y can have no meaning at all in the calculus of classes if the class denoted by *x* is not in fact a part of the class denoted by *y*. This is like the observation that the expression x/y can have no meaning in the algebra of integers if the number denoted by *x* is not a multiple of the number denoted by *y*. Secondly, the expression x/y is generally indeterminate in the calculus of classes; for there may be many different classes whose intersections with the class denoted by y are all coextensive with the class denoted by *x*. Instead of the example given above we might just as well write:

$$\frac{\text{the class of men}}{\text{the class of rational beings}} = \text{the class of primates.}$$

although the class of primates is certainly not identical with the class of animals. This is a much more serious limitation of the use of the suggested notation, and it probably accounts for Boole's statement that the expression x/y cannot be interpreted in logic.

In the algebra of classes the complex sign $x+y$ may be used to signify the class of things which belong either to the class denoted by *x* or to the class denoted by *y*. But the word 'or' has two distinguishable meanings in ordinary English; it is used sometimes in an inclusive and sometimes in an exclusive sense. Most of Boole's successors in mathematical logic have taken $x+y$ as a sign for the union, or logical sum in an inclusive sense, of the classes called *x* and *y*, i.e. so that the class called $x+y$ contains the class called xy. This convention has considerable advantages from the formal point of view, since it allows us to assert the equation $x+x = x$ and so to work out the whole calculus in accordance with a principle of duality for union and intersection. In particular we can adopt De Morgan's two rules

$$\overline{xy} = \overline{x} + \overline{y}$$

$$\overline{x+y} = \overline{x}\,\overline{y}$$

in which the sign x stands for the complement of the class called *x*, i.e. for the class of all things which do not belong to the class called *x*. But Boole assumes always that if the letters *x* and *y* stand for classes we are not to write $x+y$ unless the classes are mutually exclusive, and in order to make clear that the condition is satisfied he sometimes expresses a logical sum in the form $x+xy$, where x has the sense explained above.'[18] The effect of this restriction is to bar from his system the equation $x+x=x$ and with it the two general rules noticed above. It is not correct, however, to say that he adopts an exclusive sense for the sign +, if by this assertion it is meant that he introduces $x+y$ as a sign for the class of all things which belong to the class called x or to the class called y but not to the class called xy. Rather he assumes that, if it is correct to write $x+y$, the equation $xy=0$ must be true.

Boole's reason for adopting the restriction we have just noticed in his use of the symbol + was probably a wish to be able to use the symbol – as its inverse. We have here a situation something like that explained above in connexion with division. When x,y, and z denote classes it is tempting to suppose that from the equation $x = y+z$ we can derive another equation $x-y=z$. But there are two limitations to this usage in the algebra of classes. In the first place we can attach no meaning to the expression $x-y$ if the class denoted by y is not part of the class denoted by x. This is like the observation that the expression $x-y$ is meaningless in the calculus of natural numbers if the number denoted by y is greater than the number denoted by x. Secondly, the expression $x-y$ will be indeterminate if the symbol + is taken in an inclusive sense without the special assumption that the signs between which it occurs stand for non-overlapping classes. For the equation $x= y+z$ may then be quite compatible with the equation $x= y+w$ although the letters and w do not stand for coextensive classes. Whatever his motive, Boole adopts the convention that the symbol -+- may occur only between signs for mutually exclusive classes and makes free use of the symbol – as its inverse. In particular he writes 1–x for the complement of the class denoted by x, and introduces the sign x merely as an abbreviation. This usage enables him to express the special principle of his system in the formula x(1–x)=0. Sometimes he derives this from the equation x=x, which is a special case under his index law; but sometimes he prefers to regard it as basic, remarking that it is a formulation of the principle of non-contradiction, which Aristotle and Leibniz both described as the most fundamental of all principles.

This system of notation is sufficient, as it stands, for expression of the *A*, *E*, *I*, and *O* propositions of traditional logic, provided that *A* and *E* propositions are taken without existential import.'[19] Supposing the letter *x* to stand for the class of *X* things and the letter *Y* for the class of Y things, we have the following scheme:

Every X is Y	$x(I—y) = 0$
No X is Y	$xy = 0$
Some X is Y	$xy \neq 0$
Some X is not Y . .	$x(I—y) \neq 0$

Each of the four propositions can be represented in various other ways which are algebraically equivalent to these but not so simple. It will be noticed, however, that in this scheme particular propositions are expressed by inequalities, whereas universal propositions are expressed by equations. Boole prefers to express all the traditional types of categorical propositions by equations, and therefore writes instead of the last two lines of the scheme printed above:

Some X is Y . . . . $xy = v$

Some X is not Y . . . . $x(i— y) = v$

The letter *v*, which he introduced here for the special purpose of expressing particular propositions, seems to correspond to the English word 'some'; but it is said to stand for a class 'indefinite in all respects but one', namely that it contains a member or members (i.e. is not coextensive with the null class). This explanation is not very satisfactory. If some X thing is Y, the class denoted by *xy* does indeed contain at least one member. But we cannot assert this by equating the class called *xy* with a class whose sole defining characteristic is that of containing a member or members; for there is no such class.

Within Boole's system the letter v can be manipulated in some respects as though it were a class symbol. But this is a defect rather than a merit of the notation, because it suggests mistaken inferences. We may be tempted, for example, to suppose that the equations $ab=v$ and $cd=v$ together entail the conclusion $ab=cd$. Boole himself does not fall into such fallacies, but that is because he observes restrictions on the use of the letter v which are inconsistent with his own description of it as a class symbol. He says, for example, that we may pass from the equation $x(I—y)=0$ which means 'Every X is Y', to the equation $vx(I—y)=0$, and that the second may then be interpreted as meaning 'Some X is Y', but only on the assumption that the equations $v(I—x)=0$ and $r(I—y) = o$ are true, i.e. that the class denoted by v is contained as a sub-class in each of the two classes denoted by x and y . Since v is supposed to denote a class which has at least one member, his condition of interpretation amounts in effect to in assumption that the classes denoted by x and y are not null. Obviously his purpose in all this is to provide for those Aristotelian inferences which depend on existential import, but he has chosen an unfortunate device. If the letter v stood for a class, even in the enlarged sense in which the symbols o and I may be said to stand for classes, there would be no need to lay down special rules for its interpretation in the various contexts where it is used. It is interesting, however, to notice that at one time Leibniz had a similar idea.'[20]

For the interpretation of the system in terms of classes and operations on classes it is clear that the following formulae, which are explicitly or implicitly assumed by Boole as premisses, all express true propositions:

(1) $xy = yx$	(5) *If* $x = y$, *then* $xz = yz$
(2) $x+y = y + x$	(6) *If* $x = y$, *then* $x+z = y+z$
(3) $x(y + z) = xy + xz$	(7) *If* $x = y$, *then* $x = z\ y—z$
(4) $x(y—z) = xy—xz$	(8) $x(I—x) = o$

Of these the first seven are similar in form to rules of ordinary numerical algebra. What distinguishes the system is the eighth formula. But Boole has pointed out that even this can be interpreted numerically with a suitable restriction of the values for the variable x. He states his discovery in the following words:

'Let us conceive, then, of an Algebra in which the symbols x, y, z etc. admit indifferently of the values o and I, and of these values alone. The laws, the axioms, and the processes, of such an Algebra will be identical in their whole extent with the laws, the axioms, and the processes of an Algebra of Logic. Differences of interpretation will alone divide them. Upon this principle the method of the following work is established.[21]

This passage, and others like it, have led some commentators to describe Boole's system as a two-valued algebra. That description is a mistake; for when we treat the system as a calculus of classes, we do not assume that every class is coextensive either with the universe class or with the null class. It is possible, indeed, to turn Boole's system into a two-valued algebra by adding a new principle:

(9). *Either* $x = I$ or $x = 0$.

The resulting calculus can still be interpreted numerically (i.e. by taking the symbols I and o in their ordinary numerical senses); but it no longer admits an interpretation in terms of classes. Boole does not distinguish sharply between his original system and the narrower system which involves (9). This may be seen from the fact that he gives two other logical interpretations of his formulae without remarking that one satisfies (9) while the other does not. These other interpretations have great interest for their own sake, and deserve to be mentioned here.

In the *Mathematical Analysis of Logic* and again in the *Laws of Thought* Boole suggests a convention whereby the equation x=1 may be taken to mean that the proposition X is true and the equation x=0 to mean that X is false. In accordance with this usage the truth-values of more complicated propositions can be represented by combinations of small letters, e.g. the truth-value of the conjunction of the propositions X and Y by the combination *xy* and the truth-value of the exclusive disjunction of X and Y by the combination $x+y$. It will be seen that we have here all that is needed for an interpretation of Boole's system in terms of the truth-values of propositions with the symbols 1 and 0 standing respectively for truth and falsity. And this interpretation, like the numerical one, satisfies principle (9).

The interpretation by reference to propositions is worked out by Boole in the way just noticed, though without use of the phrase 'truth-value', which was invented later by Frege. But it is introduced on each occasion by remarks which might lead us to expect something different and perhaps more interesting. In his *Mathematical Analysis of Logic* Boole writes:

'To the symbols X, Y, Z, representative of Propositions, we may appropriate the elective symbols *x,y, z,* in the following sense. The hypothetical Universe, I, shall comprehend all conceivable cases and conjunctures of circumstances. The elective symbol *x* attached to any subject expressive of such cases shall select those cases in which the Proposition X is true, and similarly for Y and Z. If we confine ourselves to the contemplation of a given Proposition X, and hold in abeyance any other consideration, then two cases only are conceivable, viz. first that the given Proposition is true, and secondly that it is false. As these two cases together make up the Universe of the Proposition, and as the former is determined by the elective symbol *x*, the latter is determined by the elective symbol *i* —*x*. But if other considerations are admitted, each of these cases will be resoluble into others, individually less extensive, the number of which will depend on the number of foreign considerations admitted. Thus if we associate the Propositions X and Y, the total number of conceivable cases will be found as exhibited in the following scheme.

	Cases	Elective expression
1st	X true, Y true.	xy
2nd	X true, Y false.	$x(I-y)$
3rd	X false, Y true	$(I-x)y$
4th	X false, Y false.	$(I—x)(I—y)$

... And it is to be noted that however few or many those circumstances may be, the sum of the elective expressions representing every conceivable case will be unity.'[22]

In the *Laws of Thought* Boole abandons this very promising suggestion and proposes instead that the letter x should be taken to stand for the *time* during which the proposition X is true. This is a return to an unsatisfactory account of truth put forward by some ancient and medieval logicians, and it may have been suggested to him by what he read in metaphysical and theological books about eternal verities. But in both works he seems to be preparing the way for a scheme in which the symbols I and o would not stand merely for truth and falsity but represent rather necessary truth and impossibility. Like the class interpretation, this model would not satisfy principle (9), since it does not require that every elective expression be equated either to I or to o.

At the end of the *Mathematical Analysis of Logic* Boole says rather obscurely that the theory of hypothetical propositions could be treated as part of the theory of probabilities, and in the *Laws of Thought* several chapters are devoted to the application of the new algebra to probabilities. This amounts in effect to yet another interpretation of the calculus according to which the letter stands for the probability of the proposition X in relation to all the available information, say K. Adapting and simplifying Boole's symbolism we have

$$\text{Prob}_k\ (X\ and\ Y) = xy$$

if X and Y are independent, given K, and

$$\text{Prob}_k\ (X\ or\ Y) = x + y$$

if X and Y are mutually exclusive. Clearly this scheme does

not satisfy principle (9); for we cannot allow that every probability is equal to 1 or 0.

In a passage of the *Laws of Thought* which was quoted above Boole states that his method is founded on the identity of the calculus of logic with a numerical algebra of 0 and 1. Later in the same book he says emphatically:

We may in fact lay aside the logical interpretation of the symbols in the given equation; convert them into quantitative symbols, susceptible only of the values 0 and 1 ; perform upon them as such all the requisite processes of solution; and finally restore to them their logical interpretation.[23]

We have seen that the numerical algebra of o and I is a narrower system than the algebra of classes, since it involves principle (9), which does not hold for classes. But for anything which can be proved in the algebra of o and I without the use of principle (9) as a premiss there will, of course, be an analogue in the algebra of classes; and Boole does not in fact use principle (9), or anything which implies it, when he manipulates the symbols of his calculus. If he sometimes allows himself to think of his symbols as numerical, that is merely a concession to custom, something which makes him feel at home with them. The essence of his method is really the derivation of consequences in abstract fashion, i.e. without regard to interpretation. He made this clear in the opening section of his *Mathematical Analysis of Logic*, though he sometimes wrote later as though he had forgotten it.

The fundamental process in the formal elaboration of Boole's system is one which he calls *development*. Let us suppose that the expression $f(x)$ is an abbreviation for an expression involving the letter x and possibly other elective symbols but apart from them only the usual algebraic signs we have already discussed. Then for suitable coefficients a and b we have $f(x)=ax+-b(i—x)$. And in order to determine the values of a and b we need only suppose x to take the values 1 and 0. For then we obtain by substitution the equations $f(1)=a$ and

$f(o)=b$ from which we can infer

$$f(x)=f(I)x+f(0)\,(I-x).$$

This formula is said to give the development of the expression $f(x)$ with respect to x. In the *Mathematical Analysis of Logic* Boole treats it as a degenerate case under Maclaurin's theorem about the expansion of functions in ascending powers, but he relegates this rather fanciful notion to a footnote in the *Laws of Thought*.[24]

Let us now suppose that the expression $\phi(x,y)$ is an abbreviation for an expression which apart from the elective symbols x and y involves only the usual algebraic signs. Regarding this first as a functional sign with x in the argument place, we can say

$$\phi(x, y,) = \phi(I, y)\, x + \phi(o, y)\, (I-x)$$

Considering the result as a functional sign with Y in the argument place we can then go on to write

$$\phi(x, y,) = \phi(I, I)xy+\phi(I, o)x(I-y)+ \\ +\phi(o,I)\,(I-x)y+\phi(o,o)\,(I-x)(I-y)$$

which is the complete development of the expression $\phi(x, y)$. It is easy to see how functional expressions with a larger number of elective symbols may be developed in a similar fashion. If, for example, we have to do with an elective function of three arguments, the development will contain $2^3 = 8$ terms, each consisting of a coefficient equal to o or I and a product expression from the list: xyz, $xy(I-z)$, $x(I-y)z$, $x(I-y)\,(I-z)$, $(I-x)yz$, $(I-x)y\,(I-x)\,(I-y)z$, $(I-x)\,(I-y)\,(I-z)$. Those terms whose coefficients are equal to o can naturally be omitted without alteration to the sense of the whole expression.

Since any elective equation can be brought into the form $\phi(x, y, \ldots) = o$, it is clear that it can also be expressed by the equation of a sum of terms to o. From such an equation it can then be inferred that each of the terms included in the sum is separately equal to o, since terms with negative values are not admissible in this calculus. On the other hand, if we have two elective equations $\phi(x, y, \ldots) = o$ and $\psi(x,y, \ldots) = o$, their full force can always be rendered in one equation $x(x,y, \ldots) = o$ which includes among the terms of its developed form every term included in the developed form of either of the other two. It is then said that the two given equations have been *reduced* to one.

On this basis it is possible also to define another operation of importance, namely *solution*. Let us suppose that the given information is all contained in one equation $f(x) = o$, where the expression $f(x)$ is an abbreviation for an expression involving elective symbols other than x, and that it is desired to find an equation of the form $x=\phi(y, z, \ldots)$, where $y,z,$ &c., are the other elective symbols. Developing our original equation with respect to x, we have

$$f(I)x+f(o)\,(I-x) = o.$$

This can be rewritten in the form

$$[f(I)- f(o)]x+f(o) = o.$$

and it is then easy to infer

$$x=\frac{f(o)}{f(o)-f(I)}$$

It will be noticed that Boole introduces here the operation of division to which he has so far assigned no fixed interpretation in his calculus of logic. In order to make general provision for the solution of elective equations he therefore lays down some rules of decoding based on the assumption that here at least the .symbolism of division may be taken to signify abstraction. The task is not so difficult as it might appear at first sight.

When an expression of the form $\frac{f(o)}{f(o)-f(I)}$ is developed with respect to the elective symbols it involves, the result is a sum of products, and the sign of division appears only in the various coefficients, each of which must have one of the four forms:

$\frac{1}{1}, \frac{0}{0}, \frac{0}{1}, \frac{1}{0}$. The first and the third of these are fairly easy to understand, because they can be reduced to 1 and 0 respectively, not only in ordinary numerical algebra, but also in a system where the sign of division indicates abstraction. Similarly the fourth is not very troublesome, since it can be shown not to occur except as coefficient to a product which is separately equal to 0. But the second is curious. Boole says that it is a perfectly indeterminate symbol of quantity, corresponding to 'all, some, or none'. Sometimes he equates it with the symbol v which he uses in the expression of particular propositions, but this is unsatisfactory, since the letter v is supposed to stand for a class which is not null. We may perhaps use the letter w instead as an abbreviation. Thus if the application of the rules of solution has produced a result of the form

$$x=\frac{1}{1}p+\frac{0}{0}p+\frac{0}{1}r+\frac{1}{0}s.$$

where p, q, r, and s are the various product expressions to be considered for inclusion in the final expression, we can write

$$x = p + wq.$$

According to the class interpretation this means that the class denoted by x consists of the class denoted by p together with an indeterminate part (all, some, or none) of the class denoted by q. In one of the late drafts which he did not publish Boole said that the four possible coefficients noticed above should be taken to represent respectively the four categories of universality, indefiniteness, non-existence, and impossibility, which might, he thought, be adopted with advantage in place of the Kantian list.[25]

Finally, Boole lays down rules for *elimination*. Let us suppose that our information is represented in abbreviated form by the equation $f(x) = 0$ and that it is desired to find what relations, if any, hold independently of the class denoted by x between the other classes symbolized in the full version of $f(x)$. By the process of solution we get ,

$$x=\frac{f(o)}{f(o)-f(I)}$$

and from this we can obtain also

$$I-x=\frac{f(I)}{f(o)-f(I)}$$

But by one of the basic rules of the calculus we have

$$x(I—x) =o,$$

and from this, taken together with our two results of solution, we can infer according to Boole

$$-\frac{f(o)f(i)}{[f(o)-f(i)]^2}=0,$$

$$f(o)f(i)=o.$$

If the working out of the left side of this equation yields only o = o, the original equation covers no relations independent of the class denoted by *x*. If, however, it yields something of the form $\phi(y, z, ...)$ = o, we have established that the full version of the equation $f(x)$ = o covers some relation or relations independent of the class denoted by x.

This argument, given by Boole in the chapter on elimination in the *Laws of Thought*, is bewildering because it involves use of expressions for which there is no logical interpretation. But the same result can be proved by an argument which is intuitively more satisfactory. Since development of the functional expression f(x) with respect to *x* gives f(I) *x*+ f(o) (I—*x*), where f(I) *x* is short for the sum of those terms in the complete expansion which have x as a factor and f(o) (I—*x*)short for the sum of those terms which have (i—x) as a factor$f$(I) and$f$(o) must each represent a sum of terms which are expressible without the symbol *x*, and$f$(I)f(o) must be an abbreviation for their common part, i.e. for the sum of those terms which appear in both totals. If in fact the full versions of f(I) and f(o) have no common part, it is obvious that the equation $f(x)=0$ covers no relation independent of the class denoted by x. If, however, the full versions of $f(1)$ and $f(0)$ have a common part, the equation of this to 0 must indicate a relation independent of the class denoted by x.

By various combinations of these processes of calculation Boole could give algebraic representations of all the kinds of reasoning recognized in traditional logic. Syllogistic reasoning, in particular, might be presented as the reduction of two class equations to one, followed by elimination of the middle term and solution for the subject-term of the conclusion. Thus, to take a simple example, if h stands for the class of human beings, a for the class of animals, and m for the class of mortals, the premisses 'Every human being is an animal' and 'Every animal is mortal' can be replaced by the equations

$$h(1-a) = 0.$$

$$a(1-m) = 0.$$

Reducing these to none

$$h-ha+a-am = 0$$

and from this in turn by development with respect to a we get

$$(h-h1+1-1m)a + (h-h0 + 0-0m)\ (1 - a)= 0.$$

or $\quad (1-m)\ a + h\ (1 - a)= 0.$

Then by eliminating a in accordance with the rules we can conclude

$$(1-m)h = 0.$$

his equation is already in such a form that it can be interpreted to mean 'Every human being is mortal', but for an exercise in Boole's methods we may continue according to his rules for solution:

$$h=\frac{(1-m)0}{(1-m)0-(1-m)1}$$

$$=\frac{(I\text{-}I)\mathrm{o}}{(I\text{-}I)\mathrm{o}-(I\text{-}I)\mathrm{I}}m+\frac{(I\text{-}o)\mathrm{o}}{(I\text{-}o)\mathrm{o}-(I\text{-}o)\mathrm{I}}$$

$$=\frac{0}{0}m+\mathrm{o}(I\text{-}m)=wm+\mathrm{o}(1-m)$$

In words our result means that the class of human beings consists of an indeterminate selection (which may perhaps be null) from the class of mortals together with a null selection from the class' of immortals; in order to exclude the possibility of a null selection from the class of mortals it would be necessary to include among our premisses explict provision for the existential import of the term 'man'. Obviously the nut from which this kernel has been obtained could have been cracked with a lighter hammer, but it is interesting to see that the methods Boole introduced can be applied in a mechanical fashion. In effect he has given what is now called a decision procedure.

4. LATER DEVELOPMENTS OF BOOLEAN ALGEBRA

The chief novelty in Boole's system is his theory of elective functions and their development, or, as we should now say, his theory of truth-functions and their expression in disjunctive normal form. Philo of Megara discussed particular elective functions and explained how they could be developed, but Boole should have the credit of being the first to treat these two topics in general fashion. We have quoted a passage of the *Mathematical Analysis of Logic* from which it was a short step to Frege's use of truth-tables (i.e. tabulations of alternative truth-possibilities) in his *Begriffsschrift* of 1879 for the clear exhibition of Boolean developments.'[26] In a paper of 1885 the American logician C.S.Peirce added the remark that a necessarily true formula was one which remained true under all assignments of truth-values to its constituents: 'To find whether a formula is necessarily true substitute **f** and **v** for the letters and see whether it can be supposed false by any such assignment of values.'[27] And with these two notions we have all the essentials for the tabular method in primary logic which was popularized by Post and Wittgenstein in 1920.

In his *Symbolic Logic* of 1881 J.Venn, another admirer of Boole, used diagrams of overlapping regions (i.e. topological models) to illustrate relations between classes or the truth-conditions of propositions. His diagrams differ from those of Euler in that he first represents all possible combinations by distinct areas and then indicates by marks within the various areas which combinations must be null and which not null for the holding of a given proposition. Like Jevons, he thought that what he was trying to elucidate was one of the principal discoveries of Boole, and his diagrams may in fact be regarded as illustrations of the theory of development by which Boole justified his various processes of calculation. Thus the example considered at the end of the last section can be presented without Boole's fearsome apparatus of numerical coefficients by means of the figure to the right in which the square represents the universe of discourse and the areas of the three circles represent the three classes of human beings, animals, and mortals. Shading of an area indicates emptiness of the corresponding class as stipulated in a premiss, e.g. the class of human beings who are not animals, and the placing of an asterisk in an area indicates that the corresponding class is not empty. In his *Symbolic Logic* of 1896 Lewis Carroll used a somewhat similar scheme in a procedure which he introduced for determining the validity of syllogisms.

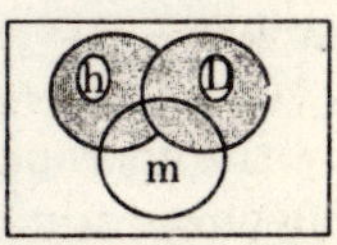

Because Boole's methods can be reduced to rules of thumb, they lend themselves to mechanization. Jevons was the first to realize this, and in 1869 he succeeded in constructing a logical machine which he exhibited next year to the Royal Society.[28] In one description he said that its appearance was like that of a very small upright piano, but to modern eyes it looks more like a cash register, since signs indicative of various possible combinations of elements (either classes or propositions)

are made to appear and disappear by the pressing of keys. In 1885 Allan Marquand suggested an electrical analogue of Jevons's machine, and in 1947 an electrical computer of different design was constructed at Harvard by T. A. Kalin and W. Burkhart specially for the solution of Boolean problems involving up to twelve logical variables (i.e. proposition or class letters).[29]

Any modern electronic computer designed for general purposes must be capable of dealing with Boolean algebra. For if it is to follow the logical articulation of ordinary mathematical calculation, it must be able to take account of conjunction, disjunction, negation, and conditional dependence. Its instructions may be, for example, that, if conditions A and B are both fulfilled in the carrying out of a certain process, it is to do C, and that then, if the result of C is either D or E, it is to go on to do F, but otherwise to do G, and so forth. All this is achieved by the use of thermionic valves or transistors, in various combinations of serial and parallel arrays, as switches for the routing of electrical impulses and it is not very surprising that the appropriate circuits can be produced, since Boolean algebra was used as early as 1936 for the study of switch and relay circuits in electrical communication engineering.'[30] If the putting-on of a switch, which must be in one or other of two states, is likened to the affirmation of a proposition, its putting-off may be likened to the denial of the same proposition, and the arrangement of two switches in series may be likened to the conjunction of two propositions, while the arrangement of switches in parallel may be likened to the connexion of two propositions by 'or'. When a complex circuit of switches and relays has been described in accordance with these analogies by the appropriate Boolean expression, it is possible to determine algebraically whether certain paths will be open in certain conditions, and through algebraic transformations of the expression it may even be possible to find a circuit that will produce the same results with less apparatus.

Although Boole's system lends itself in some ways to easy manipulation, we must admit that it contains not only a defect of elegance in the restriction whereby we may not write $x+y$ unless we know the truth of the equation $xy= o$, but also some defects of rigour such as the use of the letter v for the expression of existential propositions, the admission of numerical coefficients other than 1 and o, and the use of the operation of division to which no constant meaning has been assigned in logic. In the course of the half century after the publication of his *Laws of Thought* these shortcomings were all removed by his followers Jevons begen the reform in 1864 with his *Pure Logic, or the Logic of Quality apart from Quantity*, in which he suggested the use of the symbol + in the sense of the inclusive 'or' without any restriction on the signs between which it may occur. This made possible a great simplification, and was therefore welcomed by all later writers on the algebra of logic except Venn. As C.S.Peirce pointed out in a paper of 1867, it produces an exact parallelism between theorems including logical addition and theorems involving logical multiplication.[31] This advantage was most fully exploited by E. Schroder when he set out such theorems in parallel columns of his *Vorlesungen uber die Algebra der Logik* (1890-1905). In a later paper (c. 1880) Pcirce went even farther in the direction of simplification and showed how all the elective functions of Boole could be expressed by use of a single primitive sign with the meaning of 'neither . . . nor . . .'.[32] But like many other discoveries of Peirce, this passed unnoticed at the time: no use was made of the possibility of such reduction until it had been rediscovered by H. M. Sheffer in 1913.[33] Peirce should also have credit for the reintroduction of a sign with the sense of Leibniz's *inist*; his idea, though not his sign, was adopted by Schroder.

The most important development, however, is the presentation of the calculus in a strictly axiomatized form. Whereas Boole had been content to characterize his system by the single principle in which it seemed to differ from ordinary numerical algebra, his successors tried to make all their assumptions explicit. The , results of this endeavour can be studied best in two papers of E. V. Huntington on 'Sets of Independent Postulates for the Algebra of Logic'.[34] Although Huntington speaks of the algebra of logic, he presents his postulates in abstract fashion, i.e. without reference to any special interpretation, and it is interesting to notice that this reformed version of Boolean algebra has in fact a considerable interest for modern mathematicians apart from its use in logic. For convenience of comparison the first, second, and fourth of Huntington's sets are given below in the symbolism of Boole, so far as that is appropriate. It should be remembered, of course, that the various signs, including I and o, have only the sense assigned to them by the postulates.

Huntington's first set is adapted from one given by A. N. White-head in his *Universal Algebra* of 1898, and is the nearest to Boole's system in that it takes the two operations of addition and multiplication as primitive. These are supposed to be applicable to any pair from a class of things which may be called for short the elements of the algebra. When we wish to give a logical interpretation to the postulates we take these elements to be either classes or propositions.

Ia. *If a and b are elements, so too is* $a+b$

Ib. *If a and b are elements, so too is* $a \times b$.

IIa. *There is an element o such that* $a+o = a$ *for every element a.*

IIb. *There is an element* I *such that* $a \times I = a$ *for every element a.*

IIIa. $a+b = b+a$ *fw all elements a and b whose combinations here mentioned are also elements.*

IIIb. $a \times b = b \times a$ for all elements *a* and *b* whose combinations here mentioned are also elements.

IVa. $a+(b \times c) = (a+b) \times (a+c)$ *for all elements a, b, and c whose combinations here mentioned are also elements.*

IVb. $a \times (b+c) = (a \times b) + (a \times c)$ *for all elements a, b, and c whose combinations here mentioned are also elements.*

V. *If the elements o and I exist and are unique, there is an element a such that (i)* $a + a = \mathrm{I}$ *and* (ii) $a \times a = \mathrm{o}$.

VI. *There are at least two elements x and y such that* $x \neq y$.

It will be noticed that these postulates are framed in such a way as to bring out the correspondence between addition and multiplication in the system. The independence of each postulate from the rest can be proved by the construction of a model which satisfies all the others without satisfying the postulate under consideration. Some conditions which seem at first sight to be redundant are included for the special purpose of preserving independence. Thus IIa or IIb can be false when V is satisfied merely by the non-fulfilment of its condition.

Huntington's second set is similar to suggestions of Leibniz, Peirce, and Schroder in that it deals with a relation of inclusion between elements, as distinct from any operation on elements. The sign we shall use for this relation is employed in numerical mathematics with the sense of 'is less than', but it is to be understood here in such a sense that the formula $a < b$ does not exclude the formula $a = b$. If, as is usual, the elements of the algebra are supposed to be classes, the sign may be taken to mean inclusion in that sense in which a sub-class is included in a super-class, but *not* membership.

1. $a < a$ *for every element* a.
2. *If* $a < b$ *and* $b < a$, *then* $a = b$.
3. *If* $a < b$ *and* $b < c$, *then* $a < c$.
4. *There is an element o such that* $o < a$ *for every element* $a, \neq o$.
5. *There is an element I such that* $a < I$ *for every element* $a, \neq I$.
6. *If* $a \neq b$ *and neither* $a < b$ *nor* $b < a$, *there is an element s such that (i)* $a < s$, *(ii)* $b < s$, *and (iii) if* $y, \neq s$, *is such that* $a < y$ *and* $b < y$, *then* $s < y$.
7. *If* $a \neq b$ *and neither* $a < b$ *nor* $b < a$, *there is an element p such that (i)* $p < a$, *(ii)* $p < b$ *and (iii) if* $x \neq p$, *is such*

that $x < a$ and $x < b$, then $x < p$.

8. *If the elements* o *and* I *exist and are unique, then for every element a there is an element $\bar{a}$ such that*(i) *if $x < a$ and $x < \bar{a}$, then $x = o$, and* (ii) *if $a < y$ and $\bar{a} < y$, then $y = i$.*
9. *If postulates* (I), (4), (5), *and* (8) *hold and it is not the case that $a < b$, then there is an element x, $\neq$ o, such that $x < a$ and ,$x < b$.*
10. *There are at least two elements, x and y, such that $x \neq y$*

In this set postulates (i) to (7) are independent among themselves, and (8) and (9) are independent of the first seven, but either (6) or (7) can be deduced from the rest. Both are retained here for the sake of symmetry. The letters *s* and *p* used in the statement of them are intended, of course, to suggest 'sum' and 'product' respectively.

Postulates (4) and (8) for inclusion bring out explicitly a principle of the theory of classes which has often caused bewilderment, namely, that the null class is a sub-class of all classes. At first hearing there is something curious in any talk of a class with no members, but when once this technical extension of the use of the word 'class' has been accepted, the principle just mentioned is natural and easily intelligible. For it is a truism that the intersection of any two classes is a subclass of each of them, and from this it follows directly that the class designated by $a \times \bar{a}$, i.e. the null class, must be a sub-class of the class designated by *a*, whatever that may be.

Huntington's fourth set is constructed to show how the whole system can be formulated with the operations of addition and taking the complement as the sole undefined notions. Other notions such as the operation of multiplication and the relation of inclusion can be introduced by definition, if required.

(i) *If a and b are elements, so too is $a+b$.*

(ii) *If a is an element, so too is $\bar{a}$.*

(iii) *$a+b = b+a$ for all elements a and b whose combinations here mentioned are also elements.*

(iv) $(a+b) + c = a + (b + c)$ *for all elements a, b, and c whose combinations here mentioned are also elements.*

(v) $\bar{a}+b+\bar{a}+b = a$ *for all elements a and b whose combinations here mentioned are also elements.*

This and the corresponding set for the operations of multiplication and taking the complement are perhaps the simplest of the kind that can be constructed.

By the device of Peirce and Sheffer mentioned above it is possible, however, to produce a set of postulates which is simpler in that it involves only one primitive operation.

1. *There are at least two distinct elements.*
2. $a \backslash b$ *is an element for all elements a and b.*
3. $(a/a) | (a | a) = a$ *for every element a whose combinations here mentioned are also elements.*
4. $a \backslash \{b \backslash (b \backslash b)\} = a \backslash a$ *for all elements a and b whose combinations here mentioned are also elements.*
5. $\{a \backslash (b \backslash c)\} \backslash \{a \backslash (b \backslash c)\} = \{(b \backslash b) \backslash a\} \backslash \{(c \backslash c) \backslash a\}$ *for all elements a, b, and c whose combinations here mentioned are also elements.*

This set is to be found in the paper of Sheffer noticed above, and the expression $a \backslash b$ is often called Sheffer's stroke function. Admittedly the last three postulates seem rather complicated when written, as here, in full, but they come to seem more natural when the expression $a \backslash b$ is taken to mean either $\bar{a} \times b$ or $\bar{a} + b$ and the sign $\bar{a}$ is introduced as an abbreviation for a/a. The fact that the stroke can be interpreted equally well in two different ways is an interesting consequence of the principle of duality.

More recently A. Tarski has given several equivalent sets of postulates for an extended system of Boolean algebra in which there are two operations of a non-finitary character, namely that of taking the logical sum or union of all the elements of some specified set of elements and that of taking the logical product or intersection of all the elements of some specified set of elements.[35] This extended system is closely related to a theory of the part whole relationship developed by

S. Lesniewski under the name of 'mereology'.[36] In fact the difference is simply that Lesniewski's system excludes the possibility of a null element included in every other element.

It is a common feature of all these sets of axioms that they involve use of ordinary English words such as 'if' and therefore presuppose a system of logic containing rules for inference from one proposition or set of propositions to another. This fact is not sufficient reason for denying that Boole's algebra may itself be interpreted as a system of logic, but it suggests that it cannot be the simplest or most fundamental part of logic. If the elements of the algebra are supposed to be classes, there must clearly be a more basic theory about the derivation of propositions from other propositions. But that more basic theory cannot be Boolefan algebra interpreted in the other way with propositions for elements, because the other version of the algebra involves precisely the same assumptions as the algebra of classes. Frege's *Begriffsschrift* of 1879 was the first treatise of logic in which the science was developed in a thoroughly comprehensive fashion with a calculus of propositions, something like that of Chrysippus, at the beginning and then in due order a calculus of classes. But already in 1877 H. MacColl had put forward suggestions for a calculus of propositions in which the asserted principles would be implications rather than equations, and he should therefore have credit for priority in this regard, though the system which he produced was not complete like Frege's calculus of propositions.'[37]

5. THE THEORY OF RELATIONS: DE MORGAN AND PEIRCE

Boole's success in constructing an algebra which included all the theorems of traditional logic led some logicians to assume that all logic must be capable of presentation in algebraic form, and attempts were made in the next generation to work out a logic of relations in the same fashion as the logic of classes. The most detailed development of this line of thought is to be found in Schroder's *Vorlesungen uber die Algebra-der Logik* (vol. iii, 1895), but the original idea and most of the interesting propositions were first suggested by Peirce in a series of papers written between 1870 and 1903 which are now available in the third volume of his *Collected Papers*. Unfortunately Peirce was like Leibniz, not only in his originality as a logician, but also in his constitutional inability to finish the many projects he conceived.

In earlier chapters we have noticed a number of sporadic attempts to deal with arguments which depend on the properties of relations, but sustained interest in this subject dates from a paper written by Augustus De Morgan in 1859.[38] In this he says that the doctrine of the syllogism, which he had discussed in his *Formal Logic* of 1847 and in earlier papers, is only a special case in the theory of the composition of relations, and that he wishes to go on to a more general treatment of the subject. The canons of syllogistic reasoning are in effect a statement of the convertible and transitive character of the relation of identity. A relation is convertible when it is the same as its own converse (e.g. the relation of resemblance); and it is transitive when a relative of a relative in respect of this relation is a relative of the same kind (e.g. the relation of being an ancestor). Here the word 'convertible' expresses what is meant by 'symmetrical' in the writings of later logicians. The distinction was not new; far, as Peirce pointed out, Ockham had written of such relations as equipment in opposition to disquiparant relations like that of being father.[39] By the word 'relative' which he uses in his definition of transitive relations De Morgan means what some logicians have called a relative term, i.e. a term which applies to something only in respect of its being related to something else. He and Peirce and Schroder always think of relationships as expressed in some such form as '— is an ancestor of ...' and conceive their task to be that of showing how relative terms may be combined with each other and with non-relative terms.

In the body of his paper De Morgan suggests symbols for

the converse and the contradictory (he says 'contrary') of a relative and for three different ways in which a pair of relatives may be combined. Having shown that the converse of the contradictory and the contradictory of the converse are identical, he then goes on to set out in a table the converse, the contradictory, and the converse of the contradictory of each of the three combinations. His notation is not very satisfactory and need not be reproduced here. The three modes of combination which he discusses are those which could be expressed by phrases of such patterns as (i) *x is an l of an m of y (*e.g. 'John is a lover of a master of Peter'), (ii) *x is an l of every m of y,* (iii) *x is an l of none but an m of y.* And he shows that the converse or the contradictory or the converse of the contradictory of each such combination is itself a combination of one of the kinds discussed, but a combination in which a simple relative may be the converse or the contradictory or the converse of the contradictory of a simple relative in the original combination. Thus the converse of the contradictory of the combination 'lover of a master of' is 'non-servant of every beloved of' or 'servant of none but a non-beloved of'.

In his first paper on the logic of relatives, published in 1870, Peirce says of De Morgan's work:

'This system still leaves something to be desired. Moreover Boole's logical algebra has such singular beauty, so far as it goes, that it is interesting to inquire whether it cannot be extended over the whole realm of formal logic, instead of being restricted to that simplest and least useful part of the subject, the logic of absolute terms, which, when he wrote, was the only formal logic known. ... In extending the-use of old symbols to new subjects, we must of course be guided by certain principles of analogy, which, when formulated, become new and wider definitions of these symbols.'[40]

Possibly the idea of an algebra of relatives was suggested by De Morgan's convention of writing *Im* as an abbreviation for *I of an m of*; for Peirce continued to use juxtaposition of relative signs in this way and spoke of it as expressing a relative product. In what follows we shall use the symbol $I\times_{R}m$ instead of *Im* in order to make clear the novelty of the conception and the danger of supposing that relative multiplication is commutative, i.e. that from *x is a lover of a master of y* we may infer *x is a master of a lover of y*. Pursuing the same analogy, Peirce later introduced the notion of a relative sum. Since his special sign is difficult to reproduce, we shall express this by the symbol $I+_{R}m$. There was nothing in ordinary usage or the conventions of previous logicians to suggest an interpretation for such a sign, and Peirce's choice seems to have been guided by the desire to preserve the pattern of De Morgan's rules for logical sums and products of the non-relative kind. For he said that the relative sum of 'lover' and 'master' was to be 'lover of every non-master of'. This is a combination which would scarcely occur to anyone as a suitable candidate for the title of sum, but it has the merit of allowing us to assert the two equations ....

$$\overline{l+_{r}m}=\bar{l}\times_{r}\overline{m}$$

and

$$\overline{l\times_{r}m}=\bar{l}+_{r}\overline{m}$$

The relative products and relative sums which Peirce defines in this way must, of course, be distinguished carefully from ordinary logical products and sums of relatives. The sign $I\times m$ may be taken to mean 'lover and master', where both the relations under consideration have the same terms; but the sign $l\times_{R}m$ means 'lover of a master of', where the relations are combined only in the sense that an after-term of the first is a fore-term of the second. This distinction inevitably leads to complications in the new calculus. We have, for example, not only

$$a\times_{R}(b\times_{R}c)=(a\times_{R}b)\times_{R}c,$$

but also $a\times_{R}(b\times c)<(a\times_{R}b)\times(a\times_{R}c)$

where $<$ has the sense of 'is included in' and the terms between which it occurs are supposed to stand for classes.

Is the result a natural extension of Boolean algebra? Besides the three operations of addition, multiplication, and negation (or taking the complement) which occur in ordinary Boolean algebra, this new system contains the operations of relative addition, relative multiplication, and conversion; and although there are some analogies between the three new and the three old operations, anyone who studies the details in the work of Schröder may well doubt whether this attempt to present the theory of relations as an algebra is worth the trouble it involves. It is true, as Schröder said, that the notion of relative product is important for the study of series, e.g. in Dedekind's *Was sind und was solen die Zahlen?* (1888). For in a series each earlier object is related to each later by a transitive relation, that is to say by a relation whose powers are .all equivalent to itself because it satisfies the condition $t \times_R t = t$. But the part of the theory of rclations which can be presented in this way is only a small fragment of the whole, and even for that fragment the style of presentation seems inappropriate. When his earlier suggestions had been worked out in detail by Schröder, Peirce himself came to approiate this point.

In a paper of 1883, printed as an appendix to *Johns Hopkins Studies in Logic*, he began to use subscript indices with his relational signs to show what terms were supposed to be related by each relation and in what order.[41] Thus the compound sign l_{ij} was to mean that the person called i was a lover of the person called *j*. This notation has very great advantages. If, for example, we want to talk about a man's loving himself, we can do very simply by writing l_{ij}, where the occurrence of the same letter in the two Index places shows that we have to do with the reflexive, or, as Peirce called it, the self-relative, use of the relational sign. And if we wish to speak, as Peirce sometimes did, of relations with more than two terms, we may construct expressions such as a_{ijk} and b_{ijkl}. But the most important use of these indices is that in which they are combined with the Σ and Π which Peirce introduces in the same article. These quantifiers, as he calls them, are operators with the meanings of 'some' and 'ever Y", and they are intended, of course, to suggest logical addition and logical multiplication over all the objects of a certain range, although, as he explained later, they cannot stand for addition and multiplication in a strict sense if the individuals of the universe are innumerable.[42] With these devices it is possible to give very clear and simple definitions for the notions of relative product and relative sum, namely,

$$(l \times_{R} m)_{ij} = \Sigma_x (l_{ix} \times m_{xj})$$

and $$(l +_{R} m)_{ij} = \Pi_x (l_{ix} + m_{xj})$$

For the moment this was perhaps the chief service Peirce expected from his new notation, but he wrote of it at greater length two years later,[43] and in the course of time he came to see that it could be employed to deal with all sorts of problems which could not be expressed in the language of relative multiplication and relative addition. In 1897 we find him writing of his own algebra of dyadic relatives:

'Professor Schröder attaches, as it seems to me, too high a value to this algebra. That which is in his eyes the greatest recommendation of it is to me scarcely a merit, namely that it enables us to express in the outward guise of an equation propositions whose real meaning is much simpler than that of an equation. Besides the algebra just described, I have invented another which seems to me much more valuable.... In this algebra every proposition consists of two parts, its quantifiers and its Boolian. Its Boolian consists of a number of relatives united by non-relative multiplication and aggregation. No relative operators are required (though they can be introduced if desired). Each elementary arelative is represented by a letter on the line of writing with subjacent indices to denote the hecceities [i.e. individuals] 'which fill its blanks. An obelus is drawn over such a relative to deny it. To the left of the Boolian are written the quantifiers. Each of these is a Π or a Σ with one of the indices written subjacent to it to signify that in the Boolian every object in the universe is to be imagined substituted successively for that index and the non-relative product (if the quantifier is Π) or the aggregate (if the quantifier is Σ) of the results taken. Thus

$$\Pi_i \Sigma_i l_{ii} \cdot = (l_{11}+l_{12}+l_{13}+\text{etc.}).\ (l_{21}+l_{22}+l_{23}+\text{etc.}),\text{etc.}$$

will mean everything loves something. But

$$\Sigma_i \Pi_i l_{ij} = l_{11}.\ l_{21}.\ l_{31},\ \text{etc.} + l_{12}.\ l_{22}.\ l_{32}.\text{etc.}+\text{etc.}$$

will mean something is loved by all things.'44

In his paper of 1883 and his more detailed study of 1885 Peirce gives the credit for these new devices to O. H. Mitchell. This pupil of his had indeed used relational signs with indices and the operators Π and Σ in his contribution to *Johns Hopkins Studies in Logic*, but not in conjunction or with the senses which Peirce gave to them. What Peirce created was a symbolism adequate for the whole of logic and identical in syntax with the systems now in use. He himself called his invention the General Algebra of Logic;[45] but it is not an algebra in the same sense as Boole's, and recent custom has reserved the title 'algebra of logic' for that part of logical theory which can be presented without the use of quantifiers. This includes all primary logic and a fragment of non-primary logic which is isomorphic with primary logic, namely, the theory of attributes or of classes. When we have to deal with propositions which would be expressed in Peirce's final symbolism by formulae such as $\Pi(a_i < b_i)$, we can drop the indices and quantifiers without ambiguity; but some such devices are essential for the general theory of relations, and it is a mark of Peirce's greatness as a logician that he realized this. It is noteworthy also that he formulated some very important principles for the use of quantifiers in deduction. He saw, for example, that every proposition could be expressed in a way which brought all the quantifiers to the beginning; and he advised that existential quantifiers should, so far as possible, be brought to the left of universal quantifiers, thus anticipating in a remarkable way the advantages of what is now called a Skolem prenex normal form.[46] We cannot, it is true, give Peirce the credit of being the first to conceive a comprehensive theory of general logic; for that honour must go to Frege, who published his *Begriffsschrift* in 1879. But so far as is known, Peirce had never heard of Frege when he published his paper on *The Logic of Relatives* in 1883, and his achievement therefore deserves commemoration.

Because he had been led to his more comprehensive view of logic by his study of the theory of relations, Peirce attached special importance to the notion of a relation in his later logical writings and sometimes tried to enlarge the terminology of his theory in a slightly paradoxical way. Not content with talking polyadic relatives, i.e. relative expressions which in his notation require more than two subscripts, he went on to say that an attributive expression such as '... is wise' might be called a *monadic* relative and a complete propositional expression without blanks a *medadic* relative.[47] For certain purposes this way of talking may offer the advantage of theoretical simplification, and it has in fact been adopted for that reason by some later logicians, but it can scarcely be said to give philosophical illumination. On the other hand, there is some increase of understanding to be gained from Peirce's remarks about two different ways in which his notation of relatives may be connected with older talk of subjects and predicates:

'In the statement of a relationship, the designations of the correlates ought to be considered as so many *logical subjects* and the relative itself as the *predicate*. The entire set of logical subjects may also be considered as a *collective subject*, of which the statement of relationship is *predicate*.'[48]

Another interesting development of Peirce's theory of relations was what he called second-intentional logic, i.e. the theory of notions such as identity and inherence. He introduces it as follows:

'Let us now consider the logic of terms taken in collective senses. Our notation, so far as we have developed it, does not show us even how to express that two indices, *i* and *j*, denote one and the same thing. We may adopt a special token of second intention, say L, to express identity, and may write I_{if}. But this relation of identity has peculiar properties. The first is that if *i* and *j* are identical, whatever is true of *i* is true of *j*. This may be written

$$\Pi_i \Pi_j \left(\bar{I}_{ij} + \bar{x}_i \mathbf{x}_j \right).$$

The use of the general index of a token, *x*, here, shows that the formula is iconical. The other property is that if everything which is true of i is true *of j*, then *i* and *j* are identical. This is most naturally written as follows: Let the token, *q*, signify the relation of a quality, character, fact, or predicate to its subject. Then the property we desire to express is

$$\Pi_i \Pi_j \Sigma_k \left(I_{ij} + \bar{q}_{ki} q_{kj} \right).$$

And indentity is defined thus

$$I_{ij} = \Pi_k \left(q_{ki} q_{kj} + \bar{q}_{ki} q_{kj} \right).$$

That is, to say that things are identical is to say that every predicate is true of both or false of both. It may seem circuitous to introduce the idea of a quality to express identity; but that impression will be modified by reflecting that qkiqkj merely means that *i* and j' are both within the class or collection *k*. If we please, we can dispense with the token q, by using the index of a token and by referring to this in the Quantifier just as subjacent indices are referred to. That is to say, we may write

$$I_{ij} = \Pi_x \left(x_i x_j + \bar{x}_i \bar{x}_j \right).$$

In this passage the word 'token' does not have the special sense of 'particular utterance' which he gave to it later but means any general symbol of the sort he often calls a relative, while 'index' means any sign whose sole task is to direct our attention to something and 'icon' any sign which represents by picturing.[49] Thus when he says that a certain formula is iconical because it contains the general index of a token, he intends to convey that it gives the pattern of many possible formulae and is therefore, as we should now say, schematic. The letter *q* which he uses here to signify the relation of a character to a subject or that of a class to a member is obviously a constant sign of great importance.. He introduces it in order to allow himself to generalize over the whole range of possible predicates *of i and j.*' without departing from the convention that quantifiers refer only to subjacent indices; but he then goes on to say that we may, if we wish, abandon this convention and allow a quantifier to refer to an index of a token, which is as much as to say in modern terminology that we may employ quantifiers to bind predicate variables. In later chapters we shall have occasion to examine more carefully the implications of Peirce's two ways of generalizing over qualities or classes. For the moment we need only remark that Peirce showed remarkable penetration when he distinguished his new study from the rest of logic by calling it second-intentional. It is a beginning of what we now call the theory of sets.

Footnotes

1 T. L. Heath, *The Thirteen Books of Euclid's Elements*, i, pp. 202 f., gives an account of noteworthy attempts.

2. P. 99

3. Corrado Segre, 'Congetture intorno all'influenza di Girolamo Saccheri sulla formazione della geometria non-euclidea', *Atti della R.A. delle Scienze di Torino,* xxxviii (1903).

4. Sometimes the title 'elliptic' is reserved for a geometry in which antipodal points are identified. The system considered above is then called spherical geometry.

5. Essai sur la theorie des difinitions', *Annales de mathématiques,* ix (1818), pp. 1-35, especially p. 23.

6. *Was sind und was sollen die Zahlen?* § 10, 134.

7. 'A System of Axioms for Geometry', *Transactions of the American Mathematical Society,* v (1904), pp. 343-81.

8. *Einführung in die symbolische Logik.* § 42 c.

9. In the abstract theory of groups, where elements are not assumed to be always operations, it is necessary to specify separately that combination is associative and that there exists an identity element.

10. Ed. de Falco, 82. 10 ff., reprinted in *Greek Mathematical Works,* ed. Ivor Thomas, i. pp. 75 ff.

11. 'Report on the Recent Progress and Present State of Certain Branches of Analysis', *Report of the Third Meeting of the British Association for the Advancement of Science held in 1833,* pp. 185-352, especially pp. 198-207.

12. *Transactions of the Royal Society of Edinburgh,* xiv (1840), pp. 208-16.

13. *Transactions of the Cambridge Philosophical Society,* vii, pp. 173-87, 287-300; viii, pp. 139-42, 241-54.

14. Bolzano's proof in his eassy *Funktionenlehre* was not published until 1930.

15. W. Kneale has given an account of Boole's life in 'Boole and the Revival of Logic,' *Mind,* n.s. Ivii (1948), pp. 149-75.

16. *Studies in Logic and Probability,* by George Boole (ed. by R. Rhees), 1952, p. 14. Apart from short works published in his lifetime, e.g. the *Mathematical Analysis of Logic,* this collection contains extracts from the papers in the possession of Royal Society and in particular a draft 'On the Mathematical Theory of Logic and on the Philosophical Interpretation of its Methods and Processes.1 Apparently Boole was not sufficiently satisfied with any of these papers to send it to a periodical, and De Morgan, who saw them after Boole's death, decided against publication. We are grateful to Dr. W. Mays for copies of correspondence between Boole and Jevons in 1863 and 1864.

17. A. De Morgan, *Formal Logic,* p. 55.

18. *Mathematical Analysis of Logic*, p. 52; *Laws of Thought*, pp. 33, 48, 55-56, 119.

19. Such an account of universal propositions was given by Franz Brentano in his *Psychologie vom empirischen Standpunkt* (1874) ii, ch. 7, and the consequences were developed in detail by his pupil F. Hillebrand in *Die neuen Theorien der kategorischen Schlüsse of* 1981.

20. Couturat, *La Logique de Leibniz*, pp. 345-50.

21. *Laws of Thought*, pp. 37-38.

22. *Mathematical Analysis of Logic*, pp. 49-50.

23. *Laws of Thought*, p. 70. The whole sentence is italicized in the original.

24. *Mathematical Analysis of Logic*, p. 60; *Laws of Thought*, p. 72.

25. *Studies in Logic and Probability*, pp. 220-6.

26. In his *Elementary Lessons in Logic* of 1870 and later works, W. S. Jevons produced tabulations of permissible combinations of general terms and showed how these could be used for logical calculations.

27. *Collected Papers*, iii, § 387. In what follows this series of volumes will be cited as *C.P.*

28. *The Substitution of Similars*, 1869; 'On the Mechanical Performance of Logical Inference', *Philosophical Transctions of the Royal Society*, clx (1870), pp. 497-518. There is an account of the machine, together with a picture, in *The Principles of Science* which Jevons published in 1874. The machine itself is preserved in the Museum of the History of Science at Oxford. W. Mays and D. P. Henry have give a summary of Jevons's work in 'Jevons and Logic', *Mind* Ixii (1953), pp. 484-505.

29 B. V. Bowden, *Faster Than Thought*, pp. 333 f. This work on electronic computers contains particulars of other logical machines, but the fullest account of the subject is given by Martin Gardner in his entertaining book *Logic Machines and Diagrams*, which begins with Raymond Lull.

30. C. E. Shannon, 'A Symbolic Analysis of Realy and Switching Circuits', *Transactions of the American Institute of Electrical Engineers*, Ivii (1938), pp. 713-23.

31. *C.P.* iii, §§ 1-19.

32. *C.P.* iv. §§ 12-20

33. *Trans. Amer. Math. Soc.*, xiv (1913), pp. 481-8.

34. Ibid. v (1904), pp. 288-309, and xxxv (1933), pp. 274-304, 557-8, 971.

35. Zur Grundlegung der Booleschen Algebra', *Fundamenta*

Mathematicae, xxiv (1935), pp. 177-98. There is an English translaiton in the collection of his papers called *Logic Semantics, Metamathematics,* pp. 320-41.

36. 'O podstawach matematyki', *Przeglad Filozoficzny,* xxxiii (1930), pp. 77-105.

37. 'The Calculus of Equivalent Statements', *Porceedings of the London Mathematical Society,* ix (1878), pp. 9-10, 177-86; x (1879), pp. 16-28; xi (1880), pp 113-21.

38. On the Syllogism IV and on the Logic of Relaitons', *Cambridge Philosophical Transactions* x (1864) *pp* 331-58.

39. *Summa Totius Logicae,* i, ch. 52, quoted by Peirce in *C.P.* iii, § 136. The term *acquiparantia* occurs already in the *Summulae Logicales* of Peter of Spain (ed. Bochenski, # 3. 19).

40. *C.P.* iii, §§ 45-46.

41. *C.P.* iii, §§ 328-58.

42. Ibid., §§ 393.

43. Ibid., §§ 359-403.

44. Ibid., §§ 498-502.

45. Ibid., § 499.

46. C.P. iii, § 505.

47. Ibid., § 465.

48. Ibid., § 467.

49. *C.P.* iii, § 361. ff.

Chapter-8

Numbers, Sets, and Series

Chapter 4
Numbers, Sets, and Series

Chapter-8

I. FREGE AND HIS CONTEMPORARIES

AFTER the work of Boole the next great advance in logic was made by Gottlob Frege (1848-1925). But whereas Boole wished to exhibit logic as part of mathematics, Frege wished to show that arithmetic is identical with logic. On first consideration the two programmes seem to be opposed, and philosophers who are unsympathetic to both have sometimes pointed derisively to the apparent clash. But there is no real inconsistency. When Boole wrote of the mathematical analysis of logic, he meant only the presentation of logic as a calculus similar in certain respects to numerical algebra. Like Leibniz, he thought that the distinctive feature of mathematical science was the construction of calculi and that there might be interesting calculi which could be interpreted without reference to number or quantity. Frege did not wish to deny this. On the contrary, he went much farther than any of his predecessors in his demand for formal rigour within the study of logic, and the deductive system or calculus which he elaborated is the greatest single achievement in the history of the subject. But he tried also to show that numbers can be defined without reference to any notions other than those involved in the interpretation of his calculus as a system of logic. If he was right in this, logic includes arithmetic and with it all those branches of mathematicvs which can be reduced to arithmetic in the sence that they can be shown to involve only notions already available in arithmetic or logic.

The suggestion that arithmetic is an elaboration of logic had been made by other writers before Frege, as he well knew.[1] But no one had ever shown in detail how logic could be developed into a system which might also be called arithmetic, and Frege realized quite early that the thesis could not be satisfactorily established until two improvements had been made in the presentation of logic. First, the traditional material and the newer contributions of Leibniz and Boole must be organized in such a way as to make clear the structure of the science and the great variety of the prepositional forms to be considered in general logic. Secondly, everything which is required for the proof of the theorems must be set out explicitly at the beginning and the procedure of deduction must be reduced to a small number of standard moves so that there may be no danger of our unconscious smuggling in what we ought to prove.[2] It was in order to meet these two requirements of system and rigour that Frege in 1879 produced his *Begriffsschrift, eine der arithmetischen nachgebildete Formelsprache des reinen Denkens*. As its name implies, this pamphlet is a manual of ideography or concept-script. In his preface Frege says that the relation of the script to ordinary-speech is like that of the microscope to the eye, and claims for it the merits which had been predicted by Leibniz and others in the seventeenth century for a *calculus philosophicus et ratiocinator*. It is one of the tasks of philosophy, he tells us, to break the dominion of the word over the human mind, and his invention has already done something towards this by freeing logic from too close attachment to the grammar of ordinary language. In particular it is to be expected that the ambiguous and confusing terminology of 'subject' and 'predicate' will now give place in logic to a more satisfactory distinction of propositional forms according to the doctrine of functions. By addition of a few extra signs for intuitable relations the new script might be extended to make a geometrical calculus of the kind mathematicians desiderate when they speak of *analysis situs*; but it is his intention to show presently that it is adequate as it stands for the presentation of arithmetic, and the third part of the little book is to be taken as a preliminary communication on this programme.

Unfortunately Frege's epoch-making little book was neglected by mathematicians and philosophers alike. As he remarked later, there was no hope of understanding from the many mathematicians who, whenever they came across logical expressions like 'concept', 'relation', 'judgement', said *Metaphysica sunt, non Ieguntur*, nor yet from the many philosophers who on seeing a formula said *Mathematica sunt, non leguntur*.[3] In 1884 he therefore produced a book called *Die Grundlagen der Arithmetik* which gave an informal exposition of his views together with criticisms of current ideas about the nature of arithmetic. He did not claim here to have done more than render his thesis probable, and though he was much discouraged by the neglect of his earlier work, he still hoped to produce a rigorous demonstration of the identity of arithmetic and logic. Somewhere about the end of the decade he returned to this task, and in 1893 there appeared the first volume of his masterpiece, *Die Grundgesetze der Arithmetik*. While working on this he modified his earlier notions of the philosophy of logic in certain respects, and some of his results were published in three important articles, 'Funktion und Begriff (1891),[4] 'Uber Begriff und Gegenstand' (1892),[5] 'Uber Sinn und Bedeutung' (1892).[6] So far as they are relevant, these novelties are incorporated in his large work, but for a full understanding of his thought it is still necessary to refer back to the original publications. Again the reception of Frege's work was discouraging, and he did not produce the second volume of his *Grundgesetze* until 1903. This is concerned especially with the theory of real numbers, but a good deal of the space is taken up by criticism of current views, and at the end Frege alfaws that there is more to be done before real numbers can be properly defined. In a *Naehwort* or appendix, written after most of the work had been printed, he sadly admits the ruin of his work by Bertrand Russell's discovery of a contradiction implicit in his premisses; but he still maintains that his general conception of the relation between arithmetic and logic is correct, and considers methods by which the damage might be repaired.

In the last twenty-two years of his life Frege continued to work at the philosophy of logic and mathematics, but published little, presumably because he could find no satisfactory solution to his problems. Some articles on the foundations of geometry which he published in 1906 show a lack of sympathy, and perhaps even a lack of understanding, for the development of axiomatic method by Hilbert.[7] On the other hand, some comments which he made on Russell's work in 1910,[8] and some papers which he published in later years on cpistemological questions, show that his intellect remained vigorous and critical.[9]

We shall consider in the next chapter those logical discoveries of Frege which are respected even by his philosophical or mathematical opponents. But before entering into details it will be useful to notice here the general outlines of his programme, as he himself expounded it in his most popular work. *Die Grundlagen der Arithmetik,* and to compare it with the views of his distinguished contemporaries, J.W. R. Dedekind (1831-1916), G.Cantor (1845-1918), and G. Peano (1858-1932). Dedekind, who was the oldest and the first to attain fame, published his *Stetigkeit and irrationale Zahlen* as early as 1872, but Cantor was the only one of the group who put forward a 'logical' theory of arithmetic before Frege, and we must therefore start with him.

2. CANTOR'S THEORY OF SETS

The introduction of the theory of real numbers is a momentous step, not only because it involves talk about infinite sets of rational numbers, as we noticed in an earlier chapter, but also because it seems to require recognition of a new kind of infinity. Whereas the rational numbers can be put in one-to-one correspondence with the natural numbers and are therefore said to form a denumerably infinite set, even the sub-set of unreal numbers contained within an interval such as that from 0 to I apparently exemplifies a higher order of infinity. This was first shown by Cantor with his famous diagonal procedure. For simplicity let us think of the real numbers between 0and I as infinite decimals, taking 1/4 to be

0.249, ½ to be 0.49, &c.; and let us suppose that there is some prescription for arranging them all in an infinite table of the form

$$0\,.\,a_1\,a_2\,a_3\,\ldots\ldots$$
$$0\,.\,b_1\,b_2\,b_3\,\ldots\ldots$$
$$0\,.\,c_1\,c_2\,c_3\,\ldots\ldots$$

so that it is proper to speak of the first, the second, the third, and so on. Then it is possible to indicate a real number within the interval from 0 to I by putting in the first decimal place any digit we like except a_1, 0 or 9, in the second place any digit we like except b_2, o, or 9, in the third place any digit we like except c_3, 0, or 9, and so on. But this real number cannot be identical with any one of those in the table, because it differs from each of them in at least one of its decimal places. And this is as much as to say that the table does not contain all the real numbers in the interval, or in other words that the totality of real numbers in the interval is not denumerable.

In order to deal with this situation Cantor elaborated between the years 1874 and 1897 a new mathematical discipline called the theory of sets. His work has won passionate admiration from many mathematicians, and equally passionate condemnation from others. Since, as we shall see later, debates about the development of the theory are very closely connected with some important questions about logic, it is necessary to consider here some of the principal ideas which he put into circulation.

According to Cantor's own definition a set (*Menge*) is 'a collection into one whole of definite, distinct objects of our perception or our thought, which are called the elements of the set'[10] In his earlier papers he sometimes used instead the term 'manifold' (*Mannigfaltigkeit*) and his successors have used the words *ensemble*, 'totality', 'aggregate', and 'class'. A set is said to contain its elements (or members), and they in turn are said to belong to it. A sub-set of a given set S is one whose elements are all elements of S; and this, in distinction from the elements, may be said to be a part of S. A set may be indicated either by the listing of its elements, e.g. the set {Peter, Paul}, or by the giving of some general description appropriate to all its elements and to nothing else; but in either case sets which have the same elements are to be accounted identical, since according to the definition a set is just a collection of elements. So far Cantor's theory of sets is like Boole's theory of classes, but there are further complications to come.

Two sets S and T are said to be equivalent if there exists a one-to-one correspondence between them, i.e. if there is some relation such that each element of S is correlated by the relation with one and only one element of T and each element of T has one and only one element of S correlated with it by the relation. Thus the set of husbands is equivalent in this technical sense to the set of wives in a monogamous society.

The power (*Mächtigkeit*), or cardinal number, of a set can then be introduced as that which it has in common with all equivalent sets but with no others. According to Cantor it is 'the general concept which with the aid of our active intelligence results from a set when we abstract from the nature of its various elements and from the order of their being given', and it can be represented by the sign '$\overline{\overline{S}}$', in which the two horizontal strokes indicate the double abstraction. If $\overline{\overline{S}}$ is finite $\overline{\overline{S}}$, is some natural number; but the theory is intended to cover also infinite sets, whose powers are certainly not natural numbers, and this extension can be achieved most easily by a new definition of infinity. A set is infinite, we now say, if and only if it can be put in one-to-one correspondence with a proper sub-set (i.e. with a sub-set that is not identical with the set itself). Thus the set of the positive integers, 1, 2, 3, &c., can be put in one-to-one correspondence with the set of the squares of the positive integers, 1, 4, 9, &c., although the square numbers are only some among the positive integers. This definition was first formulated explicitly by Cantor's friend Dedekind in 1888,[11] but in 1885 C. S. Peirce had defined a finite set as one which could not be put in one-to-one correspondence with a proper sub-set,[12] and there are interesting anticipations of the idea to be found in Plutarch,[13] Proclus,[14] Adam of Balsham (who has been mentioned earlier), Galileo,[15] and Bernard Bolzano.[16]

As finite sets may be compared in respect of their cardinal numbers, so too may infinite sets. For any set S has a smaller cardinal number than a set T if S is equivalent to some sub-set of T but not to T itself. Thus N, the set of natural numbers, has a smaller transfinite cardinal number than C, the set of real numbers (sometimes called the continuum), i.e. $\overline{\overline{N}} < \overline{\overline{C}}$, because N is equivalent to a sub-set of C but not to the whole.

Next we define a number of operations by which sets may be constructed out of sets. In each case the sets to which the operation is applied may be either finite or infinite, (I) S+T, which is called the logical sum (or union or join) of S and T, contains those things which are elements either of S or of T and nothing else. (2) ST, which is called the inner product (or intersection or meet) of S and T, contains those things which are elements both of S and of T and nothing else. These are both Boolean notions, but what follows is new. (3) S×T, which is called the outer (or Cartesian or cross) product of S and T, is that set whose elements are all the ordered pairs containing one element from S and one clement from T. (4) S^T, sometimes called the insertion set of S into T, is the set of all possible arrangements (or single-valued functions) by which elements of S may be assigned to all the various elements of T, when (*a*) T is not null, (*b*) it is allowed that one element of S may be assigned to more than one clement of T, and (*c*) two arrangements are counted as different if there is at least one element of T to which they assign different elements of S. Thus if T is a set of test-tubes and S a set of chemical substances, S^t is the set of possible ways of inserting the substances into the tubes so that no tube contains more than one substance.

Among sets constituted by insertion into S there is one of special importance called the power set (*Potenzmenge*) of S. This is the set of all sub-sets of S (where among sub-sets of S we include both S it self and the null set), and it is often represented by '𝒰S', in which the letter '𝒰 is taken from the German *Untermenge*. In order to sec that 𝒰S is in fact a set constituted by insertion into S, we need only reflect that a sub-set of S is determined as soon as it has been decided for each of the elements of S whether or not it should be included in the sub-set under consideration- In short, 𝒰S={in, out}^{s}", where {in, out} is the set of possibilities open for each clement of S during the selection of a sub-set.

Now Cantor declares that 𝒰S has a higher cardinal number than S, whatever S may be; and this proposition is so important in his theory that it has been distinguished by the name 'Cantor's Theorem'. Obviously S is equivalent to a part of 𝒰S, namely to the set of all unit sets whose elements are drawn from S, and it is therefore sufficient for Cantor's purpose to prove that S is not equivalent to the whole of 𝒰S. Let us suppose for the sake of argument that S and 𝒰S are equivalent. This is as much as to say that there is some scheme of correlation in which the elements of S are correlated one-to-one with the elements of 𝒰S. Now the elements of 𝒰S are all sub-sets of S, and so we may reasonably ;ask of any element of S whether or not it is an element of its correlate in this scheme. Let us then consider the set that contains all those and only those elements of S which are not elements of their correlates. This must itself be an element of 𝒰S, say u*, and so according to the hypothesis we are investigating it must have correlated with it some element of 𝒰S, say s*. Is s* an element of u* ? If we say 'Yes', we fall into self-contradiction; for according to our definition u* contains only those members of 𝒰S which are not elements of their correlates. But if we say 'No', we fall likewise into self-contradiction; for according to our definition any element of S not contained in u* must be an element of its correlate. But this is absurd, and so we must reject the supposition that S is equivalent to 𝒰S. In short, 𝒰S>S. The proof is similar in general conception to the proof that real numbers are not denumerable, since it shows the impossibility of a certain proposed correlation of elements by showing that this would permit the definition of an element it could not cover. For that reason the argument is sometimes said to exhibit Cantor's diagonal procedure, though the extra case which it introduces to refute the hypothesis of equivalence is not literally a diagonal sequence.

As their symbols suggest, the operations by which sets may be constituted out of sets are introduced in order to prepare the way for a general arithmetic of cardinal numbers'. Thus if S and T are mutually exclusive (or disjoint), $\overline{\overline{S + T}} = \overline{\overline{S}} + \overline{\overline{T}}$ where the second use of + signifies addition of cardinal numbers. Similarly $\overline{\overline{S + T}} = \overline{\overline{S}} + \overline{\overline{T}}$ and $\overline{\overline{S^T}} + \overline{\overline{T^T}}$. So long as we confine our attention to finite sets, the results are in no way surprising. But when we take into account infinite sets, the arithmetic to which the definitions lead is inevitably different in many respects from the arithmetic of natural numbers. We have, for example,

$$\aleph_0 = \aleph_0 + n = n\aleph_0 = \aleph_0{}^n,$$

where $\aleph_0$ is the cardinal number of the set of natural numbers and n is any natural number greater than o. On the other hand $2^{\aleph_0} > \aleph_0$ just as $2^n > n$ for any natural number n; and in general $2^c > c$ for any cardinal c, whether finite or transfinite. This is an immediate corollary of Cantor's Theorem. For $\overline{\overline{s}} > \overline{s}$ and $\overline{\overline{s}} = 2^{\overline{s}}$ so that $2^{\overline{\overline{s}}} = \overline{\overline{S}}$, whatever S may be. We have therefore an unending succession of ever greater transfinite cardinals (or alephs), $_0, 2^{\aleph_0}, 2^{2^{\aleph_0}}$, &c. The first of these is by definition the cardinal number of N, the set of all natural numbers, and the second can be shown to be the cardinal number of C, the set (or continuum) of alll real numbers, which we considered at the beginning of this section. But it is not known whether $2^{\aleph_0}$ is $\aleph_1$, i.e. the *next* trasnfinite number after $\aleph_0$. Cantor conjectured that it was, and Gödel has shown that the generalized continuum hypotheses, i.e. the proposition that $2^{\aleph_n} = \aleph_{n+1}$ for any ordinal number n, is at least consistent with some widely accepted axioms of set theory;[17] yet so far no one has proved the impossibility of a set which is equivalent neither to N nor to C but has a sub-set equivalent to N and is itself equivalent to a sub-set of C.

Like all great mathematicians, Cantor thought of his work as the discovery of laws not made by man. He was, he said, only a, faithful scribe with no claim to merit except for his style and the economy of his exposition.[18] But his admirers have sometimes talked of his theory of sets as though it were a dream creation like Coleridge's *Kubla Khan*, and his enemies have treated it as a nightmare. That which above all else fascinates or repels is his doctrine of the unending succession of transfinite cardinals; and this, as we have seen, depends on his theorem about power sets. The proof of that theorem is an argument *ad absurdum* constructed by means of Cantor's characteristic diagonal procedure, and it is therefore not surprising that suspicion of the general theory has led some mathematicians to cast doubt on the unrestricted use of arguments *ad absurdum* to prove existence.

3. FREGE ON HIS PREDECESSORS

Frege was one of the few who admired Cantor's work when it first appeared. In his *Grundlagen* he writes:

'It is only recently that infinite Numbers have been introduced in a remarkable work by G. Cantor (*Grundlagen einer allgemeinen Mannichfaltigkeitslehre,* 1883). I heartily share his contempt for the view that in principle only finite Numbers ought to be admitted as actual. Perceptible by the senses these are not, nor are they spatial—any more than fractions are, or negative numbers, or irrational or complex numbers; and if we restrict the actual to what acts on our senses or at least produces effects which may cause sense-perceptions as near or remote consequences, then naturally no number of any of these kinds is actual. But it is also true that we have no need at all to appeal to any such sense-perceptions in proving our theorems. . . . While in this I agree, as I believe, with Cantor, my terminology differs to some extent from his. My Number he calls a "power", while his concept of Number his reference to arrangement in an order. . . . For us, because our concept of Number has from the outset covered infinite numbers as well, no extension of its meaning has been necessary at all.[19]

And then, after some comments on Cantor's ideas of ordinal numbers, which were not mentioned in the last section, he goes on:

'Nothing in what I have said is intended to question in any way their legitimacy or their fertility. On the contrary, I find special reason to welcome in Cantor's investigations an extension of the frontiers of science, because they have led to the construction of a purely arithmetical route to higher transfinite Numbers (powers)."[20]

These remarks are especially noteworthy because they occur towards the end of a book which contains much hostile criticism of other writers. The objections which Frege has to bring against previous accounts of arithmetic are in fact so many that it would be impossible to summarize them all here. But in order to make clear the direction of his thought and to show why he sided with Cantor we must consider what he has to say against three rival philosophies of arithmetic, namely that of J. S. Mill, that of Kant, and that of the formalists.

Since Greek times it has been accepted almost universally that ' mathematics is an *a priori* science, that is to say, a science in which all the propositions can be established without appeal to experience for information about particular objects. It was. indeed, reflection on the nature of this study which first led philosophers to conceive the possibility of learning without experience. But in the nineteenth century J. S. Mill went even beyond the empiricism of Hume and tried to maintain that arithmetic rests on inductions from facts about particular groups of things. He allowed that for proof of the equation '5+2=7' we may rely on the axiom that 'whatever is made up of parts is made up of the parts of those parts' and on the definitions '7=6+1 and '6=5+1'; but he said that the axiom, being 'obvious to the senses in all cases which can be fairly referred to their decision and so general as to be coextensive with nature itself, was to be considered 'an inductive truth or law of nature of the highest order'; and he argued that even the definitions involved assertion of physical facts about the existence of collections decomposable in certain ways.[21] Frege therefore thought it necessary to begin his *Grundlagen* by maintaining the a *priori* character of arithmetic.

Against Mill's account of definition Frege points out that, if knowledge of some special physical fact were required for correct use of the definition of each small number, such knowledge would be necessary also for the correct use of the definition of each large number. We could not, for example, put

$$1{,}000{,}000 = 999{,}999 + 1$$

unless we had observed a collection of a million things split up in precisely that way; and a man who calculated properly with nine-figure numbers would deserve the highest honour for his knowledge of nature.[22] Against the suggestion that general laws of arithmetic are inductive truths he makes the objection that induction itself seems to require some general propositions of arithmetic, since, in that usage in which it is supposed to be a method of science and not a mere process of habituation, it depends on the theory of probability.[23] But his most telling criticism of the whole empiricist theory is that it involves the confusion of supposing the plus sign to refer to physical addition.[24] When we say that 5+2 = 7, we do not mean that if we pour 2 unit volumes of liquid onto 5 unit volumes of liquid we shall have 7 unit volumes of liquid. For the latter statement is at best an application of the mathematical proposition and holds good only under the proviso that no alteration of volume occurs as a result, say, of some chemical reaction. Other applications of the formula may be to numbers of events, or virtues, or roots of equations, where there can be no question of physical aggregation.

Having disposed of the empiricist theory, Frege goes on to

consider whether the laws of arithmetic are synthetic or analytic. 'The question was raised first by Kant, and Frege regards Kant as the chief exponent of the view that mathematical propositions are synthetic, but he does not accept Kant's account of the distinction between the two kinds of judgement. According to his own account, a truth is analytic if for the proof of it we need refer back only to general logical laws and to definitions, but synthetic if for the proof of it we must use premisses which are not of a general logical nature.[25] Kant came near to suggesting this when he tried to connect the truth of analytic judgements with the principle of non-contradiction,[26] but he unfortunately worked with a conception of logic that was too narrow. When he asked whether the predicate concept was or was not contained in the subject concept of a judgement, he used a criterion that is applicable only to universal affirmative judgements of the Aristotelian scheme. For in singular and in existential judgements there is no subject concept. And he seems to have thought of the definition of a complex concept as a mere list of characters, whereas the really important definitions of mathematics, e.g. that of the continuity of a function, are not of this kind.[27] Here Frege lays his finger on a defect of the traditional logic which had not been noticed even by those among his predecessors whose interests were nearest to his own. Leibniz, for example, had thought of concepts and propositions in the way presupposed by Kant's account of analytic truths; that, as we have seen, was the main reason why he never succeeded in producing a convincing specimen of the great development that he proclaimed in his writings on logic. Boole too had been content to investigate those relatively simple patterns of structure that can be represented by Euler's circles. Frege could more plausibly make large claims for logic prcisely because he allowed for much greater complexity of logical form than any of his predecessors had been able to conceive. In his work 'analytic is to be understood by reference to his own logic, and it is by no means a synonym for Locke's 'trifling'.

Although Frege criticizes Kant's way of distinguishing between analytic and synthetic truths and rejects his account of arithmetic, he writes towards the end of the Grundlagen:

'I have no wish to incur the reproach of picking petty quarrels with a genius to whom we must all look up with grateful awe; I feel bound, therefore, to call attention also to the extent of my agreement with him, which far exceeds any disagreement. To touch only upon what is immediately relevant, I consider Kant did great service in drawing the distinction between synthetic and analytic judgements. In calling the truths of geometry synthetic and *a priori*, he revealed their true nature. And this is still worth repeating, since even to-day it is often not recognized. If Kant was wrong about arithmetic, that does not seriously detract, in my opinion, from the value of his work. His point was that there are such things as synthetic judgements a *priori;* whether they are to be found in geometry only, or in arithmetic as well, is of less importance.[28]

In an earlier passage he tells us that geometry is indeed founded on intuition, as Kant said, and that its axioms govern everything which is spatially intuitable, including even the wildest visions of delirium and the boldest inventions of poetry:

'Conceptual thought alone can after a fashion shake off their yoke, when it supposes, say, a space of four dimensions or positive curvature. To study such conceptions is not useless by any means; but it is to leave the ground of intuition entirely behind....For purposes of conceptual thought we can always suppose the contrary of some one or other of the geometrical axioms, without involving ourselves in any self-contradictions when we proceed to our deductions, despite the conflict between our suppositions and our intuition. The fact that this is possible shows that the axioms of geometry are independent of one another and of the primitive laws of logic and consequently are synthetic.'[29]

From these explanations it appears that Frege did not wish to deny the possibility of non-Euclidean geometries (in a large sense of the word 'geometry'); and if pressed, he would presumably have said that the assertions made by mathematicians who study such systems are analytic truths, since according to his account of the matter they can be no more than conditional statements guaranteed by their logical form. From this he might have been led on to admit that even Euclidean geometry, considered as a branch of pure mathematics, is analytic. For the truth, if it is a truth, that Euclid's axioms apply necessarily to relations in intuited space is irrelevant to the study of the system of order which they determine. But he followed the old fashion of using the phrase 'truths of geometry' to cover axioms and theorems as well as statements of their connexion, and this accounts for the distinction of status which he drew between geometry and arithmetic. If anyone claims to know that Euclid's geometrical axioms are necessarily true in the sense in which Euclid intended them to be taken, i.e. as general statements about relations in ordinary space, he commits himself to a doctrine of intuition such as Frege took over from Kant. Conversely, anyone who rejects all talk about intuition as a source of a *priori* knowledge should realize that he is not entitled to retain the old view of *any* of Euclid's axioms. In short, the thesis which interested Frege is not refuted by an alteration of the usage of the word 'geometry'.

It must be admitted, nevertheless, as Frege himself says, that 'we are all too ready to invoke inner intuition when we cannot produce any other ground of knowledge'.[30] And it is difficult to attach any clear sense to what Kant says about intuition in his account of arithmetic. In one of his most explicit pronouncements he asserts that in order to add together the numbers 7 and 5 we must go beyond their concepts 'by calling to our aid the intuition corresponding to one of them, say our five fingers' and concludes, 'Arithmetical judgements are therefore always synthetic, and the more plainly according as we take larger numbers'.[31] But it is surely absurd to maintain that we can establish the truth of the equation :

$$135,664 + 37,863 = 173,527$$

by calling to our aid an intuition of 173,527 fingers. Are we then to say that Kant's doctrine applies only to small numbers, in spite of his own explicit statement? But there is no fundamental distinction between small and large numbers. If formulae involving numbers from, say, 10 onwards are provable without intuition, why not those which involve smaller numbers?[32] And again what is this supposed intuition corresponding to a number? Arithmetic is not about fingers as geometry may be said to be about points, lines, and planes; and there is no intuition that can guarantee the applicability of arithmetical truths to everything numerable. Furthermore, if any truths of arithmetic were derivable only from intuition, they would presumably be independent of one another and of laws of logic, just as the axioms of Euclid have been found to be. But if we try denying any of the fundamental propositions of the science of number, the result is not an alternative system of arithmetic but complete confusion.[33]

From these considerations Frege draws the conclusion that the basis of arithmetic must lie deeper than that of any of the empirical sciences and deeper even than that of geometry as he conceives it. The domain of the numerable is the widest domain of; all for it is not confined to the intuitable, nor even to the existent, but includes everything thinkable. Is it not reasonable then to suppose that the laws of number may be connected very intimately with the laws of thought ? When Frege asks this question, he certainly does not wish to suggest that arithmetic is a branch of psychology. For again and again he insists that logic, and with it arithmetic, which he wishes to exhibit as a development of logic, is completely independent of psychology. In the Preface to his *Grundlagen*, for example, he lays it down as the first guiding principle of his work that the logical should always be, kept separate from the psychological. And in the Preface to his *Grundgesetze* he attacks explicitly all attempts to present the laws of thought as psychological generalizations, saying that he hopes his work will help to free logic from the infection which seems to have contaminated all the recent books on the subject. What he suggests by the question quoted above he expresses also in another place by saying that the laws of arithmetic are not laws of nature, but laws of the laws of nature, i.e. fundamental principles about the thinkable.[34]

Frege's thesis, then, is that truths of arithmetic are analytic because we require for their proof only laws of logic and definitions. But there were many mathematicians in his day who might have accepted this dictum and yet defended a theory of arithmetic which Frege rejected. The point at issue between them concerned the nature of definition in mathematics, and Frege evidently regarded it as of the utmost importance; for the space that he devotes to it in his *Grundlagen* and his *Grundgesetze* is more than he gives to the criticism of all other theories of mathematics.

When mathematicians of the nineteenth century surveyed the progress of their science since the Renaissance, they sometimes had the impression that the novelties were products of human construction rather than discoveries. As their name implies, imaginary numbers were conceived in this way from an early, date; but presently it occurred to some mathematicians that all' higher types of numbers, and even the natural numbers themselves, might be regarded in the same fashion. This view appealed to the positivist, or anti-metaphysical, temper of the age. In his *Theorie der complexen Zahlensysteme* of 1867 Hankel wrote:

'Number to-day is no longer a thing, a substance, existing in its own right apart from the thinking subject and the objects which give rise to it, a self-subsistent element in the sort of way it was for the Pythagoreans. The question whether some number exists can therefore only be understood as referring to the thinking subject or to the objects thought about, relations between which the numbers represent.. As impossible in the strict sense the mathematician counts only what is logically impossible, that is, self-contradictory. That numbers which are impossible in this sense cannot be admitted, needs no proof. But if the numbers concerned are logically possible, if their concept is clearly and fully defined and therefore free from contradiction, then the question whether they exist can amount only to this: Does there exist in reality or in the actual world given to us in intuition a substratum for these numbers, do' there exist objects in which they— that is, intelligible relations of the type defined—can become phenomenal?[35]

The expression of this passage is not very clear, but the seems seems to be that in pure as opposed to applied mathematics questions about existence are out of place because the whole subject is a free construction of the human mind, subject only to the restrictions of logic.

Against such teaching Frege maintains that it is absurd to talk of creative definition:

'We might just as well say this: among numbers hitherto known there is none which satisfies the simultaneous equations

$$x + 1 = 2$$

$$x + 2 = 1,$$

but there is nothing to prevent us from introducing a symbol which solves the problem. Ah, but there is, it will be replied: to satisfy both the equations simultaneously involves a contradiction. Certainly, if we are requiring a real number or an ordinary complex number to satisfy them; but then all we have to do is to widen our number system, to create numbers which do meet these new requirements. Then we can wait and see whether anyone succeeds in producing a contradiction in them. Who can tell what may not be possible with our new numbers? .. . And why not create still further numbers which permit the summation of diverging series? But that will do,— even the mathematician cannot create things at will, any more than the geographer ĉan; he too can only discover what is there and give it a name.'[36]

The source of the illusion is to be found in the history of

mathematics. When they were already familiar with the operation of subtracting 2 from 3, mathematicians began to talk of the operation of subtracting 3 from 3, and introduced the symbol '—1' for the result of this operation. And again later, when they were already familiar with the notion of the square root of a positive real number, they began to talk of the square root of a negative number, and introduced the symbol 'i' as an abbreviation for '√—1'. In each case it seemed that the scope if mathematics had been widened by the postulation of something not given before, and there was a temptation to say that new numbers had been created by the rearrangement of old signs. But this way of talking involves a serious mistake about definitions. Anyone who thinks he has fully explained his use of the symbol 'i' by writing 'i = √—1' must assume a meaning for the sign '√', and yet there was nothing in the original explanation of the use of this sign to justify its use in the new context. If, however, we say that the creative definition of imaginary numbers involves also enlargement of the definition of '√", we reduce everything to uncertainty. For this doctrine of the piecemeal definition of the mathematical signs implies that the square-root sign was not fully defined in its earlier uses. And 'so long as it is not completely defined, or known in some other way, what a word stands for, the word may not be used in an exact science—least of all with a view to further development of its own definition'.'[37]

It is easy to understand why mathematicians have retained such symbols as '+' and '–' throughout the development of mathematics, while giving them different senses at the successive stages. For each lower calculus is in a sense reproduced in each higher calculus. But the practice has led to some confusion, and in his *Grundgesetze* Frege argues that we should do well to avoid it, at least for philosophical purposes.

'Instead of first defining a symbol for a limited domain and then using it for the purpose of defining itself in regard to a wider domain, we need only choose different signs, confining the reference of the first, once for all, to the narrower domain; in this way the first definition is now complete and draws sharp boundary lines. This in no way prejudges the relation between the reference of one sign and that of another; we can investigate this, without its being possible that the result of the investigation should make it questionable whether the definitions were justified. It really is worth the trouble to invent a new symbol if we can thus remove not a few logical difficulties and ensure the rigour of the proofs. But many mathematicians seem to have so little feeling for logical purity and accuracy that they will use a word to stand for three or four different things, sooner than make the frightful decision to invent a new word.'[38]

Again those who talk of creative definition reveal the confusion of their thought when they say that we must be careful to avoid self-contradiction while introducing novelties. They are obviously on the side of the angels in their desire to avoid inconsistency, but how do they propose to prove the consistency of their constructions? 'Strictly, of course, we can only establish that a concept is free from contradiction by first producing something that falls under it.The converse inference is a fallacy.[39] And if we are in a position to indicate something that falls under a concept, it is obviously absurd to talk as though our definition of the concept were a creation. In practice, however, the mathematicians who use such language merely assume consistency because they have not hitherto found any inconsistency, and then go on to assume also the existence of examples. Sometimes indeed they try to justify the fallacy by saying that in mathematics 'existence' just means the same as 'consistency'; but if Frege is right, this defence is an aggravation of their fault, because it implies that consistency can never be proved at all.

According to his view each numerical calculus deals with a certain set of objects, not of course physical objects such as stones, nor yet psychical objects such as feelings, but nevertheless objects independent of all language. And when he speaks of the definition of a concept in mathematics, he means nothing like the constructive activity assumed by his opponents, but simply the elimitation of the field of application of a general term by means of an equivalence. Thus complex numbers may be defined as ordered pairs of real numbers, and operations on complex numbers may be defined by reference to operations on the real numbers in such pairs. That we use certain sounds or shapes as'defined terms is obviously arbitrary, but there is nothing are bitrary about the truths which we enunciate by means of them after we have defined them. For it is possible in principle to eliminate all terms which have been defined explicitly. In the practice of mathematical thinking we need them only because we should find it difficult to focus our attention properly without them. They are, so to say, instruments of selection. In the philosophy of mathematics, on the other hand, we are especially interested in definitions precisely because the setting forth of a satisfactory chain of definitions shows the possibility of eliminating all the defined terms. That which is valuable from one point of view as a licence to abbreviate is valuable also from another point of view as an elucidation. Furthermore, it is Frege's view that when a satisfactory chain of definitions has been set forth it will be clear that the only undefined notions required for the presentation of arithmetic are notions of formal logic. In particular he wishes to show that talk about natural numbers can be reduced to talk about sets, classes, or manifolds, which in the terminology of logicians are the extensions of concepts, and he says explicitly that the objects of arithmetic are logical objects.[40]

If it is allowed that mathematical symbols have meanings and that mathematical formulae are used to make statements, Frege's attack on the theory of creative definition cannot be resisted, though his attempt to reduce mathematics to logic may still be questioned. But the suggestion that mathematical novelties are creations rather than discoveries has often been coupled with a rejection of the view that mathematicians as such make statements about any objects whatsoever, and Frege therefore devotes much space to proving that mathematics cannot properly be considered as a game with meaningless marks. Naturally no one ever denied that the application of arithmetic involved assignment of meanings to the arithmetical symbols, but mathematicians who call themselves formalists have tried to maintain that in pure mathematics there is no need to go beyond the symbols and their rules of combination, that is to say, beyond material over which we ourselves have complete control. At the beginning of his *Elementare Theorie der analytischen Functionen iner complexen Veränderlichen* published, in 1898, J. Thomae expressed the view as follows:

'The formal conception of arithmetic accepts more modest limitations than does the logical conception. It does not ask what numbers are and what they do, but rather what is demanded of them in arithmetic. For the formalist, arithmetic is a game with signs, which are called empty. That means they have no other content (in the calculating game) than they are assigned by their behaviour with respect to certain rules of combination (rules of the game). The chess player makes similar use of his pieces; he assigns them certain properties determining their behaviour in the game, and the pieces are only the external signs of this behaviour. To be sure, there is an important difference between arithmetic and chess. The rules of chess are arbitrary, the system of rules for arithmetic is such that by means of simple axioms the numbers can be referred to perceptual manifolds and can thus make important contribution to our knowledge of nature. . . . The formal standpoint rids us of all metaphysical difficulties ; this is the advantage it affords us.'[41]

In the second volume of his *Grundgesetze*,, published in 1903, Frege argues against this new enemy in detail, maintaining that it is impossible to present the arithmetic we know without assuming references for its signs.[42]

In the first place, he points out that formulae which are merely combinations of meaningless marks cannot properly be said to have any applications. There would be no sense in talking of the application of chess unless we had *already* assigned a representative function to the pieces and their moves, e.g. by deciding that the movement of a pawn in a game was to represent the advance of a scouting patrol in a battle between armies. Now if, as the formalists seem to admit, it is the possibility of application which distinguishes mathematical thinking from the playing of games and entitles us to call it pursuit of knowledge, when does the assignment of meanings occur? It is presupposed in applied mathematics, and yet apparently it has no place in pure mathematics. Frege does not deny that it might be possible to carry out all the moves required for the derivation of a formula in his own deductive system without thinking of the meanings of the signs; but he says that, so far from producing a great simplification, such refusal to interpret the signs would make the problem harder. Since the interest of mathematical formulae lies in the possibility of applying them, let us be frank with ourselves and admit that our rules of calculation are not chosen arbitrarily but depend on the meanings we have assigned to our symbols. If a game were devised for playing on paper with meaningless marks according to arbitrary rules, it would certainly not be called a branch of mathematics.

Secondly, Frege draws attention to the fact that at certain critical points formalists unconsciously smuggle in meanings for marks that were supposed to be meaningless. The most interesting example of such self-deception in Thomae's work is a passage where he says that the rules for his calculating game are contained in a set of seven formulae such as 'a+b = b+a' and 'a+(b+c) (a+b) +c'. From what he does later, however, it appears that these formulae are also to be taken as initial dispositions in the calculating game, i.e. something like the arrangement of the pieces on the board at the beginning of a game of chess. But how can a rule be given by an arrangement of meaningless marks? It would be thought very odd if anyone pointed to an arrangement of pieces on a ches-sboard and said that it was one of the rules of the game of chess. Obviously Thomac intends us to understand that any combination of marks which appears on one side of an identity sign in one of his formulae may be substituted for the combination of signs which appears on the other side of the same identity sign, or rather something more complicated, namely, that every combination of marks which occurs on one side of an identity sign in a formula that is structurally, though not perhaps alphabetically, similar to any of his seven may be substituted for the combination which appears on the other side of the same identity sign. In short, the identity sign, as he uses it here, expresses the equivalence of certain things for the purposes of his game, and the letters are variables which express generality. For a proper understanding of the situation we must distinguish between the game and the theory of the game. Whereas the former may be only a manipulation of meaningless marks, the latter, which deals with the rules and their consequences, cannot be formulated without meaningful signs. Indeed it involves arithmetic of the ordinary kind, and Thomae himself seems to admit as much in a curious passage where he says that his numerals sometimes 'have more than a mere formal reference even within pure arithmetic, e.g. in the sentence "this equation is of degree three" '. Now all Thomae's *theorems* and their proofs must belong to the theory of his calculating game, not to the game itself. Why then does he think that he has escaped from the restrictions of ordinary meaningful arithmetic ?

Thirdly, Frege shows with many examples that the formalists persistently confuse numbers with numerals. Some of them explicitly identify numbers with sensible signs, and others give the same impression without committing themselves to a clear declaration. In mathematical texts we often find the authors writing as though there were no difference between 's is the smallest root of the equation' and 's designates the smallest root of the equation'. Such failure to distinguish between the *use* and the *mention* of a symbol may be harmless enough in many contexts, but in a discussion of the foundations of mathematics, and particularly in an exposition of formalist doctrine, it is extremely dangerous. For it encourages formalists to think that they can say about numerals what is significant only in reference to numbers. Thus Thomae writes about numbers at one moment as though they were marks on paper and at another moment as though they formed an infinite sequence in order of magnitude. Numbers do indeed form an infinite sequence, and this is essential for the development of arithmetic, e.g. for the theory of irrationals. But the set of particular numerals written or printed on paper is, and always will be, finite. It may be added that, if a formalist tried to answer Frege by saying that he was not thinking of what Peire would call token numerals, but rather of what Peircce would call type numerals (e.g. of '2' in the sense in which '2' can be written or printed many times),[43] he would not improve his case. For while we may say that there are infinitely many numerals in this sense, our warrant for the assertion is our understanding of the infinity of the sequence of natural *numbers*. Given any type numeral we can conceive a successor constructed by means of the suffix '+1', but only because there is no limit to the theoretically possible number of such suffixes.

Fourthly, Frege shows that the rules given by Thomae are quite inadequate for his purpose of reproducing arithmetic without reference to the meanings of its signs. The seven formulae mentioned above are supposed to cover all numerals alike, and suitably interpreted they are unobjectionable as general rules, but they provide no clue to the distinctive features of the several numerals. It is as though a writer on chess gave some rules applicable to all pieces alike but omitted mention of the existence of pawns, bishops, and the rest. True, Thomae remarks on some peculiarities of the number o, but what he has to say is very curious reading in an exposition of formalism. According to him, we must exclude combinations of marks such as '2/o', because division by zero cannot be 'performed uniquely (i.e. consistently)' and 'a quotient whose denominator is o has no meaning'. If manipulations of marks in which 'o' is allowed to appear on the right of a division sign lead to results such as 'I =2', why should this worry a formalist ? And what special objection can there be to the combination '2/o' in a system where all the combinations of marks are meaningless? For Thomae the only proper course is to introduce a new rule which expressly forbids the placing of the mark 'o' after (or under) a line. But even this is not enough. If he wishes to make his system resemble ordinary meaningful arithmetic in its external features, he must exclude also such combinations as '2/(3—3)'and '2/(2+1—3)', in short every combination in which there appears after a solidus a set of marks that can be replaced by the single mark 'o'. Clearly he cannot exclude them all separately, and yet he has given no criterion for recognizing what sets of marks can be replaced by 'o' in his system.

The criticisms are fatal to Thomae's philosophy of arithmetic, but we shall sec later that a stronger case than his can be made for some kind of formalism. In accordance with our plan we must now go on to consider Frege's own doctrine.

4. FREGE'S DEFINITIONS OF THE NATURAL NUMBERS

Frege accepts the view of Leibniz, Mill, and others that all the natural numbers greater than i are to be defined by reference to their predecessors, i.e. by equations such as '2 = 1+1', '3 = 2 + I'+ &c. But he remarks that these definitions remain incomplete so long as the number i and the notion of increase by i are themselves undefined, and he draws attention also to the fact that general propositions are needed for the full development of arithmetic.[44] In order to gain a deeper understanding of the 'subject he therefore decides to investigate the general concept of a natural number. It would take too long to notice all the confusions about this which he finds in the works of predecessors, including even those of great mathematicians from Euclid to Cantor, but he himself has summarized the results of his historical review in the following passage:

'Number is not abstracted from things in the way that colour, weight, and hardness are, nor is it a property of things in the sense that they are. But when we make a statement of number, what is that of which we assert something? This question remained unanswered. . . . Number is not anything physical, but nor is it anything subjective (an idea). Number does not result from the annexing of thing to thing.... The word "one", as the proper name of an object of mathematical study, does not admit of a plural. Consequently, it is nonsense to make numbers result from the putting together of ones. The plus symbol in 1+1 = 2 cannot mean such a putting together.'[45]

The answer to the outstanding question is revealed in the next section, where Frege says that numbers are properly assigned to concepts, not to objects:

'This is perhaps clearest with the number o. If I say "Venus has o moons", there simply does not exist any moon or agglomeration of moons for anything to be asserted of; but what happens is that a property is assigned to the *concept* "moon of Venus", namely that of including nothing under it. If I say "the King's carriage is drawn by four horses", then I assign the number four to the concept "horse that draws the King's carriage".[46]

For an understanding of this it must be remembered that in Frege's terminology a concept is something signified by a general word or phrase such as we might use in the predicate position of a statement, whereas an object is something that can be named by a proper name and said to fall under a concept or to have a concept as a property. The opposition is not that between mental and material, nor yet that between ideal and real, but more like that between universal and individual; and yet it does not correspond exactly to the last of these traditional antitheses, because the phrase 'moon of Venus' could scarcely be said to signify a universal.

There is an appearance of circularity in a definition according to which the number o belongs to a concept if no objects fall under the concept. For the word 'no' seems to be only a variant of the numeral 'o'. But we can avoid this objection by saying ' The number o belongs to the concept F if, for every x, x. does not Fall under F'. In similar style we can say also that the number n +1 belongs to the concept F if there is an object x falling under F and such that the number n belongs to the concept 'falling under F but not identical with x'. With this apparatus it is obviously possible to explain in the way suggested by Leibniz what it means to say that 1,2,3, or any other definite number belongs to a concept. But Frege is still not satisfied. It is an illusion, he tells us, to suppose that we have defined the numbers in this say. In reality we have only fixed the sense of such expressions as 'the number o belongs to ...' and 'the number I belongs to ...'. As yet we have no authority 'to pick out o and I as self-subsistent objects that can be recognized-again'. But to do so, he thinks, is essential for arithmetic, since the numerals are used there as nouns. Admittedly the numerals occur in ordinary speech as adjective. But 'Jupiter has four moons' can be replaced by 'the number of Jupiter's moons is four', where 'four' is a noun and 'is' has the sense of an identity sign; and the second expression is better articulated than the first. For although the adjective 'four' is said by the grammarians to agree with the plural noun 'moons', the moons are not severally four. There is indeed no property signified by the word 'four' which anything, whether an individual or a collection, may be said to possess. A number is not a concept but an object.

Frege is undoubtedly in the right when he maintains that we can think of objects which are neither sensible nor imaginable. But is he right when he says that numbers are objects in his special sense, i.e. not concepts? We must allow that numerical adjectives do not behave like ordinary attributive phrases: although it is correct to say that Jupiter has four moons, it is absurd to say that each of these moons is four, and also strange at the very least to say that the set of them is four. Furthermore, when the word 'four' is used as a noun, e.g. in the statement 'four is an even number', it seems to behave, as Frege says, like a proper name. It would be silly to say that the roots of two equations were both fours, though we can speak of fours in the plura when the context shows that we are talking of numerals as distinct from numbers. On the other hand, there are some definite nouns of multitude, such as 'pair' and 'dozen', which must classed among common nouns, since they can be used in the plural; and these may appear as predicates for sets. It is quite sensible to say that the group of Jesus's disciples was a dozen. Whether we express numerical propositions by this device or in one of the other ways mentioned above seems to be a matter of linguistic accident. In Latin *mille* is an adjective but *milia* is a noun, and in English 'hundred' is still a noun though 'a hundred and one' is a complex adjective. Why then should we not identify numbers with pairhood, dozenhood, &c., or, to use Frege's terminology, with the concepts 'pair', 'dozen', &c. ? This suggestion seems to be what Cantor had in mind when he talked of *Mächtigkeiten*, and it has the great merit of simplicity. Everyone must admit that there are sets of various sizes, and according to the proposed definition a number would be just the common character of all sets of the same size. Or, if it is thought better to say, as Frege does, that numbers belong to concepts, why should we not identify numbers with second-level concepts such as that of having a pair of instances ?

Frege's reason for rejecting such a view is inadequate. He writes:

'In the proposition "the number o belongs to the concept F", o is only an element in the predicate (taking the concept F to be the real subject). For this reason I have avoided calling a number such as 0 or 1 or 2 a *property* of a concept. Precisely because it forms only an element in what is asserted, the individual number shows itself for what it is, a self-subsistent object. I have already drawn attention to the fact that we speak of 'the number 1', where the definite article serves to class it as an object. In arithmetic this self-subsistence comes out at every turn, as for example in the identity 1 +1 = 2.'[47]

When he says that o is only an clement of the predicate, he seems to imply that if o were a property of the concept F it would be possible to say 'the concept F is o'. But this is a mistake. If o is indeed a concept, then to say 'o belongs to the concept F' is a perfectly proper way of saying that o is a property of the concept F. For according to this view 'o' is just an abbreviation for 'the concept of having no instances', and in certain contexts Frege allows himself to talk as though he recognized such a concept. He says, for example:

'By properties which a re asserted of a concept I naturally do not mean the characteristics which make up the concept. These latter are properties of the things which fall under the concept, not of the concept.

Thus "rectangular" is not a property of the concept "rectangular triangle"; but the proposition that there exists no rectangular equilateral rectilinear triangle does express a property of the concept "rectangular equilateral rectilinear triangle"; it assigns to it the number nought. In this respect existence is analogous to number. Affirmation of existence is in fact nothing but denial of the number nought. Because existence is a property of concepts the ontological argument for the existence of God breaks down."[48]

Since the existence of which he speaks here is not, strictly speaking, the existence of concepts, but the existence of objects falling under them, the property of concepts with which he identifies it must be that of having an instance or instances. It is probable, therefore, that when Frege refused to regard numbers as second-level concepts he was moved chiefly by the thought that numbers have a self-subsistence which is impossible for concepts. If so, he was misled by onc of his own doctrines about concepts which we shall have to examine later. But we must in any case go on to consider the nature of the objects with which he tries to identify the natural numbers.

In the introduction to his *Grundlagen* Frege had laid it down as the second of his three guiding principles that the meaning of a word was never to be sought in isolation but only in the context of a significant utterance. Following this principle, he now undertakes to obtain a definition of natural numbers in general by first fixing the sense of a numerical identity. If numbers are self-subsistent objects, but not perceptible, it is obviously of the greatest importance to make clear how we can recognize them, which is as much as to say, how we can establish numerical identities. The procedure suggested is rather like that of defining the direction of a line by first defining identity of direction, or parallelism, and then abstracting the notion of direction. Frege's main task, it seems, is to explain the sense of 'The number which belongs to the concept F is the same as the number which belongs to the concept G' without making use of such expressions as 'the number which belongs to the concept F'; and this he proposes to do by means of the notion of one-to-one correlation. The suggestion that identity of numbers could be defined in this way was at least as old as Hume,[49] but when Frege wrote it had recently become fashionable among mathematicians, as he himself remarked.[50] Cantor in particular had used it in his *Grundlagen einer allgemeinen Mannichfaltigkeitslehre* of 1883, and Frege, as we have wen, admired Cantor's work, though he sometimes found occasion to charge him, with other mathematicians, of talking loosely about 'ideal constructions'.

Now the objects falling under two concepts F and G may be said to be correlated with each other by the relation ϕ if (i) every object falling under the concept F stands in the relation ϕ to an object falling under the concept G, and (ii) for every object falling under the concept G there is an object falling under the concept F which stands to it in the relation ϕ. And it may be understood that these conditions are satisfied vacuously when no objects fall under either of the concepts. In order to make such correlation one-to-one (*beiderseits eindeutig*) we must add two further conditions: (iii) that, for any x, y, and z, if x stands in this relation ϕ to y and also to z, then y and z are the same; and (iv) that,' for any x, y, and z, if x and y both stand in the relation ϕ to z, then x and y are the same. It will be noted that all four conditions are expressed in the terminology of formal logic (if that is allowed to include 'same'), and that one-to-one correlation can be explained in this fashion without use of the word 'one'. On this basis Frege builds a structure of three definitions:

(1) 'The concept F is like-numbered (*gleichzahlig*) with the concept G' is to mean the same as 'there exists a relation ϕ which correlates the objects falling under the concept F one-to-one with the objects falling under the concept G'. ,

(2) The number which belongs to the concept F is the extension of the concept 'like-numbered with the concept F'.

(3) 'n is a number' is to mean the same as 'there exists a concept such that n is the number which belongs to it'.'[51]

In (1) the artificial word 'like-numbered' is intended, of course, to suggest identity of the numbers belonging to the concepts to which it is applied, but the meaning of the phrase 'number belonging to the concept' is not fixed until we come to (2), and so for the purposes of strict theory 'like-numbered' is to be taken as a unitary expression with just the sense given to it by (1), i.e. concepts are to be called like-numbered if their extensions are equivalent according to the technical phraseology of the theory of sets. In (2) likewise the phrase 'the number which belongs to the concept F' is intended to suggest the ordinary use of the word 'number', but there is no circularity involved in the use of the phrase before the word 'number' is defined in (3). For in the strict theory (2) is merely an explanation of the usage of the whole phrase 'the number which belongs to the concept F', and it is not until we reach

(3) that we have a rule for talking about a number without mention of this or that concept to which it belongs.

This system of definitions is a very remarkable achievement of philosophical ingenuity, and it is easy to see why Frege thought he had at least made it probable that arithmetic could be reduced to logic. But we must ask whether the definitions provide a satisfactory account of the natural numbers, and for this purpose we must consider each in turn.

If at the first step Frege were merely stipulating that the expression 'like-numbered' might be used as a substitute for a longer expression about one-to-one correspondence, there could, of course, be no objection. But it is clear from his preliminary explanation that he thinks his definition gives a correct analysis of the sense which anyone would attach to the compound adjective if he met it without a special stipulation. That is the point of Frege's statement that he intends to obtain the concept of number by first finding the sense of a numerical identity. Now when it is considered as an elucidation of ordinary usage, definition (1) involves a difficulty. For while it is obvious that any two concepts whose instances are correlated in the way described must be like-numbered in the sense that each has just as many instances as the other, it is not so obvious that there must be such a correlation between the instances of concepts which are like-numbered in that sense.

Let us consider an example supplied by Frege. He says correctly :

'If a waiter wishes to be certain of laying exactly as many knives on a table as plates, he has no need to count either of them; all he has to do is to lay immediately to the right of every plate a knife, taking care that every knife on the table lies immediately to the right of a plate.[52]

But his argument proves only that one-to-one correlation is a sufficient condition of numerical identity, not that it is also a necessary condition. Perhaps we may go farther than Frege does in expounding his example, and say that two concepts cannot he *proved* to be like-numbered unless there is a one-to-one correlation between their instances. For when we count the objects filling under each concept, we establish such a correlation by our assignments of ordinal numbers; and when in some special case we are able to recognize a numerical identity without counting, because the members of one set of things are arranged in the same pattern as the members or another, like the signs on playing cards of equal value, the important consideration is that each member of one set is related to one and only one member, the other set by the relation of similarity of position within the pattern. But even so there is no patent absurdity in the suggestion that the number of knives on a table might be the same :is the ' number of plates though the knives were not correlated one-to-one with the plates in the waiter's way for by any other method such as the drawing of lines. According to Frege's doctrine the fact, if it is a fact, that the number of knives is the same as the number of plates requires the existence of *some* relation by which the knives are correlated one-to-one with the plates; and yet it seems that correlation of any special kind we choose to mention could be lacking without any alteration of the numbers.

If the number of knives is the same as the number of plates, it is certainly *possible* that the knives should be correlated one-to-one with the plates, whereas there can be no such correlation between the objects falling under concepts which are not like-numbered. And there, no doubt, is a reason why the difficulty of Frege's definition has been overlooked by many mathematicians. For the notion of one-to-one correlation first gained serious attention in connexion with Cantor's theory of transfinite numbers, and the only sets which can be cited as plausible illustrations of that theory are from within mathematics itself, that is to say, from a realm where we do not commonly distinguish between possibility and fact. Thus, for example, it is of no importance whether we say that the rational numbers *can be* correlated one-to-one with natural numbers or that they *are* so correlated by a functional relation. Outside pure mathematics the situation is very different; and yet, if Frege is right, from the mere fact that the number of knives on a table is the same as the number of plates it follows that there is some relation by which the knives *are* correlated one-to-one with the plates and will always be so correlated, whatever may happen, provided only that their number is not changed. How can this be explained?

If indiscernibles are identical, as Leibniz asserted, the various objects falling under a concept must have distinguishing attributes. Let us suppose that the objects falling under the concept F are distinguishable by the attributes F_1, F_2, and F_3, each of which entails F, and that the objects falling under G are likewise distinguishable by the attributes G_1, G_2, and G_3, each of which entails G. Further, let us agree to say that x has the relation R to y if, and only if, x and y satisfy the condition expressed by the complex formula:

$$\text{(x has } F_1 \text{ and y has } G_1\text{) or (x has } F_2 \text{ and y has } G_2\text{)}$$
$$\text{or (x has } F_3 \text{ and y has } G_3\text{).}$$

Then the objects falling under F are correlated by this relation one-to-one with the objects falling under G. That is to say, according to the explanation given above, every object falling under F has R to one and only one object falling under G, while for every object falling under G there is one and only one object falling under F which has R to it. For simplicity we have used the same numerical subscripts to indicate the distinguishing attributes under the two concepts and have then paired attributes with the same subscript when composing the long expression by which we define R, but there is nothing essential in this use of numerals. The distinguishing attributes under each concept may be indicated in any convenient way and paired as we please with attributes under the other concept, provided each distinguishing attribute appears in one and only one of the conjunctions we take for our alternatives. It is essential to the argument, however, that the only extra-logical signs contained in the definition are expressions for the distinguishing attributes of the objects which fall under the two concepts F and G. If anyone objects that what we have defined is not what men ordinarily call a relation, we may agree, but we must insist that this is the only kind of relation which suffices in all circumstances for one-to-one correlation between the objects falling under like-numbered concepts.

It may perhaps be thought that a suitable co-ordinating relation can always be defined more simply and without assumption of Leibniz's principle of the identity of indiscernibles by some such formula as:

$$(x = A \text{ and } y = K) \text{ or } (x = B \text{ and } y = L) \text{ or } (x = C \text{ and } y = M),$$

where 'A', 'B', and 'C' are supposed to be proper names of the objects falling under F and 'K', 'L', and 'M' proper names of the objects falling under G. But there are two mistakes in this objection. In the first place, our aim is not just to define relations for the co-ordination of classes whose members happen to have been named. We wish rather to indicate kinds of relations which suffice for the co-ordination of classes even though their members have not been named and perhaps never will be. Without Leibniz's principle there can be no assurance of the existence of such relations. Secondly, even when the objects falling under a concept all have proper names, it is clear that they must be distinguishable in some way without names, since otherwise they could not have been named. And so even for this special case our assumption of Leibniz's principle is not superfluous.

At stage (2) in his systematic construction Frege undertakes to ' define the number which belongs to the concept F, and he says that it is the extension of the concept 'like-numbered with the concept F'. Since the expression 'like-numbered with tlie concept F' can be applied with truth only to concepts, the extension of the concept which it expresses must be a set of concepts. And so Frege, after objecting to the suggestion that a number is a concept, seems to have committed himself to the view that a number is a set of concepts. But this is not the only curious consequence of his definition. For he wants to say that the concept F has a number belonging to it, and according to the definition which we have quoted this is as much as to say that the concept F has a set of concepts belonging to it, namely, the set of concepts whose instances are correlated one-to-one with its own instances. It is difficult to find any usage of the word 'belong' (*zukommen*) which makes this claim seem natural. We may perhaps say that the concept F belongs as a member to the set of concepts like-numbered with itself, or that the concept 'like-numbered with the concept F' belongs as a property to the concept F, but not that the set of concepts like-numbered with the concept F belongs to the concept F in either of these senses. Perhaps Frege realized that his phraseology was curious; for he says in a footnote that he believes the phrase 'extension of the concept' could be replaced in definition (2) by the single word 'concept'.[53] It is obvious, however, that in making this concession he did not intend to retract his earlier statement that individual numbers are objects, as distinct from concepts; for he says that he is convinced he could explain away the apparent contradiction, though to do so would take him too far afield. We do not know how he would have proceeded in the alternative development of his theory, but another remark in the footnote shows what was at the back of his mind when he chose the formulation given in his text.

Apart from an apparent contradiction with his earlier statement, there is according to Frege another difficulty to be met by the alternative development, namely, 'that concepts can have identical extensions without themselves coinciding'. In order to appreciate the point of this remark we must consider what is involved in the situation where the number belonging to the concept F is the same as the number belonging to the concept G. Clearly the two concepts are like-numbered, and so whatever is like-numbered with the one is like-numbered with the other, i.e. the extension of the concept 'like-numbered with the concept F' is identical with the extension of the concept 'like-numbered with the concept G'. But this does not mean that the concept 'like-numbered with the concept F' is identical with the concept 'like-numbered with the concept G'. On the contrary, it is obvious that they are distinct. And if we define the number belonging to the concept F as the concept 'like-numbered with the concept F' and similarly the number belonging to the concept G as the concepts 'like-numbered with the concept G', we are committed to the paradoxical position that one and the same number is two distinct concepts. Obviously for one who wishes to maintain a theory like Frege's the easiest way out of the trouble is to define the number belonging to the concept F as the *extension of* the concept 'like-numbered with the concept F'. Frege admits that the definition seems strange at first, but he defends it by arguing that the *extension* to which he refers has the properties and relations expected of the number belonging to a concept.

At stage (3) in his construction Frege tries to explain how we can talk about numbers in general without referring to any particular concepts to which they belong, and for this purpose he lays it down that 'n is a number' is to mean the same as 'there exists a concept such that n is the number which belongs to it'. If we can accept what precedes, we need not cavil at this definition. For it is obvious that in order to practise arithmetic we must be able to talk about numbers without reference to particular concepts, and Frege's account of the matter shows how we can do so while retaining a connexion with the usage according to which numbers are said to belong to concepts. But the definition just quoted is not by itself enough for the foundation of arithmetic, since it provides only an explanation of the expression 'n is a number'. We still need definitions of the individual numbers, or rather a general scheme which provides for the definition of infinitely many numbers and so allows us to prove all the commonly accepted theorems of arithmetic.

Now within Frege's theory the only way of indicating an

individual number is to speak of it as the number belonging to a certain concept. But it is his intention to exhibit arithmetic as a development of logic, and so he cannot introduce the individual numbers by reference to empirical concepts, e.g. by saying that 5 is the number belonging to the concept 'continent' and 12 the number belonging to the concept 'apostle'. Furthermore, reference to empirical concepts would not guarantee the existence of an infinite sequence of numbers such as we require for the higher development of arithmetic. It is essential, therefore, that Frege should provide for definitions of the individual numbers , by reference to standard concepts from within logic itself. Taking o as the start of the series, he offers the following scheme :

0 is the number belonging to the concept 'not identical with itself'
1 " " " " 'identical with 0'
2 " " " " 'identical with 0 or withI'
3 " " " " 'identical with 0 or with 1 or with 2'
. . . .

Here the concept 'not identical with itself' is supposed to come from pure logic; and obviously there can be no object falling under it. So the first definition apparently satisfies all the appropriate requirements. But if the first definition is free from extralogical concepts, so too are all the others; and the plan according to which they are constructed allows for continuation *ad libitum*. It seems, therefore, that Frege has succeeded in his enterprise and shown how arithmetic can be reduced to logic.

In the first volume of his *Grundgesetze* Frege goes through the same argument giving references back to the appropriate passages of his *Grundlagen*. But in accordance with the general policy of his later work he formulates his definitions wherever possible by means of class signs instead of functional expressions; and although he still says in his German text that numbers belong to concepts, in his symbolism the sign which has the sense of 'the number of' always appears in front of a class sign.[54] If we allow ourselves to talk of classes, we may accept this version of the theory as a reasonable simplification. For concepts which determine the same class must obviously be like-numbered according to Frege's way of speaking, and the number which he says they have in common may more naturally be said to belong to the class they determine. This way of speaking has in addition the merit of connecting Frege's definition of number with Cantor's theory of sets or classes. For the one-to-one correlation of which Frege speaks is the relation between sets which Cantor calls equivalence, and in Cantor's language the novelties of Frege's work can be summarized very simply by the two following statements:

(i) The cardinal number of a set is the set of all sets equivalent to it.

(ii) For the natural numbers, 0, 1,2,3, etc., considered as sets of equivalent sets, we may take as exemplars, or standard members, certain sets defined in purely logical fashion, namely, for 0 the set of things not identical with themselves, for 1 the set whose sole member is the number 0, for 2 the set whose members are the numbers 0 and 1, for 3 the set whose members are the numbers 0, 1, and 2, and so forth.

It is a curious fact, however, that neither Frege nor Cantor ever committed himself explicitly to this account of numbers. In his *Grundlagen* Frege said that the *Anzahl* which he defined was the same as the *Mächtigkeit* of sets in Cantor's theory,[55] but in a review of that work for the *Deutsche Literaturzeitung* Cantor denied this and found fault with Frege's definition[56] While professing to agree with the programme of basing arithmetic on logic alone, he objected to some of Frege's subtleties and in particular to his talk of a number as the extension of a concept because, as he said, this latter might be 'quantitatively indeterminate'. It looks as though the difference was due merely to misunderstandings about technical usages. Such at least was the view of whitehead and Russell, who accepted the definition of number given above, although for reasons which will become clear in a later chapter they could not accept Frege's way of guaranteeing the infinity of the series of natural numbers.

5. THE NUMBER SERIES: DEDEKIND AND PEANO

In order to carry out his programme of exhibiting arithmetic as identical with logic Frege must first define all the notions of arithmetic in an acceptable fashion without using any extralogical terminology and then show that with these definitions all arithmetical reasoning can be reduced to logically valid patterns. In particular, he must show that nothing more than logic is required for the validity of mathematical (or recursive) induction, that is to say, the argument in which we conclude that, because a property belongs to the number 0 and also to the successor of any number which has it, it must therefore belong to all natural numbers. For those who wish to maintain that arithmetic is not identical with logic commonly point to this as a peculiarity of arithmetical reasoning, and say that it presupposes some intuition of extra-logical necessity. In his *Grundlagen* Frege did not attempt to deal with the second part of his programme in a detailed fashion, perhaps because he thought that the task was too difficult for a work of popular character. What he says about it seems, therefore, rather obscure and perfunctory. But he shows clearly enough that he is aware of the need for an analysis of mathematical induction, when, after quoting from the account of serial order which he gave at the end of his *Begriffsschrift,* he writes: 'Only by means of this definition of following in a series is it possible to reduce the argument from n to (n+1), which on the face of it is peculiar to mathematics, to the general laws of logic.[57] And he has in fact provided all that is needed for the purpose, although he has not indicated the connexions between his points in such a way as to make the reader's task easy.

First of all Frege says that 'n follows in the series of natural numbers directly after m' is to mean the same as 'There exists a concept F and an object x falling under it, such that the Number which belongs to the concept F is n and the Number which belongs to the concept "falling under F but not identical with x" is m'. This definition is easily intelligible from consideration of the definitions of particular numbers given near the end of the last section. As Frege says, it is also not difficult for the reader to see that the relation so defined is a one-to-one relation and that every number except 0 is related by this relation to some other number.[58] Then Frege goes on to sketch a proof of a proposition which he considers not so obvious, namely, that for every number in the series of natural numbers there is a number which follows directly after it; and it is while engaged on this enterprise that he mentions incidentally the possibility of reducing mathematical induction to the general laws of logic.

In the passage of his *Begriffsschrift*, to which he refers here, Frege had explained how, given a relation ϕ, we could define another relation expressible in the formula 'y follows in the ϕ series after x', e.g. how, given the relation expressed by 'y is a child of x', we could define the relation expressed by 'y is a descendant of x'. In ordinary life we should probably explain the meaning of the word 'descendant' by saying 'A man's descendants are his children and the children of his children and the children of the children of his children and so on'. But Frege was not content with this, because he thought that for his purpose of reducing arithmetic to logic it was necessary to find a way of eliminating the phrase 'and so on'. He therefore suggested in effect that 'y is a descendant of x' might be taken to mean the same as 'y has all the attributes which belong to x and are invariably transmitted to his children by a parent who has them'. At first hearing this proposal may be received with some doubt. For we are inclined to say that, while a descendant of x must undoubtedly have all the attributes which are hereditary in the family started by x, it is not obvious that anyone who has all those attributes must be a member of the family. But it can be answered that one of the attributes hereditary in the family is precisely membership of the family, so that anyone who possesses *all* the hereditary attributes must have this.

Applying Frege's technique to the number series, we may say that 'y follows in the series of natural numbers after x' is to mean the same as 'y has all those attributes which (i) belong to x and (ii) are such that if they belong to any particular number they belong also to the number which follows in the series of natural numbers directly after it'. In effect this is what Frege does for his special purpose in the *Grundlagen*. But in order to exhibit the argument by mathematical induction as a piece of logical reasoning we must go a step farther and say that 'n is a natural number' is to mean the same as 'n is identical with 0 or n has all the attributes which (i) belong to 0 and (ii) are such that if they belong to any object m they belong also to whatever follows-in-the-series-of-natural-numbers-directly-after m'. For the propriety of this definition it is essential, of course, that the words which we have hyphenated together should be understandable as one sign according to the explanation quoted above from Frege. But once this is granted, the rest is simple. For the ordinary formulation of the principle of mathematical induction can now be regarded as an abbreviation for the logical truism 'If P is an attribute which (i) belongs to 0 and (ii) is such that if it belongs to any object m it belongs also to whatever follows-in-the-series-of-natural-numbers-directly-after m, then P belongs to everything which is either identical with 0 or endowed with all the attributes which (i) belong to 0 and (ii) are such that if they belong to any object m they belong also to whatever follows-in-the-series-of-natural-numbers-directly-after m'. In other words, the validity of the principle of mathematical induction is made to depend on the fact that the series of natural numbers can be defined as the proper field for mathematical induction. It should be noticed, however, that this supposed reduction of arithmetical reasoning to logic involves talk of all the attributes or properties of numbers. In what follows we shall have occasion to return to this point.

In his little book *Was sind und was sollen die Zahlen?* first published in 1888, Dedekind reached somewhat similar conclusions, working independently from a different starting-point and using different terminology. According to his way of speaking a system (or set) of things S may be said to have another system S′ as its map or image (*Bild*) if there is a projection or rule of mapping (*Abbildung*) ϕ which assigns to every element of S something or other as its image and S′ is the totality of these images of elements of S. If the projection always assigns different images to different elements of S′ it is said to be similar (*ähnlich*). Obviously this is what other mathematicians have called a one-to-one correlation. Next a system K is said to be a chain (*Kette*) with respect to a certain projection if it contains as a part (i.e. as a sub-system) K′ which is a map of itself according to that projection, i.e. if K′CK where 'C′ signifies inclusion-in.[59] Probably Dedekind's reason for introducing this rather curious terminology was a wish to draw attention to the fact that the map contained in such a system must in turn contain a map of itself according to the same projection. For his first theorem about chains is that the map of a chain is itself a chain. Another of his theorems which can be proved very easily is that any chain which contains a system A as a part must also contain A′. Further, if A is a part of a chain S, the intersection or greatest common part (*Gemeinheit*) of all those chains, including S itself, which have A for a part is called the chain of A, or for short Ao. Again it can be shown easily that any chain which contains A as a part must also contain Ao. When A has only one element 1, Dedekind allows himself to call its chain '1o, though if he followed his own definition strictly he ought to write {1}o. But whatever A may be, it should be remembered that A' and Ao, are both determined by some particular projection ϕ. With this apparatus of technical terms we can now say that a system

N is *simply infinite* if there exists for it a projection ϕ and a basic element 1 satisfying the four conditions:

a. N′CN.

β. $N = 1_0$

γ. 1 is not an element of N′.

δ. The projection ϕ is similar.

And finally, if we concentrate attention upon the structure of the system N, disregarding the special nature of the elements in so far as that is not determined by the conditions listed above, we may say that N is the system of ordinal numbers.[60]

According to Dedekind arithmetic is just the science of the relations or laws which can be derived from the conditions mentioned above, and one of the most important of such laws is the principle of mathematical induction, for which we may write 'If 1 is an element of P and $(NP)' \subset P$, then $N \subset P'$, though Dedekind himself does not use the Boolean notation of juxtaposed letters for an intersection. To prove this theorem we argue as follows.[61] Since 1 is an element of N and by hypothesis also of P, it may be assumed that the system NP is not empty. Now evidently

$$NP \subset N$$

from which it follows in accordance with the definition of mapping that

$$(NP)' \subset N'.$$

But we know that

$$N' \subset N$$

from condition α, and so we have

$$(NP)' \subset N.$$

By the second part of the hypothesis, however, we have also

$$(NP)' \subset P,$$

and from these two relations taken together it follows that

$$(NP)' \subset NP,$$

i.e. that NP is a chain. Then since 1 is an element of this chain and 1o is the greatest common part of all chains of which 1 is an clement, we can assert

$$I_o \subset NP.$$

But by condition β

$$N = I_o,$$

and so we may conclude

$$N \subset NP,$$

which is equivalent to

$$N \subset P.$$

The basis of this proof is the fact that N, the set of numbers over which we want to generalize, has been declared to be a chain and in particular that chain which is the greatest common part of all chains having 1 as an element. As in Frege's argument, so here the validity of the principle of mathematical induction is secured by a definition of number which has reference to all properties hereditary in a series. For to say that N is the greatest common part of all chains having 1 as an element is to say in effect that N is contained as a part in every chain P which satisfies the hypotheses of the principle of mathematical induction, and this is another version of Frege's account of the matter. Dedekind himself noticed the correspondence when he first read Frege's, *Grundlagen*, about a year after the publication of his own book, and he drew attention to it in the preface to his second edition (1893). In the preface to his third edition (1911) he said that, although he still held to his original view, according to which arithmetic, algebra, and analysis are all parts of logic, he had to allow some force to objections which had been raised between 1893 and 1903. This means presumably that he made common cause with Cantor and Frege, whose work had been subjected to criticism at the time mentioned.

The chief difference between Frege's work and that of Dedekind is that the former, unlike the latter, connects number, the extensions of concepts. Although Dedekind started with general considerations about systems or sets, he ended with a purely ordinal theory of numbers. Frege was equally interesting in the ordering of the items of the number series, but though that it could be explained by the definition which he gave follows in the series of natural numbers directly after m'. It is not clear whether Dedekind wished to reject that part of Frege's theory which went beyond his own, but there are passages which suggest that he did not think it proper to make the theory of ordinal numbers rest on a theory of cardinal numbers. When he first announces that the elements of his system may be called numbers, he writes:

'If in the consideration of a simply infinite system N which is ordered by a projection ϕ we disregard entirely the special nature the elements, retain merely their distinguishability, and conceive only the relations in which they are set one to another through the ordering projection ϕ, then these elements are called *natural numbers* or *ordinal numbers* or simply *numbers*, and the basic element 1 is called the *basic number* of the *number series*. Having regard to this abstraction, or freeing of the elements from every other content, we may rightly describe the numbers as a free creation of the human mind. The relations or laws which are derived solely from the conditions α, β , γ ,δ in 71, and are therefore always the same in all ordered simply infinite systems (cf. 134), constitute the immediate object of the *science of number or arithmetic*.'[62]

In the later passage mentioned here he proves that all simply infinite systems can be mapped upon each other by similar projections, and then, with a reference back to the passage quoted above, goes on to say:

'It is clear at the same time . . . that every statement about the numbers, i.e. about the elements n of the simply infinite system N which is ordered by the projection ϕ, every statement, that is, in which the special nature of the elements is disregarded and mention made only of those concepts which have their origin in the ordering ϕ, possesses completely general validity for any other simply infinite system Ω ordered by a projection θ and for its elements υ, and that the transition from N to Ω (which is also the translaiton of an arithmetical statement from one language to another) takes place through the projection ψ..... which transforms every element n of N into element υ of Ω which is (n). this element can be called nth element of Ω and by the same token the number n is itself the nth element of the number series N.'[63]

These pronouncements suggest that Dedekind thinks of arithmetic as a science whose subject is implicitly defined by the four conditions α, β, γ, δ taken as axioms or postulates, and that he is not worried by the possibility of various interpretations for his basic signs, because he believes this has no importance for mathematics. It is true that he does not use the language of axiomatics, but he seems to say in effect that it is foolish to ask for more than a monomorphic axiom set.[64]

In his *Arithmetices Principia Nova Methodo Exposita* of 1889 Peano stated nine axioms for airthmetic. Four of these are truths about equality, but the other five are the following special postulates:

1. 1 is a number.
2. The successor of any number is number.
3. No two numbers have the same successor.
4. 1 is not the successor of any number.
5. Any property which belongs to 1 and also to the successor of any number which has it belongs to all numbers.

In later versions of this attempt to characterize the number series Peano starts, like Frege, with the number 0; but his general conception of number is always ordinal, like Dedekind's, and there is a close similarity between his axioms and the conditions stated by Dedekind. Thus (2) corresponds to α, (3) to δ, and (4) to γ, while (1) and (5) together do the work of β. The axioms are independent one of another, as may be seen from consideration of models which satisfy four but not five of them, and it can be shown by an adaptation of Dedekind's argument that they form a monomorphic set.

Peano was interested primarily in the clear presentation of mathematical results, and it was for this purpose, rather than for philosophical analysis, that he composed his *Notations de logique mathématique* of 1894. In the years 1895-1908 he produced five successive versions of a *Formulaire de mathématiques,* using his five axioms each time (but with 0 in place of 1) as a foundation for arithmetic, and in the last version, where the non-symbolic part was written in a new international language of his own invention called *Latino sine flexione*, he introduced them with the remark:

'Quaestio si nos pote defini No significa si nos pote scribe aequalitate dc forma

N_o = expressione composito per signos noto, $\cup$, $\cap$, — ...,+,

quod non es facile. Ergo nos sumc tres idea No, o,+ ut idea primitivo per que nos defini omni symbolo de Arithmetica. Nos determina valore de symbolo non definito per systema dc propositio primitivo sequente.,

The first group of signs to which he refers in this passage are of course the purely logical signs of his *Arithmetices Principia* and later works, while the other three mean respectively 'number', 'nought', and 'successor'. It is clear, therefore, that at this date Peano still had an open mind about the project of Frege, but thought it possible to proceed without waiting for a settlement of the question about ultimate foundations.

Although their diction was sometimes loose and extravagant, the formalists of the nineteenth century made an interesting suggestion when they said that arithmetic should be presented as an axiomatized system in which the characteristically arithmetical notions receive implicit definitions from the formal conditions to which they are made subject. Admittedly Thomae's pronouncements were unsatisfactory in detail for the reasons given by Frege, but we may well feel that in this contest Frege triumphed too easily; for at the time he wrote Peano had already carried out Thomae's programme in a much more impressive fashion. On the one hand, Peano's set of axioms is not open, like Thomae's, to the charge that it fails to provide for the several natural numbers, since we can introduce 1 as the successor of 0, 2 as the successor of 1, and so on. On the other hand, Peano's axioms, taken together with suitable definitions of the operations of addition and multiplication, are sufficient for the proof of all the general laws of number set out by Thomae. Thus, for example, we may define addition recursively by the two stipulations:

$$\text{(i) } a+0 = a,$$
$$\text{(ii) } a+n' = (a+n)',$$

where 'n′' is an abbreviation for 'the successor of n', and then prove the associative law for addition as follows. First we show that

$$a+(b+0) = (a+b)+0.$$

This is done by successive applications of (i) above; for

$$\begin{aligned} a+(b+0) &= a+(b+0) \\ &= a+b \\ &= (a+b)+0. \end{aligned}$$

Next we show that if

$$a+(b+n) = (a+b)+n$$

it must also be the case that

$$a+(b+n') = (a+b)+n'.$$

This is done by successive applications of (ii) and by use of the hypothesis; for

$$\begin{aligned} a+(b+n') &= a+(b+n') \\ &= a+(b+n')- \\ &= [a+(b+n')]- \\ &= [(a+b)+n']' \\ &= (a+b)+n'. \end{aligned}$$

And finally from these two results taken together with Peano's fifth axiom we get the conclusion that

$$a+(b+c) = (a+b)+c.$$

Why then should we not be content with Peano's formulation of arithmetic and say that his primitive notions are sufficiently defined by the axioms in which they are mentioned?

If the suggestion is sound, the mathematician need worry himself no more about the metaphysical question 'What is a number? 'When teased by a philosophical colleague or by his own conscience, he can reply that he regards mathematical axioms as implicit definitions and that all his professional demands are included in Peano's set. The proposal is, nevertheless, unsatisfactory, because it does not provide for that connexion with the ordinary use of numerals which is essential to any formal system worthy of the name of arithmetic. If the signs for 'number', 'nought', and 'successor' have only the sense required by Peano's axioms, they are in effect variables for which we may substitute any expressions that turn all the axioms into true statements. Now the axioms are all verified when the signs '0' and 'number' are taken in their usual senses and 'successor' is understood to mean the same as Frege's 'following in the series of natural numbers directly after'; but, as Peano himself remarked, they can all be verified by many other interpretations.[65] Thus the formal conditions arc satisfied when we put the numeral '1' for '0', 'member of the sequence 'number', and 'half' for 'successor'. In short, Peano's set of axioms, considered as an implicit definition, gives only the common logical characteristics of all progressions. In spite of all that Dedekind and Peano say in defence of their approach, we cannot be wholly satisfied with a basis for arithmetic which does not distinguish the sequence of natural numbers from any other progression. Even within pure mathematics we have occasion to use the numerals in their normal sense, as for example when we say 'There are *four* prime numbers less than 10'.

Nor is this the only reason for saying that Peano's axioms are inadequate by themselves as a foundation for arithmetic. The system which they form is monomorphic, as we have seen, but for this merit it seems to be essential that the fifth axiom contains a generalization over all properties. Such a generalization amounts in effect to assumption of the wide notion of a property or set used by Cantor in his theory of sets, and it must therefore be regarded with suspicion by those who are sceptical about Cantor's theory. Furthermore, it is apparently the breadth of this talk about all properties which allows for interpretation of the axioms by reference to progressions other than the natural number series. If we wish to avoid the dangers of over-wide generalization and to direct attention to the number series as distinct from other progressions, it seems, therefore, that we must try to replace Peano's single axiom of mathematical induction by a sequence of inductive axioms each dealing with some specified property of numbers. But the Norwegian mathematician Thoralf Skolem has shown that even with a denumerably infinite sequence of such axioms our new system must remain as a whole polymorphic (i.e. non-categorical). In his own words:

'The number series is completely characterized ... by Peano's axioms, if we regard the concept "set" or "propositional function" as something given in advance with an absolute meaning independent of all principles of generation or axioms. But if one wishes to carry the axiomatic treatment through consistently, so that reasoning with sets or propositional functions is also axiomatized, then the unique or complete characterization of the number series is impossible.[66]

This discovery is closely akin to Gödel's theorem on the incompletability of formal arithmetic, which we shall have occasion, to notice later, and it was, of course, unknown to Frege. But Frege had no sympathy for the postulalional approach, because he was convinced that rules for the use of numerical expressions should be derived from definitions of the numbers and not vice versa. It was this conviction which inspired his efforts to present arithmetic as an extension of logic.

Footnoes

1. *Die Grundlagen der Arithmetik*, §§ 15-17. This work, which will be cited ax *Gl.*, has been translated by J. L. Austin under the title *The Foundations of Arithmetic.*
2. *Gl.*, §§ 90-91.
3. *Grundgesetze der Arithmetik,* i, p. xii. This work, which has not been translated in full, will be cited as *Gg.*
4. *Berichte der jenaischen Gessellschaft für Medizinische and Naturwissenschaftliche Forschung*, 1891,
5. *Vierteljahrsschrift für wissenschaftliche Philosophie*, vci (1892), pp. 192-205.
6. *Zeitschrift für philosophie and philosophische Kritik*,c (1892), pp. 25-50. These articles have been translated into English by P. Geach and M. Black in *Translation from the Philosophical Writings of Gottlob Frege.* These translation contains the original page numbers, which will be used in later references.
7. 'Uber die Grundlagen der Geometrie,' *Jahresbericht des Deutschen Mathematiker Vereins*, xv (1906), pp. 293-309, 377-403, 423-30.
8. P.E.B. Jourdain, 'The Development of the Theories of mathematical Logic and the Principles of mathematics' *The Quarterly Journal of Pure and Applied Mathematics*, xliii (1992), pp. 237-69.
9. For alll papers published during his lifetime see his *Kleins Schriften*, ed. I. Angelelli, and for those he left unpublished his *Nachgelassene Schriften*, ed. H. Herme et al.
10. 'Beiträge Zur Begrndung der transfiniten Mengenlehre', i, *Mathematische Annalen*, xlvi (1895), pp. 481-512, reprinted in *Gesammelte Abhandlungen*, ed. Zewrmelo, p. 282.
11. *Was sind und was sollen die Zahlen?*, § 5, 64.
12. *Collected Papers,* iii, § 402.
13. *De Communibus Notitiis,*§ 38 (Moralia 1079A)

14. *In Primum Euclidis Elementorum Librum Commentarii,* Def. xvii.

15. *Discorsie dimostrzioni matematiche intorno a due nuove scienze,*i (*Opere*, ed. nazionale, vo. viii. p.78).

16. *Paradoxien des Unendlichen,* § 20. The historical introduction to the English translaiton of this work by D. A. Steele contains some interesting material, including the references to Plutarch and Proclus given above.

17. *The Consistency of the Axiom of Choice and of the Generalized Continuum-hypothesis with the Axioms of set Theory (Annals kof Mathematics Studies,* no. 3)

18. *Gesammelte Abhandlungen,* pp. 282, 477, 480.

19. *Gl.*, § 85.

20. *Gl.*, § 86.

21. A System of Logic, III, XXIV, § 5.

22. *Gl.*, § 7.

23. *Gl.*, § 10.

24. *Gl.*, § 9.

25. *Gl.*, § 3.

26. *Gl.*, § 88.

27. *The Critique of Pure Reason,* B. 191

28. Gl., § 89.‘

29. Gl., § 14.

30. Gl., § 12.

31. *Prolegomena to any Future Metaphysic,* § 2.

32. Gl., § 5.

33. Gl., § 14.

34. *Gl.*, § 87.

35. Pp. 6-7, quoted by Frege in Gl., § 92.

36. *Gl.*, § 96.

37. Gl., ii, § 57.

38. *Gg.* ii. §60.

39. *Gl.* ii. § 95.

40. *Gg.*, ii § 147.

41. *Gg.*, ii § 88-89.

42. *Gg.*, ii § 86-137.

43. C. S. Peirce, Collected Papers, iv. 537.

44. *Gl.* §18

45. *Gl.* § 45-

46. *Gl.* §46. When Frege wrote 'the concept "moon of Venus"', he meant presumably to refer to the concept expressed by the words 'moon of Venus'; for he certainly did not think that the concept was a set of words.

47. *Gl.* §57

48. *Gl.* §53.

49. *Treatise,* I. iii. § I.

50. *Gl.*, §63.

51. *Gl.*, §72.

52. *Gl.*, §70.

53. *Gl.*, §68.

54. See, for example, the definition of o in *Gg.* i, §41.

55. Gl., § 85.

56. *Gesammelte Abhandlungen,* ed. Zermelo, p. 440.

57. *Gl.*, § 80.

58. *Gl.*, §§76-78

59. Dedekind himself uses a variant of te sign '<' which looks something like the numeral '3'

60. *Was sind und was sollen die Zahlen?*, § 6, 71-73

61. Ibid., § 4, 59-60, and § 6, 80.

62. *Was sind und was sollen die Zahlen?,* § 6, 73.

63. Ibid., § 10, 134.

64. For the development of Dedekind's thought see Hao Wang, 'The

Axiomatiration of Arithmetic', *The Journal of symbolic Logic*, xxii (1957). pp. 145-158.
G. Peano, *Formulaire de mathematiques*, iii. p.44.

65. *Formulairo de mathématiques*, iii p. 44.

66. Cber die Nicht-charakterisierbarkeit der Zahlenreihe mittels endlich oder abzählbär unendlich vieler Aussagen mit ausschlie Blich Zahlvariablen', *Fundamenta Mathematicae*, xxiii (1934), pp. 150-61.

Chapter-9

The Philosophy of Mathematics after Frege

Chapter-9

I. THE PARADOXES OF THE THEORY OF SETS

As early as 1895 Cantor found that his theory of sets contained an antinomy. This was the paradox published two years later by Burali-Forti, and it concerns transfinite ordinals, which we have not considered in our sketch of his system. Then in 1899 Cantor discovered the simpler and more fundamental paradox about sets which goes by his name. Let us suppose that S is the set of all sets. By his own theorem about power sets $\overline{\overline{S}} > \overline{\overline{S}}$. But since $\mathscr{P}$S is a set of sets (namely the set of all subsets of S), it must be part of the set of all sets, that is, of S. And from this it follows that $\overline{\overline{S}} \leq \overline{\overline{S}}$, which is contradictory to the result we have just obtained.

Clearly there was something wrong with the rather naive way in which Cantor assumed the existence of sets, but it was not until 1903 that the trouble became widely known. In that year Frege published the second volume of his *Grundgesetze* with a Postscript (dated October, 1902), which began:

'Hardly anything more unfortunate can befall a scientific writer than to have one of the foundations of his edifice shaken after the work is finished.

This was the position I was placed in by a letter of Mr Bertrand Russell, just when the printing of this volume was nearing its completion. It is a matter of my Axiom (V). I have never disguised from myself its lack of the self-evidence that belongs to the other axioms and that must properly be demanded of a logical law. And so in fact I indicated this weak point in the Preface to Vol. I (p. vii). I should gladly have disp-ensed with this foundation if I had known of any substitute for it. And even now I do not see how arithmetic can be scientifically established, how numbers can be apprehended as logical objects and brought under review, unless we are permitted—at least conditionally—to pass from a concept to its extension. May I always speak of the extension of a concept—speak of a class? And : not, how are the exceptional cases recognized? Can we always infer from one concept's coinciding in extension with another concept that any object that falls under the one falls under the other likewise? These are the questions raised by Mr Russell's communication.

Solatium miseris, socios habuisse dolorum. I too have this comfort, if comfort it is; for everybody who has made use in his proofs of extensions of concepts, classes, sets, is in the same position as I. What is in question is not just my particular way of establishing arithmetic, but whether arithmetic can possibly be given a logical foundation at all.

But let us come° to the point. Mr Russell has discovered a contradiction which may now be stated.

Nobody will wish to assert of the class of men that it is a man. We have here a class that does not belong to itself. I say that something belongs to a class when it falls under the concept whose extension the class is. Let us now fix our eye on the concept: *class that does not belong to itself.* The extension of this concept (if we may speak of its extension) is thus the class of classes that do not belong to themselves. For short we will call it the class K. Let us now ask whether this class K belongs to itself. First, let us suppose that it does. If anything belongs to a class, it falls under the concept whose extension the class is. Thus if our class belongs to itself, it is a class that does not belong to itself. Our first supposition thus leads to self-contradiction. Secondly, let us suppose that our class K does not belong to itself; then it falls under the concept whose extension it itself is, and thus does belong to itself. Here once more we likewise get a contradiction.'

In the same year Russell gave his own account of the contradiction when he published his *Principles of Mathematics*, and two years later J. Richard announced yet another paradox which is especially interesting because it apes the diagonal procedure of Cantor.[1] First we consider all decimal fractions that can be defined by means of a finite number of words. Although they form an infinite set, they can be ordered in such a way that there is a first, a second, and so on. For we can sort them into groups according to the number of words used in defining them and then arrange them within these groups by the alphabetical order of their definitions. But when they are so arranged, it is possible to define a decimal by saying that its nth figure is the immediate successor in the ordinary scheme of figures to the nth figure of the nth decimal in the sequence or o if the nth figure of the nth decimal is 9. Obviously this new decimal is not identical with any of those in the sequence, and yet it ought to be included, since it is certainly defined in a finite number of words.

In an attempt to get out of the very unsatisfactory situation revealed to him by Russell, Frege considered first the suggestion that there might be concepts with no corresponding classes. If the concept of a class which is not a member of itself were such a one, Russell's paradox would naturally disappear, since there would then be no class of all classes which are not members of themselves. But Frege could not reconcile himself to this revolutionary novelty, and tried instead to evade the contradiction by a modification of his fifth axiom, about which he had always felt some misgivings. What he now proposed was that two concepts should be said to have the same extension if, and only if, every object which fell under the first *but was not itself the extension of the first* fell likewise under the second and vice versa. In an appendix to his *Principles of Mathematics* Russell recommended the suggestion to serious consideration; but he did not recur to it in his other writings, presumably because he became dissatisfied with it on closer examination, and later logicians have in fact proved that the modification is not enough to free Frege's system from inconsistencies.[2]

When he had time to think about the problem more carefully, Russell came to the conclusion that Frege's first suggestion was better. There were, he thought, some propositional functions which did not determine genuine classes, and the problem for the logician was to give rules by which these *non-predicative* functions, as he called them, could be distinguished from others. The contradictions seemed to result from the fact that logicians had incautiously admitted classes which turned out to be in a curious way *self-reproductive*. Perhaps such monstrosities might be excluded by special limitations on the use of the class notation, but he was strongly inclined to think that the problem could never be solved completely until all classes were eliminated from logical theory in the way in which infinitesimals had been eliminated from the theory of the differential calculus, and he therefore considered it important to find out how much of mathematics could be presented without the class notation.[3]

If Frege's symbolism for logic had been generally accepted, elimination of talk about classes would have been effective as a cure for the paradoxes by which mathematics was then afflicted. For his distinction of levels of functions makes it impossible to reproduce in his script any paradoxes about functions analogous to Cantor's and Russell's contradictions about classes. His disaster was due indeed to the self-indulgence by which he allowed himself to use a class notation without distinction of levels as a device for evading the complexities of his own theory of propositional functions. This is a very important point to which we must return later, but for the present it is enough to notice that when Russell put forward his 'no classes' theory he had already discovered a paradox which could be used to show that talk of classes was not the sole cause of difficulty. Instead of the class which is supposed to contain all classes that are not members of themselves let us consider the property of being a property which does not exemplify itself. If this property exemplifies itself, then it cannot exemplify itself; and if it does not exemplify itself, then it must exemplify itself. Clearly the nature of the trouble is the same here as in the original paradox, and yet there is no talk of classes.

When Russell published his suggestion that some propositional functions were non-predicative, Henri Poincaré was engaged in a hostile survey of the attempts by Peano and his followers to explain mathematical reasoning by the methods of symbolic logic.[4] He held that mathematical induction was the source of all excellence in mathematics and that it depended on an intuition of the possibility of infinite recurrence, i.e. on something that could never be reduced to a formal rule. Finding a new opponent in the field, he promptly produced another article, designed to show that the paradoxes resulted from a wrong conception of mathematics. Accepting Russell's distinction between predicative and non-predicative propositional functions, he said that the true explanation of the difference was to be found in Richard's note of the preceding year. After reporting his paradox Richard had gone on to say that there was really no contradiction, since the set of decimals definable in a finite number of words could not properly be understood to contain any decimal definable only by reference to the whole set. Generalizing from this Poincaré wrote: 'Ainsi les définitions qui doivent être regardées comme non-prédicatives sont celles qui contiennent un cercle vicieux'. In later literature the expression 'non-predicative' (or 'impredicative') has frequently been used as though it were *defined* by this remark, i.e. as though 'non-predicative definition' were equivalent to 'definition which purports to distinguish an object under a concept by means of a reference to the totality of all possible objects falling under that concept'.[5] But it is clear from the context that Poincaré intended only to *explain* why some phrases which looked like definitions failed to define anything. It is clear also that in his view the vicious circle which gave rise to the paradoxes of the theory of sets was of a special kind and connected with the attempt to treat of an infinite set as a completed whole. For he went on to say: 'Il n'y a point d'infini actuel. Les Cantoriens l'ont oublié, et ils sont tombes dans la contradiction.'

In a reply published in the same year Russell agreed that the paradoxes were all due to vicious circles, and laid it down as a principle for the avoidance of such circles that 'whatever involves all of a collection must not be one of the collection'. But he said that Poincaré did not properly appreciate the difficulties of applying such a principle, and that Poincaré was wrong in supposing the source of the trouble to be some mistaken doctrine of infinity introduced by Cantor. He himself believed the contradictions of set theory must be logical rather than mathematical (in any sense in which the mathematical might be distinguished from the logical), since they were essentially of the same kind as the old paradox of Epimenides (or the Liar); and he thought it interesting to notice that the vicious circle in that example had been diagnosed already in the Middle Ages, according to the article on *Insolubilia* in Baldwin's *Dictionary of Philosophy and Psychology.*[6]

These exchanges led to α renewal of interest in logical paradoxes of all kinds, and in 1910 the Liar of Eubulides received the dignity of a whole treatise,*Der Lügner, Theorie, Geschichte und Auflösung,* by A. Rüstow. Among the new paradoxes invented at this time or shortly afterwards those of Berry and Grelling are perhaps the best known. Berry's paradox concerns *the least integer not nameable in fewer than nineteen syllables.* Although it seems obvious that any name of this integer must contain at least nineteen syllables, the words printed above in italics amount to a name for it and they contain only eighteen syllables. Grelling's paradox has to do with a newly invented word. Some adjectives such as 'short' and 'English' apply to themselves, others such as 'long' and 'German' do not. Let us call those of the second group *heterological.* Is the adjective 'heterological' itself heterological? If it is, then according to the definition just given it does not apply to itself, and so it cannot be heterological. On the other hand, if it is not hetcrological, then according to the definition it does apply to itself, and so it must be heterological. Since these sophisms bear a resemblance to the contradictions of Cantor and Russell but have nothing to do with infinity, their appearance did something to strengthen Russell's contention against Poincaré.

In his *Principles of Mathematics* published in 1903, Russell had arrived independently at a view of mathematics similar to that of Frege,and although he found the paradoxes disturbing, like Frege, he still hoped for a satisfactory demonstration of the identity of arithmetic and logic. This was the reason why he thought it important to show that the paradoxes arose from a defect in the presentation of logic.It would not be sufficient to explain away the contradictions of the theory of sets by reflections on the peculiarity of infinite aggregates, nor yet to exclude them by *ad hoc* legislation about the use of symbols. For if he adopted either of these courses, he would no longer be able to say that arithmetic was identical with pure logic, and he would have no guarantee against the appearance of new contradictions. The only satisfactory solution of the problem would be to eliminate the paradoxes by a reform which recommended itself as a self-evident necessity of logic, once it had been propounded; and this, as we shall see, is what Russell attempted in his Theory of Logical Types. But in 1908, the year in which he gave the first account of this theory, there appeared also two other papers which suggested new ways of dealing with the crisis and new doctrines about the relation of mathematics to logic. In the next three sections we must consider these three proposals and their relations one to another.

2. RUSSELL'S THEORY OF LOGICAL TYPES

In his article of 1908 with the title 'Mathematical Logic as based on the Theory of Types[7] and again two years later in the second chapter of the introduction to the first edition of *Principia Mathematica* Russell presented his theory of logical types as a consequence of his vicious-circle principle and necessary for the solution of the paradoxes, but he recommended it also as consistent with common sense and inherently credible. Let us consider first the argument by which it was introduced and the form which it took when fully developed.

According to Russell a propositional function presupposes the totality of its values for a reason which he states as follows:

'When we speak of "ϕx"' where x is not specified, we mean one value of the function, but not a definite one. We may express this by saying that "$\phi.x$" *ambiguously denotes* ϕa, ϕb, ϕc' etc., where ϕa, ϕb, ϕc' etc., are the various values of"ϕx".... It follows that "ϕx" only has a well-defined meaning (well-defined, that is to say, except in so far as it is of its essence to be ambiguous) if the objects ϕa, ϕb, ϕc, etc. are well-defined. . .. It follows from this that no function can have among its values anything which presupposes the function, for if it had, we could not regard the objects ambiguously denoted by the function as definite until the function was definite, while conversely, as we have just seen, the function cannot be definite until its values are definite. This is a particular case, but perhaps the most fundamental case, of the vicious-circle principle. A function is what ambiguously denotes some one of a certain totality, namely the values of the function; hence this totality cannot contain any members which involve the function, since if it did, it would contain members involving the totality, which, by the vicious-circle principle, no totality can do.[8]

The phraseology of this passage is unfortunate. A function, not being a sign, cannot denote anything, and even a functional expression, which is indeed a sign, cannot properly be said to denote the values of the function, whether ambiguously or unambiguously. But the conclusion to which the argument leads is very interesting:

'Hence there must be no such thing as the value for ϕx with the argument ϕx, or with any argument which involves

ϕx. That is to say, the symbol "$\phi(\phi x)$" must not express a proposition, as "$\phi(a)$" does if ϕa is a value for ϕx. In fact "$\phi(\phi x)$" must be a symbol which does not express anything: we may therefore say that it is not significant Thus given any function ϕx, there are arguments for which the function has no value, as well as arguments for which it has a value.[9]

In his first article about the theory Russell says that a type may be defined as a range of significance, i.e. as the collection of arguments for which a given propositional function has values; but he also says later that propositional functions may be classified in types according to the entities which they admit as proper arguments. These two ways of describing matters are equivalent; for Russell's considerations require us to assume a hierarchy of entities. Thus if we take men as our individuals, or entities of type o, wisdom, or being wise (i.e. the propositional function expressed by *x is wise*), is of type I, because it can be asserted significantly, though not perhaps truly, of Socrates or Alcibiades, while being a cardinal virtue is of type 2, because it can be asserted significantly of wisdom; and in general every attribute is of a higher type than the entities of which it can be asserted or denied significantly. It is true that Russell's argument from his vicious-circle principle does nothing to prove that an attribute must always be of the *next* higher type to the entities of which it can be asserted or denied significantly; but this is what he assumes in the development of his theory, and it is necessary if, as he obviously Thinks, entities of the same type are to be universally interchangeable in the sense that what can be asserted or denied significantly of one can be asserted or denied significantly of each of the others.

So long as we deal only with attributive functions, we may think of the various types as arranged hierarchically in a simple ascending order; but when we take account also of relational functions, we must allow for a much greater complexity which cannot be represented adequately by the use of ordinal numbers alone. Thus a two-termed relation may perhaps hold between entities which are both individuals, and so may perhaps be said to be of the same level as an attribute of in dividuals, but it must be distinguished in type from such attributes and also from three-termed relations which hold between individuals. And again there may be relations, such as exemplification, which hold between entities of different types. Using the numeral 'o' still to represent the type of individuals, we may perhaps say that functions which take only individuals as proper arguments are of types (o), (o, o), (o, o, o), &c., that an attribute of an attribute of an individual is of type ((o)), that an attribute of a two-termed relation of individuals, as for example, the transitivity of the relation of being an ancestor, is of type ((o, o)), that an uneven relation such as exemplification may be of type (o, (o)), and so forth. It is a general rule, however, that no propositional function may take arguments from any but the appropriate lower type or types, i.e. from the type or types whose sign or signs in the notation just explained would be found by removing the outer brackets from the sign of the type of the propositional function in question.[10]

This theory is sufficient to exclude the paradox of the property of being a property which does not exemplify itself. For if the letter *F* is supposed to signify the paradoxical property it must be introduced by some such definition as $F(gx) =_{\text{def}}$.. $\sim g(gx)$, where the combination of signs on the right-hand side is obviously at fault. In order to exclude the paradox of the class of all classes which are not members of themselves Russell finds it necessary, however, to use also his 'no classes' theory. This latter is rather unfortunately named, and it may perhaps be objected that the project of getting rid of paradoxes about classes by getting rid of classes is extravagant in the same way as a proposal to get rid of children's diseases by getting rid of children. But what Russell intends is something much more reasonable than his phraseology suggests. He holds that designations of classes are incomplete symbols, that is to say, symbols which cannot be defined alone but may be defined in company,since all the complexes in which they occur significantly can be replaced by equivalent complexes in which they do not appear. Thus whenever we have an expression of the form A$\varepsilon x(Fx)$, we may replace it by an expression of the form FA, and so too in more complicated cases class signs may be eliminated without loss. Sometimes he expresses all this by saying that classes are fictions which disappear on analysis, but such remarks are to be interpreted by reference back to what he says about incomplete symbols: they are suggested no doubt by lawyers' talk about the fictitious personality of corporations.

Now according to Russell's explanation, when we try to translate his paradox about classes in the manner required by the 'no classes' theory, the result to which we are led is a combination of symbols forbidden by the theory of types, and so it is evident that the paradox arises from the failure of ordinary grammar to meet all the requirements of logic. In his own words:

'A proposition about a class is always to be reduced to a statement about a function which defines the class, i.e. about a function which is satisfied by members of the class and by no other arguments. Thus a class is an object derived from a function and presupposing; the function, just as, for example, $(x).\phi x$ presupposes the function ϕ. Hence a class cannot, by the vicious-circle principle, significantly be the argument to its defining function, that is to say, if we denote by "$z(\phi z)$" the class defined by ϕz, the symbol "$\phi\{z(\phi z)\}$" must be meaningless.[11]

For the solution of other paradoxes, such as Berry's and the Liar, a further development is necessary, but one which seems to be required in any case by the vicious-circle principle. This is the ramified theory of types or the distinction of orders within types, and Russell explains the need for it as follows:

'Let $f(\phi z, x)$ be a function of two variables ϕz and x. Then if, keeping x fixed for the moment, we assert this with all possible values ϕ, we obtain a proposition (ϕ)-$f(\phi z, x)$. Here, its is variable, we have a function of.*, but as this function involves a totality of values for ϕz it cannot itself be one of the values included in the totality, by the vicious-circle principle.It follows that the totality of values of ϕz concerned in $(\phi)\ f(\phi z, x)$ is not the totality of all functions in which x can occur as argument, and that there is no such totality as that of all functions in which x can occur as argument.[12]

For the sake of simplicity in our distinction of orders we may begin by supposing that we have to do only with functions which take individuals as proper arguments. If any such function can be defined without the application of quantifiers to any variables other than individual variables it may be said to belong to the first order. Taking men once more as our individuals, we may give as examples the functions expressed by *Socrates loves x* and *Everybody loves x*. Then according to Russell 'second order functions are such as contain variables which are first order functions but contain no other variables except (possibly) individuals'.[13] Strictly speaking, it is a functional sign, not a function, which contains a variable, but the sense of the definition is clear. Thus the phrase *x has all the first order qualities that make a great general* expresses a function of the first type but of the second order, because it takes individuals as its proper arguments but is equivalent in sense to $(f)[(y)(y \textit{ is a great general} \supset f!y) \supset f!x]$. In general, if the variable of highest order occurring in the expression of a function is one marking a gap for signs of functions of the nth order, then the function so expressed is of the (n+I)th order. And according to Russell's usage in *Principia Mathematica*, a function denoted by $F!x$ is to be called *predicative* if, and only if, it is of the lowest order compatible with its having the argument or arguments it has.[14] Thus a predicative function in this new sense of the word involves no totality except the totality of its possible arguments and any totalities they presuppose.

The distinction of orders of functions helps to a solution of paradoxes like that of Berry by enabling us to split up illegitimate totalities. Thus we can say that in Berry's paradox the word 'name' is incorrectly taken to cover not only proper names in the ordinary sense, i.e. designations which involve no functions, but also descriptions involving functions of *all* orders. If we wish to talk correctly of descriptions, we must be prepared to specify the order or orders of functions which they involve. But then any description which refers to descriptions involving functions of order n will itself involve a function of order n+I and so fail to apply to itself. Similarly the paradox of the Liar can be exposed as an attempt to use the description 'what I say' without regard to the need for a distinction of propositions by orders. These results of the ramified theory of types are very satisfactory, but unfortunately the limitation of discourse by which they are achieved is very drastic. Perhaps it does not matter that we must not say 'Napoleon had all the qualities that make a great general' unless we are prepared to add that the qualities in question are those of the first order, or at any rate of some finite set of orders. But it is important that we are apparently forbidden to formulate some well-known mathematical theorems and in particular the theorem that any non-empty set of real numbers with an upper bound has a least upper bound.

It will be remembered that, according to the theory of Eudoxus and Dedekind, a real number is a cut or section among the rational numbers, or more precisely the lower of the two infinite sets into which the array of rational numbers may be divided by a cut. From this it follows that a set of real numbers is a set of sets of rational numbers. Now if S is a non-empty set of real numbers with an upper bound, the least upper bound of S is supposed to be a real number which is also the union or logical sum of all the real numbers in S, i.e. which has for its members all those rational numbers which are members of any of the members of S. Here there is something which looks like a violation of the ramified theory of types. For the set of rational numbers which constitutes a real number, being infinite, cannot be specified except by mention of a propositional function which all the members satisfy, and the functional expression which is supposed to specify the least upper bound of an infinite set of real numbers must apparently involve reference to the totality of propositional functions that specify real numbers, *including that function which it expresses*. If it is said that the least upper bound must belong to an order of real numbers distinct from the numbers of S and that there can be no completely general theorems about real numbers without restriction of order, mathematical analysis, as ordinarily understood, becomes impossible. How, if at all, can Russell evade this unpleasant consequence, while continuing to use his ramified theory of types for the exclusion of paradoxes ?

He tries to have the best of both worlds by introducing the Axiom of Reducibility. This is the assumption that for every propositional function there is some predicative function (in the sense of *Principia Mathematica*) which is satisfied by all the same arguments and by no others,[15] or in symbols

$$(f)\ (\exists g)\ (x)\ [fx \equiv g!x]$$

If this is admitted, the difficulty about orders of real numbers can be overcome. For it may be said that the prepositional functions specifying real numbers do indeed fall into distinct orders, but that for every propositional function of higher order specifying a real number there is a corresponding predicative function which specifics the same real number, because it is satisfied by the same rational numbers and by no others. We are still forbidden in principle to make generalizations about all propositional functions without regard to order, but in contexts like this we can be confident that if we talk of all predicative functions we shall not leave anything unsaid which needs to be said. Another example of the advantages to be drawn from the axiom is the possibility of defining identity (as we saw in the last chapter) by reference to predicative functions alone. At the same time paradoxes of the familiar kinds remain excluded, because they cannot be recast in terms of predicative functions alone. Thus if we try to reconstruct Berry's paradox, while talking only of integers nameable by first-order names (e.g. by names composed of English numerals in arrays such as 'five two nine'), we find that what we say gives rise to no contradiction.

Is there any reason, apart from convenience, for accepting the axiom of reducibility? Russell admits that it can scarcely be said to be a self-evident truth of logic, but he tries to explain it and render it plausible by showing its connexion with what logicians have said about classes. In his article of 1908 he suggests that it might be called the Axiom of Classes, but in the introduction to *Principia Mathematica* he writes more cautiously:

'If we admit the existence of classes, the axiom of reducibility can be proved. For in that case, given any function ϕz of whatever order, there is a class α consisting of just those objects which satisfy ϕx. Hence "ϕx" is equivalent to "x belongs to α". But "x belongs to α" is a statement containing no apparent variable, and is therefore a predicative function x. Hence if we assume the existence of classes, the axiom of reducibility becomes unnecessary. .. . However, both on the ground of the contradictions, which require a more complicated treatment if classes are assumed, and on the ground that it is always well to make the smallest assumption required for proving our theorems, we prefer to assume the axiom of reducibility rather than the existence of classes.'[16]

When Russell says here that 'x belongs to α' is a predicative function of x because it contains no apparent variable, he seems to be making no distinction between a function and a functional expression. But he can scarcely wish to suggest that introduction of the Greek letter α as an abbreviation for Z (ϕz) is enough to give us all the benefits of the axiom of reducibility, and so it must be assumed that he thinks of α as a designation introduced without the help of ϕx or any other functional expression of the same kind. It is not clear, however, why without assumption of the axiom of reducibility he should suppose it must be possible to provide such a new designation for the class previously designated by Z (ϕz), unless indeed he mistakenly takes it for granted that every class can be indicated by enumeration of its members.

In a later paragraph Russell produces another line of argument:

'The axiom of reducibility is equivalent to the assumption that any combination or disjunction of predicates (given intensionally) equivalent to a single predicate, i.e. to the assumption that' if we assert that x has all the predicates that satisfy a function f ($\phi!z$)' ....there is some one predicate which x will have whenever our assertion is true 'and will not have whenever it is false' and similarly if we assert that x has some one of the predicates that satisfy a function f ($\phi!z$). For by means of this assumption' the order of a non-predicative function can be lowered by one; hence' after some finite number of steps' we shall be able to get from any non-predicative function to a formally equivalent predicative function.[17]

In effect this explanation amounts to the suggestion that an expression with a universal quantifier should be regarded as an abbreviation for a conjunction and an expression with an existential quantifier as an abbreviation for a disjunction, even though it may be impossible to write out either conjunction or disjunction in full. Thus 'Napoleon had all the qualities that make a great *general* is to be taken as short for 'Napoleon was clever, alert, able to inspire confidence quick at guessing the thoughts of others. . . etc.' If we accept this account of the matter, we can go on to say that the distinction of orders of functions is not, like the hierarchy of types, something imposed by the nature of things, but rather a complication introduced by the exigencies of our language and useful only in connexion with problems concerning language. This is in fact the conclusion of F.P. Ramsey in his paper of 1925 on 'The Foundations of Mathematics',[18] and it has been accepted by most (but *not* all) of those who try to follow in the line of Frege, Whitehead, and Russell. As Ramsey pointed out, the simple theory of types is sufficient for exclusion of those paradoxes which are of special importance to the logician and the mathematician (e.g. Cantor's and Russell's), and the ramifications of the theory of orders are not strictly necessary for the purposes of *Principia Mathematica*, because their only service is to exclude paradoxes about semantic or linguistic notions such as naming and defining, with which the mathematician has no concern in his professional capacity.

When Ramsey's point has been conceded , it seems more natural to deal with the semantic paradoxes by special semantic measures, and the suggestion which has won most favour is the distinction of language and metalanguage introduced by Tarski in his work on 'The concept of Truth in Formalized Languages.'[19] According to this no consistent language can contain within itself the means for speaking about the meaning or the truth of its own expressions, and paradoxes such as the Liar and Berry's contradiction arise from failure to appreciate this limitation. If, for example, we speak of *the least integer not nameable in fewer than nineteen syllables*, it must be supposed that we are talking with reference to the resources of some particular language or languages. When this is understood, it will become clear that the phrase italicized above is not constructed out of the resources of the language or languages under reference, but belongs to a metalanguage which is essentially richer; and with this clarification the paradox will disappear. Unfortunately we often fail to understand the distinction when we talk of the use of a natural language such as English, because we are accustomed to think of it as omni competent, and this is the source of our troubles. If we wish to avoid contradictions, we must insist that what we ordinarily call English is in reality an infinite sequence of languages, namely, $English_1$ in which we can discuss sticks and stones and many other things but not $English_1$, $English_2$, in which we can discuss all the things we can discuss by use of $English_1$ in but in addition $English_1$, $English_3$ in which we can discuss all the things we can discuss by use of $English_2$, but in addition $English_2$ and so on. Within this scheme $English_{n+1}$ is a metalanguage in relation to English_n.

Tarski recommends his distinction as necessary for the solution of the paradox of the Liar, but it is interesting to show that it can be derived from the simple theory of types. Let us suppose first that we try to use the words 'designate' and 'designation' without implicit reference to some particular language, and that we construct with their help the formula:

'Designation' designates designation.

Here there is an obvious violation of the simple theory of types, inas much as a relation is said to be one of its own terms. It is not enough, however, to say that in future we will always talk of designation-in-English. For precisely the same trouble arises when we construct the formula:

'Designation in English' designates in English
designation in English.

But the trouble ceases if we recognize the stratification explained in the last paragraph and write:

'Designation in English_1' designates in English_2
designation in English_1.

For then we make clear that the relation of which we speak is of a higher type than its terms. And this, it seems, is the only way out of the difficulty.

If we reject the distinction of orders we must reject also the vicious-circle principle from which it is derived. To do so is a relief rather than a loss, since the principle is dubious and difficult to apply. Why, for example, should we say with Russell that a function presupposes its values? But if we propose to retain the simple theory of types, while abandoning the vicious-circle principle with which Russell connected it, we must consider very seriously whether the simple theory has the intrinsic plausibility which he claimed for it, i.e. whether it is a theory we want to retain on its own merits, once we have realized its content. In order to prepare for a decision on this question, let us try once more to make clear what it involves and how it is related to the theory of propositional functions introduced by Frege.

The essential novelty of Russell's theory is a tightening of the rules of significance by which he excludes from the domain of well-formed formulae some combinations of signs that would otherwise pass for grammatically correct sentences, and in particular all combinations of the form $F(Fx)$, or $F(\S xFx)$ in our notation. Instead of discussing whether these express true propositions or false propositions, he asserts that they express no propositions. In his account of functions of different levels Frege anticipated Russell's distinction of types, but it seems to be no more than an accident that his rules for the use of functional signs made it impossible to construct in his system the paradox of the property of being a property which does not exemplify itself. For he held that any *object* could occur as argument to any prepositional function of the first level, so that the worst to be said of the complex '7 is wiser than the moon' would be that it expressed a false proposition; and if he could have satisfied himself that it was possible to talk about *functions* by means of designations which did not contain gaps, he would probably have been prepared to treat them in the same way. But he was convinced that any sign we use to talk of a function must contain a gap (which he marked by means of a small Greek consonant, not itself part of his script), and he therefore assumed that one function could occur as an argument to another function only if the expression of the second, say $-\!\smile^{a}\!\smile\!-.\phi(\alpha)$ would provide for the closing of the gap in the expression of the first, say $\Phi(\beta)$.. and so produce a complete propositional expression, say $-\!\smile^{a}\!\smile\!-\Phi(a)$... This is clear from the way in which he deals with functions of the second level in his *Grundgesetze.*

If the only signs for functions were expressions such as' . . . is wise', considerations of ordinary grammar would be enough to guarantee the truth of the theory of types. For '. . . is wise is wise' is certainly not an English sentence, and no one will worry himself about the question whether it expresses a true proposition or a false proposition. When we write in our logical symbolism *F(Fx)*, we may perhaps be inclined to suppose for a moment that this can express a proposition, but we see that it is not a well by formed propositional expression when we remember that the letter *x* is a mere gap sign. So far we may agree with Frege, and it has sometimes been suggested that this is the whole theory of types.[20] But in ordinary English we have gapless nouns such as 'wisdom' to designate functions, and it is possible, as we have seen, to introducé signs of the same kind *into* the symbolism of logic. The important question is whether any complex of the form *F(§xFx)* can express a proposition, and to this we can get no clear answer either from academic grammar or from a study of common usage. For 'Wisdom is wise' is not obviously ungrammatical,' and although no one, except perhaps Plato, wants to offer it as a true statement, many may wish to say 'It is not the case that wisdom is wise', as though they thought that 'Wisdom is wise' had some meaning. How if at all can we settle the question?

Very often a sentence which contains a designation of a function can be replaced without loss by a sentence of a different shape in which there occurs no such designation but only an expression for the function. Thus instead of 'Socrates had wisdom' we can say 'Socrates was wise', and instead of 'The fear of the Lord is the beginning of wisdom' 'If a man fears the Lord he has already begun to be wise'. If it could be established that all significant sentences which contain designations of functions must be reducible in some way to sentences which contain no such designations, we could dismiss 'Wisdom is wise' and all similar complexes as insignificant, since it seems clear that they cannot be reduced. But no one has proved that it must always be possible to eliminate designations of fucnitons from significant discourse, and it is not sufficient for our purposes to cite a multitude of examples in which they have been eliminated successfully, because those who find the theory of types unplausible will retort that the question at issue cannot be settled by the methods of the natural sciences. The most we can achieve, then, by this line of argument is to show that the kind of complex to which the theory of types denies significance is in any case very peculiar. This consideration may well dispose us to accept the theory as a way out of our perplexities, but it is important to realize that there is a price to be paid for the advantages which it offers, and that it has its own difficulties.

In the first place, the theory produces an enormous complication in our account of logic, and not least in what we say about numbers. For we must not only distinguish in type between complex numbers, real numbers, rational numbers, signed integers, and natural numbers, but also between the natural numbers applicable to sets of different types. Thus according to Russell's elaboration of Ferge's theory the number four which is the number of the cardinal virtues must be an entity of a different type from the number four which is the number of the English kings called William. Virtues are qualities which may belong to men, and so a set of virtues, determined by a character applicable only to such qualities, cannot properly be said to be in the same class with a set of men, determined by a character applicable only to men. It may be that, as Frege said, entities of all thinkable kinds can be counted, but it seems that there must be a different arithmetic for every distinguishable type, i.e. that the numerals in the equations *2 men +2 men = 4 men and 2 virtues + 2 virtues = 4 virtues* cannot signify the same numbers. Russell tries to get over this difficulty by saying that he uses the symbols of logic and mathematics with *systematic ambiguity*. According to him there are indeed different types of natural numbers (and so different types of rational numbers, &c.), but in the development of pure arithmetic we can safely overlook this complication because our formulae will be applicable without alteration to any type that may come under discussion in applied mathematics or even in those branches of pure mathematics where we count numbers themselves.

Secondly, the theory of types rules out the possibility of providing for the definition of an infinity of natural numbers in any way like that suggested by Frege. If o is said to be the set of all sets equivalent in Cantor's technical sense to the set of things not identical with themselves and I the set of all sets equivalent in the same sense to the set {o}, it must be wrong to say that 2 is the set of all sets equivalent to the set whose members are o and I. For according to the first two definitions I is of a higher type than o, and so there can be no set of which these are both members. Frege made no distinctions of levels when dealing with the entities which he called objects; but if Russell is right, his definition of 2 is as curious as the assumption that Socrates and wisdom can have a character in common, and so his method of providing an infinity of natural numbers must be abandoned. It is essential for mathematics, however, that there should be no end to the sequence of natural numbers, and so Russell finds himself driven to introduce a special Axiom of Infinity, according to which there is some type with an infinity of instances, and that presumably the type of individuals, which comes lowest in the hierarchy. Without this axiom, he tells us, we should have no guarantee against the disastrous possibility that the supply of numbers would give out at some highest number, i.e. the number of members in the largest admissible set.

There is something profoundly unsatisfactory about the axiom of infinity. It cannot be described as a truth of logic in any reasonable use of that phrase, and so the introduction of it as a primitive proposition of arithmetic amounts in effect to abandonment of Frege's project of exhibiting arithmetic as a development of logic. Nor is it a sufficient defence to suggest, as Russell has sometimes done, that we may treat it as a postulate or hypothesis rather than as an axiom in the old sense. For we want to assert that the series 1/2 1/22 1/23+... converges to I as a limit, not that it converges to I if there happens to be an infinity of individuals in the world. But even if we abandon all hope of carrying out Frege's programme in full and say boldly that Russell's axiom is required as an extra-logical premiss for mathematics, how can we justify our acceptance of it? What are the individuals of which Russell speaks, and how can we tell whether there are infinitely many of them? Russell says that he intends to refer to those things, whatever they may be, which can be named by logically proper names and cannot occur in propositions except as subjects. But he admits that it is difficult to indicate such things directly, and he even suggests that there may possibly be none because everything which appears to be an individual is in fact a class or complex of some kind. With regard to the second possibility, which seems very mysterious, he adds cheerfully that if it is realized the axiom of infinity must obviously be true for the types which there are in the world. But he does not profess to know for certain what the situation is, and he ends by saying that there is no known method of discovering whether the axiom of infinity is true or false.[21]

Apart from these troubles, which even the simple theory of types involves for those who try to follow Frege in logicizing arithmetic, there is the more fundamental difficulty that it seems impossible to formulate the theory without violating its own provisions because words like 'function', 'entity', and 'type' must always remain free from type restrictions. If, for example, we say that no function may be asserted significantly of all entities without distinction of type, our own statement involves the unlimited generality which it declares to be impossible. And again there must be something wrong with any definition of a type according to which two entities are of the same type if a propositional function which can be affirmed or denied significantly of either can also be affirmed or denied significantly of the other. For when we try to apply such a definition in a particular case, and say, for example, that Plato is of the same type as Socrates but wisdom not of the same type, we find ourselves involved in a contradiction. From our pronouncement it follows that Plato is not of the same type as wisdom, and yet the pronouncement itself shows clearly that there is at least one function which can be affirmed truly of Plato and denied truly of wisdom, namely being of the same type as Socrates.

Such criticisms as these have led Russell to admit that he should have distinguished types of *symbols* rather than types of entities.[22] The words 'Plato' and 'wisdom', he now tells us, belong to different types because they are not interchangeable without loss of significance. For while 'Plato was younger than Socrates' makes good sense, 'Wisdom was younger than Socrates' is nonsense. On the other hand, when we construct names for these words by printing them within quotation marks, our new signs belong to the same type, because they are interchangeable without loss of significance. Thus if we replace 'Plato' by 'wisdom' in the sentence ' "Plato" is of the same type as "Socrates"', the result is still meaningful though the proposition which it expresses is false.

With care this new version of the theory of types can be made to yield all the advantages that are derivable from the original, and it may perhaps be an improvement, not only because it saves us from new paradoxes, but also because it seems to offer better hope of an understanding of the situation. It is wrong, however, to suppose that by speaking about words instead of things we can escape from all metaphysical entanglements and base our distinctions on simple considerations of grammar. In particular it is a mistake to assume that difference in type is always an affair of syntax according to the ordinary understanding of that grammatical term. There is indeed a syntactical difference between 'Plato' and '... is wise', since the first is a designation and the second a functional expression; but there is no such difference between 'Plato' and 'wisdom', and it is by no means obvious that all significant remarks must be translatable into a simplified language which contains only designations of one type.

For the solution of the paradoxes which afflicted mathematicians and logicians at the beginning of this century, the important distinction of type is that between words like

'Plato' and words like 'wisdom' which may be said to stand for possible characters and relations of Plato. But under the influence of Russell it has become common for philosophers to talk of type or category distinctions in their attempts to solve problems of very different kinds. It has been suggested, for example, that there is a confusion of categories in talking of interaction between mind and body.[23] Whether such an extension of the theory of types is justifiable must be settled in each particular case by detailed examination of the ways in which we think and speak when we are at our best, but there are two general cautions to be borne in mind.

In the first place we must not assume that words of ordinary language are interchangeable *salva significatione*! either in all contexts or in none. Although we cannot substitute 'wisdom' for 'Plato' in the sentence 'Plato was wise' without producing non-sense, we can make such a substitution in 'Socrates loved Plato' without evoking even a feeling of surprise. We must therefore be content to say that a difference of type is shown by failure of interchangeability in *some* context, and from this we may perhaps be led to doubt whether any two words are of the same type.

Secondly, when we leave the realm of logic and pure mathematics for the study of thoughts expressed in ordinary language, it is not always clear where we should draw the line between nonsense and scientific impossibility. Consider, for example, the following series of sign-complexes:

1. The parson believes in original sin.
2. The baby believes in original sin.
3. The cat believes in original sin.
4. The chair believes in original sin.
5. The rent believes in original sin.

Obviously the first may be uttered for the purpose of making a statement. And it seems reasonable to say that the last is nonsense. But what of the others ? We have all heard of precocious children: might not some child be so precocious that the parson felt obliged to instruct it in the doctrine of original Sin while it was still a baby? Then, Since some cats are more intelligent than others, might not the cat of this household, overhearing the parson's instruction, come to believe in original Sin? And finally might not the chair on which the parson sat be all the while a true believer suffering from the enchantments of a wicked magician? Or at least does not all this make some sort of sense? Shall we then say that the line comes between the fourth and the fifth of our examples? But what sort of discovery is this? Suppose someone tells us that in Coptic fairy stories true believers are often said to be changed into rents and that Coptic children do not find such stories unintelligible. Shall we admit that any collection of words which is permissible according to customary syntax may make some sort of sense to someone? Or shall we reply dogmatically that we are not interested in Coptic fairy stories because we know a *priori* that there is a line to be dwawn between the fourth and the fifth of the examples given above? In any case it seems clear that in contexts of the kind we have been considering the theory of types does not provide a simple rule for detecting otherwise unsuspected nonsense.

If our concern is solely to save the theory of sets from antinomies, we can get the benefit of Russell's theory of types without some of its difficulties by the technique of standardization noticed in the last chapter. That is to say, we can present the many-sorted theory of sets with variables which range over a single universe of discourse (containing entities of all types), provided (i) we qualify our theorems by conditions which distinguish entities according to their types and (ii) we introduce the new axiom schema

$$(x)\ (y)\ \{x \in y \supset [T_n\ (x) \equiv T_{n+1}\ (y)]\}$$

in which the *T*-signs are supposed to be category or type predicates, themselves definable in terms of membership.[24]

3. THE INTUITIONISM OF BROUWER

In his controversy with Russell at the beginning of this century Poincaré suggested that the paradoxes of the theory of sets were due to the fundamental mistake of assuming actually infinite aggregates. He did not explain in detail why that assumption gave rise to contradictions; but he was right, of course, in thinking that if mathematicians abstained from talking of infinity in the manner of Cantor they would not have to face Cantor's peculiar puzzles, and he might perhaps have argued that it was useless to spend time on the detailed discussion of an assumption whose absurdity could be seen without reference to the paradoxes. In such an attitude he would have had the support of many distinguished mathematicians. At the beginning of the nineteenth century Gauss had said that there was no place in mathematics for talk of a completed infinity,[25] and more recently Kronecker had conducted a campaign against the Cantorian programme. But none of these had realized the full consequences of refusing to admit any infinity other than the potential infinity of a sequence winch can be continued *ad libitum*, and it was not until the work of L.L.J.Brouwer in this century that the issue became clear—or at least clear enough to interest most mathematicians.

Like Kant and Poincaré, Brouwer holds that mathematical theorems are synthetic *a priori* truths. In his inaugural address of 1912 at the University of Amsterdam he admits that the development of non-Euclidean geometry has discredited Kant's view of space, but in opposition to Frege, Whitehead, and Russell he maintains that arithmetic, and with it all mathematics, must be derived from the intuition of time. In his own words, 'neo-in-tuitionism considers the falling apart of the moments of life into qualitatively different parts, to be rebyunited only while remaining eparated by time, as the fundamental phenomenon of the human intellect'. From this 'intuition of the bare two-oneness' we get first the notion of the sequence of ordinal numbers, and then the notion of the linear continuum, i.e. 'of the betweenness which is not exhaustible by the inteposition of new units and therefore can never be thought of as a mere collection of units'. In so far as it assumes continuity, even geometry is dependent on the same intuition. There are no sets except the denumerable, and so there are no transfinite cardinals except No the cardinal of a set whose members can be correlated one-to-one with the sequence of natural numbers. In particular, there is no meaning to be given to any phrase such as 'the set of all real numbers between o and I.[26]

What Brouwer has to say about intuition in this manifesto is obscure, and his other papers do not give much more light on that topic, interesting as it may be to philosophers; but he leaves no doubt that he repudiates everything connected with the notion of an actual (or completed or extensional) infinite, including even the liberty of talking about the set of real numbers in an interval. In his view even the sequence of natural numbers is to be conceived as an open manifold, always in growth and never brought to a finish: we can comprehend it only by understanding the law of its construction.

Sometimes Brouwer and his pupils say that the intuition of which they speak is just the mind's clear apprehension of what it has itself constructed, and they frequently assert that in mathematics all satisfactory proofs are constructive. It is difficult to know exactly what they mean by 'construction' and 'constructive' in this context, but the fact that they often deny the dependence of mathematical thought on any special sort of language and express distrust of the technique of formalization by which some other mathematicians hope to get security suggests that they think of a constructive proof as one which consists of the performance of an experiment in imagination. A. Heyting, who is a leading member of the school, has even gone so far as to say

'Intuitionistic mathematics consists...in mental constructions; a mathematical theorem expresses a purely empirical fact, namely the success of a certain construction.

"2+2 = 3+1" must be read as an abbreviation for the statement "I have effected the mental constructions indicated by '2+2' and '3+1' and I have found that they lead to the same result".[27]

But it can scarcely be his intention to reduce mathematics to psychological autobiography.For he quite obviously thinks that the theorems he has proved by reflection on his own powers of mental construction can be proved by anyone else who is sufficiently intelligent, and that it is not proper to say that each man has his own mathematics (unless that phrase means simply the stock of theorems he has personally discovered or verified). Presumably modern intuitionists agree with Kant that mathematical theorems are objective in the sense of being valid for all intelligent beings. If this is right, the symbolic expression of a theorem may perhaps be replaced in certain contexts by a statement that something is *provable*, but it cannot be treated as a record of the empirical fact that something has been *proved* by the writer. No doubt the writing of the symbolical expression can be cited as evidence of a mental achievement by the writer, but that is not sufficient reason for saying that the expression means something about the writer.

In practice the most important requirement of the programme of constructive proof is that no existential statement shall be admitted in mathematics unless it can be demonstrated by production of an instance. In Brouwer's view anyone who fails to observe this caution has only himself to blame if he falls into paradox; for he talks without insight. But it must be admitted that Brouwer too has been led to some surprising conclusions in his attempts to apply his programme rigorously. As early as 1908 he published a paper on the unreliability of the principles of logic,[28] and from 1918 onwards he produced a number of papers against the use of the principle of excluded middle in mathematics. In these he holds that mathematics, being derived directly from intuition, does not presuppose a system of logic, but is rather a source of logical principles, since these latter may be enunciated in general fashion only after their validity has been established by the appropriate intuition. There is, and can be, no completely safe language for mathematics, that is to say, no language which will eliminate all possibility of misunderstanding; and it is therefore vain to hope for a complete formalization of mathematics. This is shown strikingly by the history of the principle of excluded middle. In their daily concerns men commonly have to do with finite sets, and intuition shows that the rules of their ordinary logic are appropriate for reasoning about such sets. But these rules have been taken as absolute and applied without the warrant of intuition to reasoning about infinite sets. In this new context the principle of identity, the principle of non-contradiction, and the principle of syllogism are in fact once more appropriate; but the principle of excluded middle and the associated principle for the elimination of double negation are no longer sound.[29]

Let us consider an existential statement *(∃x)[Fx. ~ Gx]* and the universal statement *(x)~[Fx ~ Gx]* which is ordinarily supposed to be its contradictory. If the set denoted by xFx is finite, it is possible in principle to examine all the members, one after another, and so to decide in favour of one or other of the two statements. The task may be technically impracticable, but we have a clear conception of a method for deciding which of the alternatives is true. If, however, the set denoted by *xfx* is denumerably infinite, the situation is different. Systematic enumeration is still quite satisfactory for proving the existential statement, since it must lead to a favourable instance in a finite number of steps if there is such an instance; but it is no longer an effective method of proving the universal statement, since it is senseless to talk of going through all the members. Thus anyone who succeeds in demonstrating Goldbach's conjecture that every even number greater than two is the sum of two primes must do so by showing that it is in the nature of a multiple of two to have this property. Now Brouwer and most intuitionists are prepared to concede that one way of proving a universal statement of this kind is to show, if we can, that the existential statement involves a contradiction and must therefore be rejected, i.e. they allow the logical thesis

$$\sim(\exists x)[Fx.\sim Gx] \supset (x)\sim[Fx.\sim Gx.],$$

On the other hand they do not admit the thesis

$$\sim(x)\sim[Fx.\sim Gx] \supset (\exists x)\ [Fx.\sim Gx],$$

because they say that, if we succeeded in refuting the universal statement by showing that it involved a contradiction, we should be no nearer to discovering a thing called *A* of which we could assert *FA.* ~ *GA*, and so should not be entitled to assert the existential proposition. In short, reasoning which involved the second thesis would be non-constructive, and anyone who asserted the existential proposition as a conclusion of such reasoning would be in intellectual danger, just as a man who runs in the dark is in physical danger. But rejection of the second thesis amounts in effect to abandonment of the principle of excluded middle and the associated principle for the elimination of double negation.

This conclusion is surprising enough to make many suspect a mistake in the intuitionistic philosophy of mathematics, but its oddity is somewhat disguised when Brouwer identifies it with rejection of the assumption that every mathematical problem is soluble.[30] For we must admit that problems about infinite sets cannot all be solved by a rule of thumb like that which leads infallibly to a solution of problems about finite sets. Although we can say something about the general form which a proof of Goldbach's conjecture must take, if one is ever obtained, we are unable to give effective instructions for the finding of such a proof. But why should Brouwer suppose that unqualified assertion of the principle of excluded middle is equivalent to claiming possession of a universal method for solving mathematical problems? One reason may be that his programme of constructive proof commits him to the view that it is improper to assert any disjunctive statement unless one is prepared to assert one of the disjuncts. For according to this very strict way of understanding a disjunction a person who writes $p \vee \sim p$, using the letter p as a free variable, gives it to be understood that he is in a position to assert or deny every proposition that may be suggested for consideration. It seems likely, however, that Brouwer is influenced also by the thought that in intuitionistic mathematics there is no difference to be drawn between $.\sim(\exists x)\ [Fx.\sim Gx]$ and $(x)\sim[Fx.\sim Gx]$. when Δ is used as an abbreviation for 'it is demonstrable that'. We have noticed already that intuitionists talk of theorems as statements of provability, and it is easy to see that any one who dwells, as Brouwer does, on the requirements of constructive proof may wish to assert emphatically that there is no place in mathematics for merely accidental universality. Heyting has said 'In intuitionistic mathematics only falsity *de jure* can play a part: the introduction of mere *de facto* falsity would conflict with the principle of constructivity[31], and from this the view just mentioned could easily be derived.

Whatever the precise meaning of his more philosophical pronouncements may be, there can be no doubt that for Brouwer they have serious consequences in mathematics. For methods which he calls non-constructive are unfortunately very common in the theory of real numbers. It is difficult, indeed, to see how any substantial part of classical analysis can be presented without them. In Dedekind's theory a real number is considered to be an actually infinite set of rational numbers, and even the simplest theorems are then proved by the assumption of the principle of excluded middle in relation to such sets. When, for example it is desired to prove that for any two real numbers x and y either x > y or x = y or x < y, it is first asserted that there either is or is not a rational in x which does not belong to y. Brouwer and his followers reject all this and try to reconstruct mathematics in accordance with their own stricter standards of proof. The subtlety and ingenuity which they bring to the work give aesthetic pleasure to some mathematicians, but it is clear already that the structure which they build must inevitably be more complicated than the classical edifice which it is intended to replace.

For the study of intuitionistic logic, which especially concerns us, the most important development within the school has been the formulation of a calculus by Heyting in 1930.[32] Since it is one of the intuitionistic tenets that there can never be any guarantee of the finality of a formal system, Heyting does not suggest that mathematical reasoning must be confined for all time to arguments of the patterns he records; but his system has been accepted by Brouwer as a correct digest of the logical principles used in intuitiouistic mathematics at the present time, and it therefore deserves close attention. Its rules of deduction are the same as those of Principia *Mathematica*, but it has two distinctive features. In the first place the various logical signs (conjunctive, disjunctive, conditional, negative, universal, and existential) are all taken as undefined primitives;[33] and secondly the various sets of axioms given by Frege and others for the propositional calculus are all abandoned in favour of the following set of eleven:

1. $p \supset (p.p)$
2. $(p.q) \supset (q.p)$
3. $(p \supset q) \supset [(q.r) \supset (q.r)]$
4. $[(q \supset q).(q \supset r)] \supset (p \supset r)$
5. $q \supset (p \supset q)$
6. $[p.(p \supset q)] \supset q$
7. $p \supset (p \vee q)$
8. $(p \vee q) \supset (q \vee P)$
9. $(p \supset r).(q \supset r)] \supset [(p \vee q) \supset r]$
10. $' p \supset (p \supset q)$
11. $[(p \supset q).(p \supset \neg q)] \supset \neg p$

It will be noticed that in the last two formulae the new sign $\neg$ occurs where we might have expected ~. But apart from this, each of Heyting's axioms is similar in appearance to a thesis of classical logic, and together with the rules of substitution and detachment they allow for many of the ways of reasoning recognized in classical logic; but it is not possible to derive from them either of the two principles rejected by Brouwer, namely those expressible by the formulae p V 'p.. and ' '$p \supset p$ Furthermore, the system has the peculiarity of admitting no disjunctive proposition unless one at least of its disjuncts is separately provable. An equivalent system of rules of 'natural inference' can be obtained by omitting rule (6b) from the version of Gentzen's system given in an earlier section.

What are we to say of Heyting's calculus? It is presented as though it were a formalization of that part of classical logic to which Brouwer raises no objection; and considered from one point of view, it is just that. On the other hand, it is not possible to abandon principles of classical logic, while giving all the logical signs their usual senses, since the sense of a logical sign is determined by the logical formulae in which it is introduced. And the intuitionists are not content to ignore the formula $p \vee' ,p$, but say explicitly that it has no place in their calculus of propositions. It seems, therefore, that if the sign V retains its usual sense in intuitionistic logic, 7 must mean something different from ~. In his exposition of his theory Brouwer frequently writes 'it is absurd' where he might have been expected to say 'it is not the case', and Heyting, as we have seen, says that there is no merely *de facto* negation in intuitionistic mathematics. So it is not surprising that many critics here supposed the so-called negation sign of the intuitionistic calculus to be really a sign of impossibility and said in consequence that what is rejected is not, properly speaking, the principle of excluded middle but the obviously unacceptable thesis that every proposition is either true or impossible.'[34] But this cannot be a sufficient account of the matter; for the last of the formulae of Heyting listed above is not a truth of logic if ' is taken to mean 'it is impossible that' and the other signs retain their usual senses. In reality the situation is more complicated, as K. Gödel showed in two papers of I932.[35]

If Heyting's calculus is supposed to be part of classical logic, then paradoxically that part can be shown to contain in a certain way the whole. For although Heyting says that his signs are all to be taken as undefined primitives, there is nothing to prevent us from introducing a new disjunction sign, say →, and a new implication sign, say → defined by the equivalenes:

P ⊕ Q = ' (' P. 'Q)
P → Q = ' (P. 'Q).

And from these, taken together with the axioms and rules of inference given by Heyting, it is possible to obtain all the theses of the classical logic of propositions, including the principle of excluded middle in the form *p* ⊕ '*p* and the principle for the elimination of double negation in the form ¬¬P → ¬P. For the two formulae just mentioned are merely abbreviations for '' *p*.'' *p*) and ''' *p*. ' *p*, which can both be proved within Heyting's system. It should be noticed, however, that the new signs ⊕ and →, are not to be equated with the intuitionist signs V and ⊃, and that the formulae '' *p* → *p* cannot be used in the intuitionist calculus for the elimination of double negation, since the rule of detachment, *or modus ponens*, for that calculus refers to ⊃, not to →. By an extension of the same procedure it has been shown that the classical version of the restricted calculus of functions and classical elementary arithmetic can both be reconstructed within the corresponding intuitionistic systems, and it has even been conjectured that the same may be done for classical analysis.[36] Such reproduction of classical calculi within those of intuitionism amounts to relative proof of consistency for the former, just as the modelling of a non-Euclidean geometry within Euclidean geometry proves that the former cannot be inconsistent unless the latter is so too. If intuitionistic mathematics is free from contradiction, then so too are those parts of classical mathematics which can be translated into parts of intuitionistic mathematics.

In the first of the two papers mentioned above Gödel draws the conclusion that the restrictions which Brouwer imposes on proofs in analysis and the theory of sets are not due,as Brouwer himself says, to abandonment of the principle of excluded middle, but rather to rejection of impredicative definitions (i.e. definitions which contain a vicious circle of the kind noticed by Poincaré). Whether this is correct or not, he has certainly proved that on the simplest interpretation Heyting's calculus includes the whole of classical logic, and that intuitionists who accept this interpretation cannot properly say that they have abandoned the principle of excluded middle, except in the sense of not using it for their own reasoning in mathematics.

It may be replied, however, that intuitionistic formulae always mean something different from classical formulae of the same shape, and there is good reason, as we have seen, for believing that this is true of Heyting's logical formulae. Here again Gödel has an interesting suggestion.[37] Starting from the intuitionists' own hints, he supposes in the second of the papers mentioned above that all four signs of Heyting's propositional calculus are different in sense from the signs of the classical calculus, but that expressions containing them may be regarded as abbreviations for more complicated expressions according to the following scheme in which Δ has the sense of 'it is demonstrable that' and the signs with which it occurs are classical:

Heyting Expression	Classical Expansion
$\urcorner P$	$\Delta{\sim}\Delta\ P$
P.Q	$\Delta P.\ \Delta Q$
P v Q	$\Delta P \vee \Delta Q$
$P \supset Q$	$\Delta P \supset \Delta Q$

The result is that all Heyting's axioms become theses in a system which differs from Lewis's modal system S_4 only by its use of 'demonstrable' in place of 'necessary'. Moreover the thesis which Brouwer rejects under the name 'principle of excluded middle' turns out to be a version of the strong reduction principle. For its expanded form is $\Delta p \vee \Delta\Delta{\sim}\Delta p$ and this is equivalent to ${\sim}\Delta p \supset \Delta{\sim}\Delta p$ With the suggested interpretation it is easy to see why Brouwer says that the rejected thesis is equivalent to the principle of the solubility of all mathematical problems, and much easier to understand why he is prepared to reject it. For even those who believe in the strong reduction principle of ordinary modal logic do not all say that it seems to them as intuitively obvious as the principle of excluded middle, properly so called; and according to the suggested interpretation the rejected thesis is not concerned with the necessity of ordinary modal logic but with demonstrability in mathematics by constructive methods.

It is the basic idea of intuitionism that we should seek security in mathematics by accepting only constructive proofs, and it is therefore quite fitting that Heyting's calculus should be interpreted as an axiomatic theory of the notion of provability by constructive methods. So understood, it makes good sense;for we certainly do not wish to maintain that every mathematical conjecture is either demonstrably true or demonstrably indemonstrable by constructive methods. But according to this interpretation Heyting's calculus is not a system of logic in the strict sense, because it does not fix the sense of the logical signs that occur in its full formulation. On the contrary, it presupposes a classical calculus of logic, and it has only been mistaken for an alternative logic because of the intuitionists' unfortunate custom of talking of theorems as statements of provability. No doubt there may be theorems about the provability of theorems, but there must be others which are not of this kind although they involve logical notions such as those of conditionality and universality.

In practice anyone who decides to accept only constructive proofs in mathematics may have to reject arguments which employ the principle of excluded middle in relation to infinite sets (i.e. if he cannot explain the unsatisfactoriness of all nonconstructive arguments in the way suggested by Gödel). But he should then content himself with the remark that such arguments do not yield the insight which he wants.

4 HILBERT'S PROGRAMME OF METAMATHEMATICS

In the year 1908, in which Russell published the first version of his theory of types and Brouwer first wrote against the reliability of the principles of logic, E. Zermelo produced a set of axioms designed to save the theory of sets from paradoxes.[38] Regarding this theory still as the most fundamental part of mathematics, he suggests that it should be rebuilt by the laying down of principels which are sufficient to support the generally accepted doctrine but so chosen that they do not give rise to contradictions. He admits that he cannot prove the consistency of his axioms, but he claims that he has at least excluded the antinomies discovered in recent years. The essential feature of his method is that he no longer talks of sets with the freedom of Cantor but admits in his theory only those sets whose existence is guaranteed by his axioms.

First in his Axiom of Definiteness (I) he lays it down that two sets are identical if whatever is a member of one is a member also of the other. Then in a number of axioms hie provides for derivation of sets from others assumed to be given. Thus in his Axiom of Subsets (III) he says that if there is a property such that for every member of a set S it is a determinate question whether that member has the property or not then there exists a second set whose members are just those members of S which have the property; in his Axiom of the Power Set (IV) that for any set S there exists a second set whose members are all the subsets of S; and in his Axiom of the Union Set (V) that for any set S there exists a second set whose members are all the members of the members of S. These last three all correspond to implicit assumptions of Cantor, but Zermelo adds to the group a new assumption of his own called the Axiom of Choice (VI) according to which for every set S whose members are mutually exclusive sets all alike distinct from the null set there exists at least one subset of its union set which contains a single member from each of the members of S.The independence of this axiom and even its admissibility have been much debated by later mathematicians. Finally, since none of the axioms mentioned so far provides *unconditionally* for the existence of any sets, Zermelo lays it down in his Axiom of Elementary Sets (II) and his Axiom of the Infinite (VII) that there exists in the domain of sets atleast oneset which contains the null set as a member and is so constructed that the inclusion in it of any member A implies also the inclusion in it of the unit class {A}, i.e. the class of which A is the sole member. Thus, to use a loose expression, all the sets required in this axiomatic presentation of the theory are generated in one way or another from the null set, and provision is made for infinity in the same way as by Frege. There is no distinction of types, but the known contradictions are avoided by the device of limiting talk to sets which are *not too large*. In particular the domain (*Bereich*) of sets is not itself admitted as a set. But J. von Neumann, who has himself produced a revised set of axioms for the theory of sets, argues conclusively that there is no additional danger in admitting very large sets such as this, provided always that no set as large as the set of everything in general is supposed capable of being a *member* of any set.[39]

Apart from the fact that it does not incorporate any distinction of types, Zermelo's version of the theory of sets differs from that of Whitehead and Russell in the role which it assigns to axioms. In *Principia Mathematica* the axioms are all supposed to be necessary truths, and the whole structure is conceived by its authors in the same way as Euclid conceived his *Elements*. That is to say, there is no suggestion that there could be any alternative, except possibly a system of the same content in which some of the present axioms appeared as theorems and some of the present theorems as axioms. Admittedly Russell has misgivings about his axiom of reducibility and his axiom of infinity, but he still thinks that if they are to be accepted at all they are to be accepted as truths, and he therefore puts forward such considerations as he can produce to convince the reader or at least make him sympathetic. Zermelo, no doubt, also wishes that the axioms in his set should appear plausible, but he presents them rather as a modern geometer might present a set of axioms for a non-Euclidean geometry. If they are consistent, they delimit a system for study and provide an implicit definition of the membership sign which is used as a primitive symbol in the formulation of them.

The notion of implicit definition is as old as Gergonne, but the importance which formal, as opposed to material, axiomatics has in the thought of modern mathematicians is due largely to the work of Hilbert. In his *Grundlagen der Geometrie* of 1899 he produced the first really satisfactory set of axioms for Euclidean geometry, and in a paper of 1904 on the foundations of logic and mathematics he suggested a programme for eliminating the newly discovered paradoxes by axiomatizing logic, arithmetic, analysis, and the theory of sets.[40] He did not think that arithmetic could be reduced to logic, but rather that they should be developed together in order that the whole system might then be shown to be free from inconsistency. The paper is a mere sketch, but it shows already some of Hilbert's guiding principles and in particular that faith in the axiomatic method which he expressed more fully in his later work and particularly in a paper of 1922:

'The axiomatic method is now and for all time the instrument suited to the human mind and indispensable for every exact enquiry, whatever its field may be. It is logically unassailable, and at the same time fruitful. It also preserves for the enquirer the most complete liberty of movement. To proceed axiomatically in this sense is simply to think with knowledge of what one is about. In earlier times, when they did not use the axiomatic method, men believed in various connexions with naive dogmatism. Axiomatics removes this *naiveté*, but leaves us nevertheless the advantages of belief.'[41]

The explanation of the last-quoted sentence and the motive of all Hilbert's work on the foundations of mathematics can be seen most clearly in his essay of 1926 'On the Infinite'.[42] He tells us there that the role of the infinite in mathematics is that of an Idea of Reason in the Kantian philosophy: it transcends all experience and in a way completes it. That is to say, the theory of the actual infinite is radically different from constructive mathematics, but we must not reject it on that account. On the contrary we must welcome it as 'the most admirable flowering of the mathematical spirit' and try to preserve it by the greatest intellectual care. In short, 'we must let no one drive us from the paradise that Cantor has created for us'. These remarks are clearly directed against Brouwer, and so also is the assertion later in the same article that every mathematical problem is soluble. But for all that, Hilbert agrees with Brouwer about the primacy of intuition and constructive argument. He thinks that in mathematics the basic reasoning, which he calls *finitary,* is a kind of 'direct reflection on content that proceeds without axiomatic assumptions but by means of thought-experiments on objects imagined in full concreteness' and by use of mathematical induction, or the argument from recurrence to which Poincaré attached supreme importance.[43] Where he differs is in thinking that classical mathematics, with its 'ideal' theorems unattainable by finitary methods, may nevertheless be preserved as a valuable possession if the consistency of the axioms from which it is derivable can be proved by means of finitary argument. His programme has been described as a plan for reducing strict intuitionism to absurdity,[44] but it is not intended to be merely a polemic. On the contrary, according to Hilbert, the need for using intuitionistic methods in proving the consistency of classical arithmetic arises from the nature of the problem.

A system which is to be sufficient for the derivation of number theory, classical analysis, and the theory of sets must contain not only the rules and axioms of the restricted calculus of propositional functions, but also Frege's axioms of identity, axioms of number like those of Peano, and axioms of membership like those of Zermelo, or at any rate axioms equivalent in force to all these. Hilbert does not think it reasonable to call the whole amalgam logic, but it is clear that the name we use is of minor importance, and it is not even of very great concern that the axioms should all be independent. What is essential is that the system as a whole should be proved consistent, and for this purpose ordinary methods are useless. Since the system is intended to deal with the properties of actually infinite sets, we cannot give an absolute proof of its consistency by producing a set of objects whose relations satisfy all the conditions laid down in the axioms. For although our mathematical notion of continuity was originally suggested by reflection on continuity in the perceptual world, we have no guarantee that the requirements of the mathematical notion are all satisfied by any perceptibly continuous expanse or duration, and there is no other datum of experience in which it is even plausible to look for an actually infinite set of elements. Nor can we give a relative proof of the consistency of the set of axioms by showing that they can all be translated into statements of some other system, as axioms of non-Euclidean geometry may be translated into statements of Euclidean geometry. For there is no other system of known consistency which seems comprehensive enough to provide such a translation.[45] But we may conceivably be able to attain the goal in another way. To say that the system is consistent is to say that application of the rules of inference to the axioms can never lead to a pair of consequences one of which is the negation of the other. May it not be possible to prove this by reasoning at a higher level, i.e. not within the system but rather about the system, or to speak more strictly about the formulae in which the system is expressed? The axiomatic formulae are finite in number, and a derivation must be a finite sequence of steps taken in accordance with one or other of a finite number of rules; so it is not on the face of if absurd to suppose that the proof of consistency which we need may be attainable in this way by the use of finitary methods of argument. For just as in elemenetary number theory these methods are sufficient to prove the impossibility of finding two natural numbers m and n such that m^2 $2n^2$ so in this new study called *theory of proof or metamathematics* they may be sufficient to prove the impossibility of finding two derivations which lead from the given axioms to contradictory conclusions.

From 1917 onwards Hilbert worked on this project with various colleagues, and in 1934 and 1939 he published with P. Bernays the two volumes of *Grundlagen der Mathematik*, which explain the situation and set forth the results achieved up to the time of publication. In this work the authors admit that they are still far from a solution of the fundamental problem, and we shall presently sec reason to believe that that problem can never be completely solved as it was originally conceived, but there is no doubt that the study started by Hilbert has been extremely fruitful. For, apart from the problem of consistency, there are many questions about deductive systems for which the technique he suggested seems appropriate, in particular questions about the completeness of axiom systems and about the possibility of devising decision procedures, or rules of thumb, for the solution of problems in various branches of mathematics. In all such investigations it is essential that the theory under investigation should be formalized by the help of a strict logical symbolism, and so it may be said that here at last the work of Leibniz and Frege has produced results of importance to the progress of mathematics, though not perhaps the results they expected.

Sometimes Hilbert's philosophy of mathematics is called formalism, and just as nineteenth-century formalists were attacked by Frege, so Hilbert is attacked by Brouwer for failure to appreciate the real *content* of mathematics. Frege's opponents maintained that new kinds of numbers could be introduced by creative definitions, and that if the definitions led to no self-contradictions it was pointless to ask for any further proof of the existence of the numbers. To this Frege replied that there could be no proof of freedom from contradiction except by production of an example, and that the converse inference was a fallacy. Hilbert now argues that the consistency of a postulate system may be established without the production of a model. To this Brouwer replies that intuitionism does not assume an inconsistency in the application of the principle of excluded middle to infinite sets, and that even if Hilbert succeeded in his enterprise he would have done nothing to prove the truth of his 'ideal' statements, because there is a vicious circle in the attempt to justify formalist mathematics through a proof of its consistency. We are asked to accept the correctness of a system of postulates when it have been shown that they do not lead to self-contradiction; but according to Brouwer this justification is of no value unless we can already accept the principle that the correctness of a proposition follows from the absurdity of its absurdity, and that is just another version of the law of excluded middle.'[46] In his view a theory has no more title to be called true because it has been proved free from inconsistency than a wrongdoer has to be called an honest man because it has been found that his act cannot be punished by the existing law of the land. As Fraenkel has written

'To the thoroughgoing believer in axiomatics Hilbert's question counts as the supreme problem of all mathematics, and in the answer to it he would see one of the boldest, most original, and most profoundly important steps in the development of the problem of knowledge; but to the thoroughgoing intuitionist it is entirely without significance on the only point that matters.'[47]

This is a very curious dispute in which the parties seem to be arguing at cross purposes. Brouwer talks as though Hilbert were trying to prove the truth of his axioms, and so of what follows from them, by proving that they are self-consistent. But when Hilbert undertakes to axiomatize all mathematics he presumably thinks of his axioms as postulates which determine the sense of the otherwise undefined symbols which he uses. If this is right,a mathematical entity must be for him just what his axioms allow, neither more nor less, and every mathematical statement must have the same status as a statement of pure geometry, e.g. as the assertion that a Riemannian triangle has interior angles greater than two right angles. So interpreted, Hilbert's axiomatized mathematics is not open to Brouwer's objections. For anyone who talks of real numbers in the way Hilbert proposes will use the phrase 'real number' to mean any object satisfying certain conditions, and so his statements will be in effect assertions that his axioms have certain consequences in virtue of their form. In short, they will be truths of pure logic. On the other hand, it is not clear whether Hilbert is content with this conclusion, nor yet what he thinks about the ultimate relation of axiomatized. mathematics to constructive mathematics. Sometimes it seems that after a proof of the consistency of his axioms by constructive methods he would be content to forget the difference and treat non-constructive mathematics as a continuation of constructive mathematics. But this can scareely be a correct attitude to adopt, if he and Brouwer are right in thinking that constructive mathematics involves insight into a special subject-matter. For there seems to be no guarantee that the theorems attained without this insight are about the same subject-matter. Thus a theorem which purports to be about natural numbers but is proved non-constructively (e.g. by a detour through classical analysis) may not really be about natural numbers in the original sense. This seems to be what Heyting has in mind when he says that the subject of intuitionistic mathematics, namely, constructive mathematical thought, 'places it beside, not interior to classical mathematics, which studies another subject, whatever that may be'.'

As we have already noticed, there is reason to believe that Hilbert's programme can never be carried out in full, but the stimulus which he give to the study of axiom sets has led to some very interesting discoveries about the properties of logic and various other deductive systems. These will provide the subject for our last chapter.

Footnotes

1. 'Les Principes des mathématiques et le probléme des ensembles', *Revue génerale des sciences* xvi 1905), p. 541, reprinted in *Acta Mathematica,* xxx (1906), p. 295.

2. W.V. Quine, 'On Frege's Way Out', *Mind,* N.S. Ixiv (1955), pp. 145–59.

3. 'On Some Difficulties in the Theory of Transfinite Numbers and Order Types' *Proceedings of the London Mathematic-al*

Society, iv (1906), pp. 29–53.

4. 'Les Mathématiques et la logique', *Revue de métaphysique et de morale,* xiii (1905), pp 815–35; xiv (1906), pp. 17- 34 and 294-317. The series is reprinted with some modificaitons in *Science et Méthode.*

5. See for example, A. Fraenkel, *Einleitung in die Mengenlehre,* p.248.

6. 'Les Paradoxes de la logique', *Revue de métaphysique et de morale,* xiv (1906), pp. 627–50. The article on *Insolubilia* in Baldwin's *Dictionary* was by C.S. Peirce.

7. *American Journal of Mathematics,* xxx (1908), pp. 222–62, reprinted in *Logic and Knowledge,* pp. 59–102.

8. *Principia Mathematica,* vol. i, p. 39.

9. Ibid. p. 40.

10.. R. Carnap, *The Logical Syntax of Language,* § 27.

11. *Principia Mathematica,* vol. i, pp. 62–63.

12. Ibid., pp. 48–49.

13. Ibid. p. 52.

14. Ibid., p. 53. This sense of 'predicative' is different from that noticed in the last section.

15. *Principia Mathematica,* vol. i, p. 56.

16. Ibid., p. 58.

17. *Principia Mathematica,* vol. i, p. 59. The phrase 'given intensionally' which is printed here within brackets occurs in a footnote.

18. *Proceedings of the London Mathematical Society*, ser. 2, xxv (1926), pp. 338–84. reprinted in the volume *The Foundations of Mathematics and other Logical Essays, pp. 1–61.*

19. *Logic, Semantics, Metamathematics*, pp. 152–278.

20. This may perhaps be the sense of Wittgenstein's remarks in his *Tractatus Logico-philosophicus,* 3.332.

21. *Introduction to Mathematical Philosopy,* p. 143.

22. See Max Black's criticism and Russell's reply in *The Philosophy*

of Bertrand Russell, edited by P.A. Schilpp, pp. 235 and 691.

23. G. Ryle, *The Concept of Mind.*

24. W.V. Quine, 'Unification of Universes in Set-Theory', *Journal of Symbolic Logic,* xxi (1956), pp. 267–79. Cf. Hao Wang, 'Logic of Many-Sorted Theories', *Journal of Symbolic Logic,* xvii (1952), pp. 105–16. A more conservative treatment of the purely logical antinomies is suggested by W. Kneale in 'Russell's Paradox and some Others', *The British Journal for the Philosophy of Science,* vol. xxii (1971).

25. *Werke,* vol. viii, p. 216.

26. 'Intuitionism and Formalism', Inaugural Address at the University of Amsterdam in 1912, translated and published in *The Bulletin of the American Mathematical Society,* vol. xx (1913), pp. 81–96.

27. *Intitionism, An Introduction,* p.8.

28. 'De onbetrouwbaarheid der logische principes', *Tijdschrift voor wijsbegeerte,* ii (1908), p. 152, reprinted in *Wiskunde, Waarheid, Werkelijkkid.* We have not seen this paper.

29. See espécially 'Mathematik, Wissenschaft und Sprache', *Monatshefte für Mathematik und Physik,* xxxvi (1929), pp. 153–64.

30. 'Intuitionistische Betrachtungen über den Formalismus', *Sitzungsberihte der Preußischen Akademic der Wissenschaften, Phys.-math. klasse,* 1928, pp. 48-52.

31. *Intitionism, An Introduction,* p. 18.

32. 'Die formalen Regeln der intuitionistische Logik', *Sitzungsberichte der Preu Bischen Akademie der Wissenschafte, Phys.-math. Klasse,* 1930, pp. 42–56. See also *Intuitionism, An Introduction,* ch. vii.

33. J.C.C. Mckinsey has shown that none can be defined by reference to the others without alteration of the system, 'Proof of the Independence of the Primitive Symbols of Heyting's Calculus of Proposition', *Journal of Symbolic Logic,* iv (1939), PP. 155–8.

34. See, for example, W. Kneale, 'Are all Necessary Truths True by Convention?', *Aristotelian Society Proceedings,* sup. vol. xxi (1947), pp. 118–33.

35. 'Zur intuitionistischen Arithmetik und Zahlentheoric' and 'Eine

Interpretation des intuitionistischen Aussagenkalküls', *Ergebnisse eines mathematischen Kolloquiums*, Heft iv (1932), pp. 34–38 and 39–40.

36. S.C. Kleene, *Introduction to Metamathematics*, § 87, and A. Heyting, *Intuitionism, An Introduction*, pp. 112–14.

37. Cf. also J.C.C. McKinsey and A. Tarski, 'Some Theorems about the Lewis and Heyting Calculi', *The Journal of Symbolic Logic*, xiii (1948), pp. 1–15. The interpretation given has is the second of two suggested by Gödel.

38. 'Uber die Grundlagen der Mengenlehre', *Mathematische Annalen*, lxv (1908), pp. 261–81.

39. 'Uber eine Widerspruchsfreiheitsfrage in der axiomatischen Mengenlehre', *Journal für die reine und angewandte Mathematik*, clx (1929), pp. 227–41. In some later writings, e.g. *Axiomatic Set Theory* by P. Bernays and A. Fraenkel, 'set' is reserved for entities capable of membership, though 'class' is used in a wider way.

40. 'Uber die Grundlagen der Logik und Mathematik', *Verhandlungen des dritten internationalen Mathematiker-Kongresses in Heidelberg* (1904), pp. 174–85.

41. 'Neubergründung der Mathematik', *Abhandlungen aus dem mathematischen Seminar der Hamburgischen Universität*, i (1922) pp. 157–77.

42. 'Uber das Unendliche', *Mathematische Annalen*, xcv (1926), pp. 161–90.

43. D. Hilbert and P. Bernays,*Grundlagen der Mathematik*, vol i, p. 20.

44. J. von Neumann, 'Zur Hilbertschen Beweistheorie', *Mathematische Zeitschrift*, xxvi (1927), pp. 1–46.

45. D. Hilbert and P. Bernays, *Grundlagen der Mathematik*, vol. i, pp. 14 ff. See, however, the conjecture of Kleene and Heyting mentioned in the last section.

46. 'Intuitionistische Betrachtungen über den Formalismus', *Sitzungsberichte der Preu Bischen Akademie Phys.-math. Klasse*, 1928, pp. 48–52.

47. *Einleitung in die Mengenlehre*, p.381.